Mad Dogs and the Englishman

Confessions of a Loon

David English

For my family: Robyn, Amy Rose and David English Junior
In loving memory of Ben Hollioake,
a very special Bunbury
who will remain in our hearts forever

Dedicated to Beefy, Barry, Linda, Maurice, Robin, E.C., Sir Viv,
Sir Tim, Miami Johnny, Stewie, Rory, Dicky-Boy, Jane Cruder
and all the Bunburys – one love xxx.

First published in Great Britain in 2002 by
Virgin Publishing Ltd
Thames Wharf Studios
Rainville Road
London W6 9HA

A catalogue record for this book is available
from the British Library.

ISBN 1-85227-952-4

Typeset by Phoenix Photosetting, Chatham, Kent

Printed and bound in Great Britain by Mackays of Chatham

CONTENTS

We are buccaneers of the past …
Maybe we have been here before …
Cavaliers of fortune,
Living from one day to the next
But living it as though every second counted
And could be our last.
Rapier thrust …
A bond of trust.
Velvet plumes, a strong charger
And the clear road ahead.
Although reality sometimes ties us down,
Our imagination has no bounds.
A quality of hearts,
Where one is hurt,
Both will bleed.

   … We come, we go and in between
We leave our mark.

(DAVID ENGLISH, 1980)

FOREWORD

David English. Former film actor (starring role, a dead German in *A Bridge Too Far*); the manager of the Bee Gees; President of RSO Records; creator of the Bunbury cartoon cricketers and the charity cricket team of the same name; massive supporter and organiser of the English Schools Cricket Association and the Under-15 World Cup; master of ceremonies for many of my road show expeditions – and the funniest man I have ever met.

I first came across 'the Loon' during my days on the MCC ground staff at Lord's in the mid-1970s when English was a good club player with nearby Finchley. He has told me the same joke every time I have been in his company since then and one day he will finish it. In the meantime he will continue to absolutely live for the game of cricket.

The list of young players who appeared in the ESCA Under-15 Festivals who then went on to play first-class and Test cricket, is impressive indeed. Stars like Mike Atherton, Alec Stewart, Nasser Hussain, Marcus Trescothick, Andy Flintoff and Graham Thorpe all owe Dave a great debt of gratitude for the drive that ensures the event continues to go from strength to strength. Those who run the English Schools Cricket Association will tell you that the Festival would have died a death had it not been for David banging the drum to raise sponsorship, interest and awareness.

As for Dave's other passion, the Bunbury XI itself, surely the only way to explain how he has persuaded some of the biggest names from the worlds of entertainment, sport and public life – from Eric Clapton to John Major, from Joanna Lumley to Viv Richards, from Gary Lineker to Rory Bremner – to give up their time on a Sunday afternoon to bat at number 17 out of 29, or to bowl 12th change out of 27, field at 11th slip to a new-ball bowler running in off twenty paces and sending down a real Jaffa – as in a real Jaffa orange, peel and all – is his puckish enthusiasm.

English has the knack of grinding down resistance with a feather duster. He's just too nice a bloke and too sincere in his support for the causes to turn down. Once he even persuaded me to go against my word and my better judgement to make a brief cricketing comeback. Time and again since my retirement from first-class cricket in 1993, various offers and requests have come my way to take up bat or ball once again, many for worthwhile causes. After having made my decision never to play cricket in any form once I stopped playing it professionally, the answer has always been thanks but no thanks and that position was non-negotiable. Except for once when I was forced to join the Loon in a game of beach cricket, just to get him off my case.

Humour is always round the Loon, whether he motivates it or is the butt of it. He will never forget the first question he pulled out of the hat on the inaugural 'Beef and Loon' road show; it read 'My name is Kate Williams, I live at 96 Cambridge Street, is it true you are hung like a rhino?' It came out 'My name is Kate, I live at 96 Cambridge Street, was Michael Holding the quickest bowler you faced?' Such ability to think on his feet made him the perfect MC for the shows I did with Viv Richards and Allan Lamb, and from time to time helped take my mind off the pressure of performing at the highest level of the game.

I have to admit that David has often had the misfortune to be on the wrong end of one of my practical jokes. Perhaps the most memorable took place on an unsuccessful fishing trip in Ullapool in the north-west tip of Scotland. Bored with the lack of fish coming our way I grew restless. Stand by your beds. After having come across a dead seagull on one of my trips I decided to give it a proper Christian burial so I took it back to the house we were staying in and placed it carefully under the covers of David's four-poster. It wasn't until about 3 o'clock the following morning that David noticed he wasn't sleeping alone.

He too has been known to get up to some tricks, particularly in the field of labour-saving. On my inaugural walk for Leukaemia Research in 1985, one of the many traditions was that the first person to complete the day's march was awarded the coveted yellow jersey. Bearing in mind his flat feet and the oxygen treatment he requires on completing the 300 yard trip from his house to the tube, when David picked up the treasured garment for the third day in succession I began to grow suspicious. While I weaved in and out of traffic on the fourth day, something in the aroma of cigar smoke wafting out from behind a newspaper in the back of a stationary black cab rang a bell. Out of curiosity I opened the door, pulled down the paper and found him pulling on the end of a large Havana.

But give him a charity cause and you'll find no one better to fight it as he proved when organising the memorial march in aid of Malcolm Marshall's family at the Honourable Artillery Club ground in the city of London in 2000. The zeal and imagination he demonstrates time and again in this environment persuaded me long ago that if any county wanted to take a punt on his marketing skills they would certainly get more than they bargained for, and some of it would even be beneficial.

Ian Botham
February 2002

INTRODUCTION: PLAYING FOR ENGLAND

To play for England, there is no greater honour. To fight in the middle, the Three Lions roaring on your chest. The pride, the passion, the sweat, the toil, the mind games and physical exertion, the aggro before the calm in front of a packed crowd.

INTRODUCTION: PLAYING FOR ENGLAND

To play for England, there is no greater honour. To fight in the middle, the Three Lions roaring on your chest. The pride, the passion, the sweat, the toil, the mind games and physical exertion, the aggro before the calm in front of a packed crowd.

'Morning, Gus, good day for it.'

It's 9 a.m. As I drive into Lords through the North Gate, Gus Farley, Ground Superintendent, is making his final patrol; dog at his heel to make sure all is perfect for the Big Day.

I walk to the dressing room, a spring in my step charged with nerves and adrenaline. Past the draymen filling the bars and Big Dave in the Clerk of the Works Office.

'It's a green 'un,' smiles Jim Fairbrother, the groundsman. 'The ball will skid through. Be sure to get right behind it, Dave.'

The turnstiles are creaking into action as the spectators surge in, vying for their favourite seats. The tops of the red buses can be seen passing along St John's Wood Road as the MCC colonels and wingcos with handlebar moustaches arrive on bicycles in perfect formation to pass through the W.G. Grace Gates.

Don Wilson, the Head Coach, marshals his blazered young professionals to sell scorecards and bowl to us in the nets.

'Strap 'em on, David lad, you're batting at four,' orders the Don of Yorkshire and England.

In the score box Harry Sharp sharpens his pencil and stares at the blank page.

At 31 for 2, I walk to the wicket. There is a buzz around the ground. I take guard and stand perfectly still. Feet, three inches either side of the crease, weight evenly balanced. If it's up I can go forward; if it's short, I'll be back. But I hope it's up, I love to drive off the front foot. I was taught by the master, Jack Robertson, one-handed with a bat sawn in half. I grip the bat, long handled for leverage, the 'V' made between the forefinger and thumb going down the back of the blade, and I wait. Like Alec Stewart, I'll try and score off every ball.

I put 10 on the board then 20, driving, cutting, hooking and ducking, sweating and cursing, playing and missing.

The bowler's fired up. You can feel the burning desire in both teams to win. I reach 50 and raise my bat to the lads perched on the player's balcony; 60, 70, 80, still the red buses pass. You can see the faces of the passengers straining for a free glimpse of play. Ninety-nine, the bowler charges in, hits me on the pads and appeals madly for an LBW. I take off for a single and as the umpire starts to raise his finger I scream 'Not Out! Not Out! I'll never score another century at Lords!' and down comes his finger, the bowler goes mad, so do the crowd who surge on to the field . . . all four of them, five, if you include Gus's dog.

For my 100 was scored on the Nursery End, not for England but the Cross Arrows vs Brondesbury . . . but it still felt special to me.

THREE STUMPS ON THE WALL

The headmaster was a man called Bowden whose face resembled an ordnance survey map, with its rivers of scarlet blood vessels surrounding a monumentally dark purple nose. Each day as us Highwood Boys would Start Rite in crocodile fashion up to the Old Forge for lunch, Mr Bowden would frequent the Three Hammers public house to hose down brandy in huge quantities. Emsley, the blond head prefect and a sadist of Gestapo proportions, would line up 'the Miscreants' outside Bowden's study, ready for his return. The inebriated Beak would take off his Harris Tweed coat and grey felt trilby, and roll up his sleeves ready to cane us. As the Courvoisier coursed through his veins his aim failed to hit the mark. Very often, I returned to class having received six of the best, or should I say three of the best and three of the worst, one on my wrist, one on my shoulder and one which failed to make any contact at all, sending Bowden, catapulted by his own momentum, lurching to the floor.

1 THREE STUMPS ON THE WALL

He is a disturbing influence on all ages of the school. His act of innocence on being reproved has long failed to deceive us, if it ever did, and his desire for social pursuits is insatiable.

(My final report, Hendon County Grammar School, September 1963,
Head Master E.W. Maynard Potts)

This message may have destroyed my father's confidence in my educational ability, but to me it was a tribute, one I'd like etched on my tombstone.

What if I wrote my own school report, now, nearly forty years later? What would I say about myself? I'm not sure who I am, really. I don't know if I've ever been myself. I've always felt alone, even when I'm with people; living in my own world, propelled on a wave through a timeless sea. Living from one moment to the next, driven by my instincts into a life of spontaneous combustion. It's funny how people either reminisce or look forward. They seem to neglect the present. Well, I live for the present, keeping an eye open for the chance, an opening, then whoosh, grab the opportunity, seize the moment because it may never come again.

The great thing about the present is making live decisions. No safety net. It's no good looking back and saying I should have done this or I should have done that. At the time you do what you think is right, and, believing in your convictions, simply do your best.

Every day I wake up enthusiastic, wanting to help others. To entertain them, to fulfil their dreams. I have always believed that fantasy can become reality. In fact other people's fantasies have always seemed like reality to me. Believe me, everything in life is possible.

I have always been driven by a very strong imagination. The beauty of this is that you really don't have to go anywhere; you can just sit down and dream your dreams, then put them into practice. There is a downside. Two fish rule us Pisceans, both swimming in opposite directions. In theory they should balance themselves, resulting in a thoughtful and considered final decision. One fish is positive, the other can make you imagine things that are not there, sending you on a negative wave. Pisceans are extremely sensitive and intuitive – we see things much quicker than anybody else. The secret is to back your first impressions instinctively and swim with the positive fish. Do not be pulled back by the negative.

The uncertainty of life, the feeling of insecurity drives you on. The desire to be loved and admired, which inspires you to greater heights. Fear is a great motivator. Being self-employed, a free spirit, is wonderful. As long as you can put bread on the table and look after your loved ones, then you can enter the realms of fantasy. In my case fantasy has given me my living. What is unconventional? What is the norm? Eccentric or visionary? I just want to make people's dreams come true.

Anyway I think you'll figure out more about me if I tell you about my life, so let's get on with the story!

My earliest recollection of life on this planet was being tucked up in my Silver Cross pram and being pushed by my mother through Hendon Park. My eyes beneath my bobble hat surveyed the green expanse with interest. In the far distance, I was conscious of the underground train rattling on into the city. Dotted about the park, I was aware of different groups running, leaping and hitting a ball. Little did I realise that this freedom of body and spirit was to become the very foundation of my life – the game of cricket.

I loved my mother very deeply. Three times a week she would push me through Hendon Park, past the fountain, over Queens Road and the alley-ways, which thread their way to the Burroughs Town Hall. There we would stock up on Seven Seas cod liver oil, orange juice and powdered milk. From my pram, I would gaze adoringly at my mother. Dressed in a camel coat, belted to fit her tall, slim figure, she resembled Lauren Bacall, or a bosomy Forties sweetheart.

My dad was a deeply sensitive artistic soul. He had travelled the world with his father on the cruise ships, playing in the band on the cello, double bass and saxophone. They made an intriguing couple and soon became the toast of the P & O Lines with their exhilarating performances. My grandpa resembled Noël Coward in both appearance and singing style and my father looked like Douglas Fairbanks. From India to Canada and back again, they charmed the ladies and led the lives of dashing troubadours. My dad actually crossed the Atlantic Ocean 78 times, carousing and cruising, aboard the decks of the *Empress of Britain*.

During the war my father was stationed at RAF Leconfield in Yorkshire, where he met my mother, who was a sergeant in the WRACS working on the ACK ACK guns at nearby Beverley. In the evenings my father would play in the Air Force band. He had noticed my mum from the stage as she danced with some young officer types.

It was wartime, and people really did live for the day. My dad asked my mum for a date and from that day Kenneth Frederick English and Joyce Nottingham Scoffin started courting, clinging on to every precious moment as if it were their last.

Rumour has it that I was conceived in a furrowed field just outside York. My father, giving my mother a lift on his bicycle back to HQ, flung her into a ditch and jumped on top to cover her, shielding her from the fire of a lone Messerschmidt which'd lost its way. I don't know who was more surprised, the 'Sour' Kraut or my father. Anyway, the combined feeling of relief and togetherness must have thrilled my dad into a moment of unadulterated lust and desire, straddling my mum into submission.

Yes, it's true that those RAF types did live for the day even if they were just a humble radio operator!

Nevertheless, my dad, the hopeless romantic, married my mum, the down-to-earth realist. A marriage, not made in heaven, but blessed by the uncertainty of war.

When the war ended, my mum very quickly laid down the law, pointing out that my dad's gigs would not pay the bills. Sadly, his cello and saxophone found their way to the back of the wardrobe, to be replaced by a badly fitting pinstripe suit which would take him into the unknown world of Fleet Street as an advertisement sales executive.

I loved my dad, although he tickled me unmercifully and sent me to Bell Lane Primary School at the age of 4½. It was like entering the world of the Bash Street Kids. Quickly, I learnt the art of survival in the playground using the weapon of humour and mimicry to get me through the day.

On the playground wall were three chalk stumps. It was there that I had my first taste of cricket, bowling with a shabby tennis ball, batting with a piece of wood taken from an old orange box. Bell Lane's most famous old boy was Denis Compton (who went on to be a real hero and one of the all-time greatest cricketers in the world) so unbeknown to me I was following in the footsteps of a real master.

D.C.S. Compton:	Middlesex CCC: 296 matches 21,781 runs, ave. 49.95
	England 78 matches, 5807 runs, ave. 50.06
D.S. English:	Middlesex Second Eleven, 2 matches, 64 runs, ave. 32

At the age of five my father plucked me away from the killing fields of Bell Lane and placed me in the sedate, safe haven of Alma White Junior Pillar of Fire College, tucked behind Brent Green.

It was run by the Methodist fathers from America's Midwest. I soon found myself excelling at spelling and quickly falling in love with my English mistress, Miss Lowe.

Each day, I would parade my skills in elocution and spelling from the classroom on the corner of the quadrangle before wearily heading for home, proudly wearing my brown cap and blazer. You know that end-of-the-day feeling, tie undone, socks down, exhausted, the day well and truly seized.

It was upon this journey homeward bound that I put away my childish feelings for Miss Lowe, and first encountered true love. Hilary lived at 5a and Valentine at Number 30 Shirehall Park.

I remember the nervous tingling feeling of expectancy at seeing Hilary (a mature 6-year-old) and Valentine (7½) a bit further down the road.

The thing was I made them laugh. I have never considered myself handsome or debonair. Brad Pitt and my son aged six are handsome. Maybe I was quite tasty but I've never relied on my looks to capture a girl's heart. Best to get out there and make them laugh. I have never taken myself too seriously or looked too deeply inside. I learned then, with Hilary and Valentine, that a love affair must be the linking of hearts, a togetherness of spirits looking out at the world through the eyes of one. The true test of love is when you are apart from that person; the fire of love will flicker in your tummy at the sense of missing. For me, to this day nothing has changed.

So after my daily romantic dalliance through Shirehall Park I'd arrive home to my mother's warm embrace and a plate of biscuits and glass of milk. I would then scale the tree outside my house to wait for my dad's return from work. As he walked under the tree, I would drop on him screaming like a banshee. He, as always, pretended to be surprised as his son and heir leapt on him Zorro-like, wearing a Robert Hurst Mac, top-buttoned, as a cape.

On 8 October 1953 my sister Annie was born. It was like a breath of fresh air and a sense of relief for my parents. Years before, when I was only three, I had a brother, Nigel Barrington, who had died just after birth. My mother always said it was through the neglect of the doctors. To compensate for the loss of their son my parents had adopted a little girl called Penny. I can only remember her very vaguely. She didn't stay for long, I'm not too sure why but I think she needed medical help. However, I do remember playing in the street after the road had been freshly tarmacked. Penny then went inside and daubed the wardrobe door with her tarry fingers. Years after she had gone the tar marks remained on that door as a memory.

Sadly, at the age of eight, I left Alma White to enter the purple, black and white striped blazer brigade of Hendon Preparatory School. I missed the warm embrace of the Methodist Mothers and Fathers at Alma White but my dad decided it was time to be propelled upwards.

It was at this time that I first met 'Uncle' Ron Downes who regularly visited my mother, especially during the daytime. He always seemed to arrive when she was ironing, standing there in her apron, the view from the kitchen one of domestic bliss. Ron Downes was a salesman through and through. A loveable roguish chap, possessed by a demon tailor, always nattily turned out with his suede Chukka boots and an engaging smile.

Ron knew how to charm my mum. He made her laugh and when 'Auntie' Ruby and Blind Uncle Lionel came in from next door, the place was in an uproar. I watched Ron hold court and learned from the experience.

Every day, I walked to Hendon Prep, about five miles there and back. I quickly showed a natural flair for cricket and football, with my fitness certainly enhanced by my daily journey. When I talk to my pal Tim Selwood, a sports master at Belmont School, he tells me that kids today are so unfit, they cannot even climb over a wall. Driven to and from school, they return to the comfort zone of the couch and computer games – mesmerised by Mr Sony – the kiss of death for our young sporting youth. Years later, when I asked Viv Richards and Ian Botham how they kept fit they replied, 'Quite simply, by walking.' Viv had no choice as his dad didn't drive, so he walked to school and back. After school, he went on to the beach and the playing fields, always on the move, flexing his muscles and exercising his limbs. And 'Beefy' Botham? Well, it's not for nothing he's known as the King of the Walks, having tramped 5,000 miles so far, raising £5 million for Leukaemia Research, an incredible 'feet' indeed! Neither Ian nor Viv have ever used weights in their career, preferring the natural exercise of walking and running to keep them fit. I do understand a parent's concern for their children's safety, but there is no doubt that the Range Rover Run to and from school has seriously damaged our emerging sporting talent.

So there I stood in the snooty confines of Hendon Prep among future prime ministers and heart surgeons and those 'financial' people who earn millions behind oak-beamed offices and chandeliered splendour. Dave English, an actor in real life – I loved school for its theatre. Every lesson, among the ink wells and the Flashman feel of Latin declensions and French verbs, I would tell my gags and play the fool, ribbing the masters in their sports jackets with leather patches, 'Educating Rita' prototypes. Every lesson was a performance and an opportunity to entertain my fellow conker champions and teachers alike. There's nothing like a challenge.

Every now and again, I would overstep the mark and a well-aimed blackboard duster would arrest my show in mid flow, especially from the geography master who had a lethal right arm.

Sometimes my cheek would land me in the study of Mr Williams, the handsome headmaster who resembled a cross between Gary Cooper and Gregory Peck. With a resigned sigh tinged with sadness the head decreed, 'I hear you've been up to your tricks again, English, I'm afraid it's the cane for you!'

As Mr Williams landed his whipping bamboo six times on my outstretched palms, three strokes on each hand, I sensed he didn't enjoy the task. He was far too elegant for this world. He would have been better off in Hollywood than nearby Cricklewood!

I enjoyed Hendon Prep. I excelled at the arts and sport, though maths, physics and chemistry presented a mental block. Football, played in all weathers at Copthall playing fields, was fantastic, and as for cricket, the magic web was already spun. I played in the First X1 team and clearly recall hitting 105 not out, one fine summer's day. My best pals were Donald Grant, feted by the boys because his dad had won the Monte Carlo Rally, and a boy called Tulloch, popular not least because, on the long trek home, his mother would invite us in for cream cakes.

Then just as I had learnt to swerve the prefects on patrol and the playground bullies and 'my manor' was set and settled, we were on the move again. I was ten years old.

My mother had this obsession of keeping up with the Joneses. The problem was that her sense of where we should be living and 'what finances should be flowing into the domestic coffers' left my father and his earning powers sadly behind.

Believe me, family life should be built on love and togetherness, encouragement and support, working and living as a team through good times and bad. But my mum thought differently. When I heard them fighting I used to disappear to Hendon Park with my cricket bat under my arm. Always Hendon Park. Poor old dad, the sensitive artist in the foreign field of advertising, never seemed to come up to my mother's standards and expectations.

This time we were off to Virginia Water in Surrey. Very upmarket, very stockbroker belt.

I admired my dad for what he was. His watercolour work for my geography homework assured me of a 'ten out of ten' mark every week. His humour and charm and his ability to hold court, especially in the company of women, made him very special and his kindness was matched only by his generosity. For instance, when I was three years old, I suffered from serious sinus trouble. I had to go to the children's hospital in Great Ormond Street Hospital to sort out my ears, nose and throat. My ward was on the top floor. Every evening my dad walked from Fleet Street to stand there far below in the broken light of Bloomsbury to wave to me. Always wearing his trilby hat, navy blue Crombie coat and kid gloves. He would stand there looking up, smiling and waving, a solitary figure in his own pool of light.

To move to Virginia Water, my father had obviously borrowed from Peter to pay back Paul. He was living horribly beyond his means. At the age of ten I knew little about hire purchase, but I did become aware of knocks on the door at different times when men in suits, clutching briefcases, would stand and make their demands. Meanwhile I had been inserted into the Manor School, Egham where I quickly fell in love with Heather Tilbury, first heard Bill Haley sing 'Rock Around The Clock' and managed to fail my 11-Plus exams at the first attempt.

My mother had hoped that I would pass and go to Strodes Grammar School. My dad had promised me a new bike, a shiny red and silver Raleigh, with Sturmey Archer three-speed gears if I passed. But I had failed. From that day, I was doubly determined to succeed. I now saw life as a blank page, each page to be filled with honest endeavour, and a profusion of ideas and images. By nightfall, exhausted, when I lay my head back on the pillow, I wanted to feel a sense of achievement, however small, because that page would turn, never to reappear. My parents' reaction was exactly as I expected: 'As long as you did your best, never fear, because your day will come.'

Some of my classmates sailed through the 11-Plus. Richard Slatter, the brainy one on the corner of Trotsworth Avenue, passed, so did my mate Morgy, the soapbox king. It was with Morgy that I experienced my first brush with the law. Near where I lived was the Sandy Path where people poodled along by the Green before entering the silver birch wood.

Morgy and I filled a brown paper bag full of dog turds and stuck it above the laurel leaves, which hung over the path. We tied a piece of string to the bag and waited in the bushes until a poor unsuspecting soul passed under the laurels. Then, whoosh, we would jerk the string, depositing the crap on to the victim's head.

We got away with this act of reckless joy for over a fortnight. The curious tale of the phantom turds was the talk of Virginia Water, until one Sunday morning we came a cropper. We could hear a bicycle coming down the path without being able to see the rider.

'Pull it!' whispered Morgy. I duly obeyed, emptying the contents over the village bobby's head. 'The Laurel Hill Mob' had been twigged; propelled by fear we legged it home. That morning there was a door-to-door search. When the doorbell rang at Number 8 Trotsworth Avenue, I was nowhere to be seen. Ensconced in my bedroom cupboard I could hear the ruffled tones of my dad, 'Sorry, officer, I haven't seen him all day.'

A few months later I again unwittingly brought my dad in contact with the Old Bill. Near where we lived, along a gorse drive and beyond the woods, was a sandpit, a massive expanse of dunes. So realistic was this Surrey desert that many war films were made there. Richard Burton's *Tobruk* and *Rommel* were 'filmed on location'. Just think: Virginia Water, twinned with Tripoli. To show how realistic a desert place this was, the tank regiment itself used the place for exercises.

One day, Morgy and I got off our soapbox, bow and arrow in hand, and made our way through the dunes. There, we found this old shell, put it carefully on our trolley and took it home to dad. My dad, displaying his 'good citizen of the neighbourhood watch', wrapped it in a blanket and took it to the police station. There the kindly desk sergeant informed him that it was an unexploded 3½ lb anti-tank shell; quite lethal, and if my dad's yellow Ford Consul had gone over a bump, he really would have ended up in Tripoli.

Strangely enough, some forty years later when I went back to Virginia Water (throughout my life, I have always returned down memory lane), I retraced my steps along that path and beyond the wood to take another glimpse of the sandpit. However, when I got there it had disappeared into thin air . . . amazing.

By now, my dad was finding the pressures of Virginia Water and marriage etc. all too much. Sometimes, I would go into his bedroom to find him in bed with his head under the pillows.

Despite failing my 11-Plus, school remained the same, a playground of pleasure. I joined the Christ Church choir and sang in harmony with Vanessa Ann Taylor, a really beautiful girl who rode her mum's bicycle with a basket on the front. Even at 12, Vanessa Ann Taylor was the perfect girl. Beautiful but a tomboy, the perfect combination. She quickly fitted into our gang, like Bonnie with Clyde, and willingly accompanied us on all our adventures.

Two years passed and we were off again. My mother never explained why but very quickly we packed and left the splendour of our show house in Virginia Water to return to Station Road, Hendon and rented accommodation.

I was 13 when I was first introduced to the magic of Mill Hill. Highwood Prep stood on a hillside just off Lawrence Street. Although it carries an NW7 postcode, Mill Hill could be a little town in the depths of Gloucestershire. I still marvel at the Ridgeway with its string of convents and priories, riding schools, a village pond and the long sweep of the picturesque Totteridge Valley. However, Highwood School was Dickensian in its appearance and approach.

The headmaster was a man called Bowden whose face resembled an ordnance survey map, with its rivers of scarlet blood vessels surrounding a monumentally dark purple nose. Each day as us Highwood Boys would Start Rite in crocodile fashion up to the Old Forge for lunch, Mr Bowden would frequent the Three Hammers public house to hose down brandy in huge quantities. Emsley, the blond head prefect and a sadist of Gestapo proportions, would line up 'the Miscreants' outside Bowden's study, ready for his return. The inebriated Beak would take off his Harris Tweed coat and grey felt trilby, and roll up his sleeves ready to cane us. As the Courvoisier coursed through his veins his aim failed to hit the mark. Very often, I returned to class having received six of the best, or should I say three of the best and three of the worst, one on my wrist, one on my shoulder and one which failed to make any contact at all, sending Bowden, catapulted by his own momentum, lurching to the floor.

The French master was called Monsieur Maison – just imagine being called Mr House. He had two sons, Jean Philippe and Claude, whom he used to beat senseless. He would make us sing the verbs – *Je suis, tu es, il est, nous sommes* – and then *Arrête!* By the harmony of the singing he could tell which *étudiants* had not done his homework by his singing out of tune. The penalty for hitting the wrong note was to be hit by Maison who would make you kneel in front of him where he would ask you again to repeat the verb. Failure to do so would result in a full-blooded smack around the face, forehand, back hand and so on . . . Fear for me was and still is a great motivator, as I have said. Suffice to say my French and Latin were perfect!

Monsieur Maison seemed to take a shine to me. Chain-smoking his *Celtiques* cigarettes clenched between brown teeth, he would smile as in a Sergio Leone film, '*Monsieur Anglais*, you are *très comique, oui?*' A rhetorical question. Never has my gift for comedy been exercised so strongly for the sake of survival. Bowden and Maison got away with their cruelty for years. It amazed me that none of the pupils ever grassed them up to their parents.

Until one day, Maison lifted his hand to a boy called Ginger Clarke. Clarke took the smack on his face, and then replied with a spirited right-hook which lifted Maison clean off his feet, sending him sprawling over the desks. Clarke piled in like 'Enry Cooper, raining blows on the astonished Frog. Upper cuts, right crosses and darting jabs sent Maison into a bleary-eyed submission. Clarke went home cheered on by the boys. Within the hour he had returned with his parents and the police. Maison and Bowden were taken away in a squad car.

Two days later Highwood School was closed down forever. Three months later it mysteriously burnt to the ground. Today, if you travel down Lawrence Street, you will see a grand house called Greenfield's, built in the woods where Highwood School once stood. Sometimes, I cut across the fields and look down on those woods. As the wind whips through the trees, if you listen closely you can still hear the eerie anthem of those French verbs being sung . . . *Je suis, tu es, il est* . . .

Fourteen, and it was the entrance of the Magnificent Seven. My seventh academy of learning, Whitefield Secondary Modern School, encompassed all the elements that the dear Lord had put on this earth. Six years in all, six forms in each year. Students from 6I could go to Oxford or Cambridge. But pupils from 6VI would almost certainly end up in HMP Pentonville or Wormwood Scrubs. Never was there such a cross section of society. A mix of religions, sexes, riddled with fear, joy, racism, mob rule and genius. A pot-pourri of society, a kaleidoscope of culture.

I can tell you now; I was to learn more about life during my stay at Whitefields than at any time before or after till the day I leave this mortal earth.

Day one. Baptism of fire. I was taken by my mother past Clitterhouse and the Claremont Road Estate, through Tintown to the portals of Whitefields. Along with some other internees I stood in the headmaster, Mr Haley's study. Over his shoulder, through the window, I could see a group of boys tending an allotment. Not quite ball and chain, but certainly 'Cool Hand Luke'.

'These boys are on probation,' boomed Haley in husky tones. 'Let it be a warning to you.'

'The playground is run by the gangs from the estate,' pointed out Haskell, a genial Pakistani lad wearing rimless glasses. 'Watch out for the Fletcher brothers, the Driscolls and Butler. They'll have you away.'

My gentle upbringing, through the sheltered cloisters of Alma White and Hendon Prep, had not really prepared me for the naked truth of the Whitefield Ghetto. There I stood in my new uniform, my brand new cap perched proudly on my bonce. The next thing I knew, I was being dragged through the nettles, past the long jump pit behind the gym before being deposited unceremoniously into the River Brent. As I surfaced from the grimy waters next to an old pram and an Express Dairy milk crate I could see the perpetrators of my christening, a motley crew of gangsters indeed. 'Oy, toffee nose, welcome to f***in' Whitefields, Geezer!'

I think the only thing that saved me from the ignominy of my ducking was that I didn't cry. The mob had waited for my reaction. They expected me to cry but I didn't. I knew all about bullying, having experienced the Monsieur Maisons of this world, and I certainly wasn't going to break down in front of these tossers. Not until it was time to go home and then, when I was on my own, I confess I did shed a tear.

I felt as though I had arrived at a crossroads. I didn't know where I was going to in life. With my entry to Whitefields we had moved yet again, ironically back to Shirehall Park, Hendon. We had gone from Number 49 to Number 43 Shirehall in ten years. All these different schools and homes, my mum and dad seemingly poles apart. All I had was my little sister who I loved. And now, day one, at my new school, I had entered the gates of hell.

Still bedraggled from my ducking, I stood by my favourite 'dropping on dad' tree and made a decision, which would last me my lifetime. My 14 years so far had given me the roots to grow and the wings to fly. Clearly, to win without hardship was to triumph without glory. We all came into this life alone and we'd leave alone. In between times we were here to help each other. I would rise and fall on my wits and merit, following my intuition and relying on any natural ability that I might possess. We would all go down that one road but even then I sensed that everything in life was possible.

The playground at Whitefields taught me to be streetwise. I saw it all, anti-Semitism, paki-bashing, pregnant girls, terrible fights – and my first taste of physical love.

Up till then that exquisite sensation of the wet dream had been all I had experienced and then ... it was the last morning of our school skiing trip to the beautiful canton of Valais in Switzerland. We had enjoyed a raucous week in Champery, skiing and having a real hoot. On the day we were to return to England, I was doing my last-minute present shopping. Down in the valley I could see our train, and Mr Vincent, our maths master and tour director, waving his arms about, yelling, 'Come on English, we're waiting to go!'

As I legged it down the road past the chalets, clutching cuckoo clocks and Swiss army penknives, the friction on my trousers rubbed against 'my old boy' and began building to a climax. Suddenly that wet dream sensation returned to fill me with a blissful tingling orgasm, stopping me in my tracks, and rendering me weak at the knees. I looked up at the mountains left and right of the valley. They seemed to avalanche, making me oblivious to Mr Vincent's ranting from the station. I was in a soft-focus film, in slow motion. I could see Vincent waving, but my legs were like cotton wool, unable to move any quicker in the after-glow.

'Come on, English, climb aboard, what's the matter boy?'

Exhausted and concerned I locked myself into the toilet to examine my underpants. They were filled with gloy. What was it? Nobody had ever taught me the birds and bees, and I had been too busy playing cricket. There in the well of my pants was my first sight of able-bodied semen freshly discharged. From that day I learned to play with my pink trombone, making wonderful music non-stop. Here, there and everywhere I took myself in hand. It was fantastic.

It was the Jewish students that I most admired at Whitefields. The boys were always sharper academically and in the way they dressed, and their bravery against the anti-semitics was incredible. I remember a lad called Paul Boxer, dressed in drain-pipe trousers and Italian shoes, taking on eight thugs; and then there was Boris Arwas, standing up for his rights against the bullies. They were jealous of the Jews. The Jews were brighter and one thing was for certain: the girls – Linda Zetland, Jennifer Gunstock and Pat Lewis – were much prettier. As with all women, they were more mature than us boys and used to flirt with us mercilessly. I listened to them and learned, marvelling at their beauty.

It was Pat Lewis who first pulled me to paradise, thrusting her hand down my grey worsted trousers behind the air-raid shelters in my beloved Hendon Park. She showed me the way and educated me with her pleasure chest. Pat was like an adventure playground. We lay there fondling and kissing oblivious to the park keeper and his gang of mowers. Time simply stood still . . . funny to think we were just sixty yards from the path where my mother had pushed me in my pram.

I also fell head over heels for Jenny Gunstock. Everyday I would take her to the top of her road but never to her home because I was a gentile. Her parents would not approve of their Jewish princess fraternising with a 'Goy'. Forever, the forbidden fruit. The hopelessness of love; although it's written on the sign, 'Do not pick these flowers', it is useless to the wind, for the wind cannot read.

For me there is no greater pleasure than the company of a beautiful girl. The first sight, the chase, the talk, the eyes meeting, the smile, the laugh, exchanging numbers, hoping they'll phone. Will it lead to two hearts beating

MAD DOGS AND THE ENGLISHMAN

as one? I'm probably better off chasing Polish countesses and yet I always end up with 21-year-old out-of-work dancers. I love their spirit, their youth, and their hunger to learn. Their vulnerability . . . I like to guide them, to see them succeed. Trips to seaside towns, out of season, to watch the anglers cast their lines into the wintry seas. To cling together, camel-coated, and walk past the beach huts, empty shells of summer dreams. The uncertainty of love, the fragile fingers of fate, the tingle in the belly at the sense of missing. A weekend in Prague or maybe Ross-On-Wye. The Malverns in spring, Miami in December, Stockholm in the dark . . .

Mr Ransome, the metalwork master, wasn't handsome but we called him 'Handsome Ransome'. Mr Norman taught woodwork; Big George Graves, geography; Mr Slim, history; Miss Coombes, the beatnik, took us for art; Miss Greenaway, the French mistress, drove us crazy by sitting on the table with her long Cyd Charisse legs perched on the stool; the elegant Mr Vincent, mathematics; Mr Norman Dodd, a wonderful man with a permanent sniffle and small moustache, coached us at cricket in his own time after school. There was 'Baldy' Lewis, the science master; Les Hill, a very distinguished ex-squadron leader who educated us in technical drawing and football; Miss Crump, English; Miss Hardman (boy was she hard), the assistant head who walked with a stick; Mr Edmundson, dapper, ex-Olympic gymnast from New Zealand; and Mr King, owner of a beloved Hillman California, took PE. There was Mr Tudor 'Ginger' Lewis, who was rugby mad; Mr John Stacey, music; and a rotund caretaker whose name slips my memory. He wore the same ill-fitting brown overalls all year round, chain-smoked, and had a scrawny mongrel who pissed on the hour every hour up against the bicycle sheds.

They were a wonderful staff of teachers who performed under great duress. Mr Wills, a slightly camp master who doubled in English and flower arranging, was instantly locked into his own cupboard by the marauders of 4VI. Mr Ransome's handsome features became even more finely chiselled when he was tied up, vicelike, and stuck in the corner for two hours of double metalwork. The gang would then relax with a brew up, put a kettle on the Bunsen burner, have a portable radio blaring out Radio Caroline's hits, and take to the windows where they'd try to shoot the caretaker's dog up the arse with their air rifles, BSA 22s and 177s.

Meanwhile, the academics scholared away thinking of Oxford's dreamy spires and a release from this Dante's Inferno.

The teaching was good, if you wanted to learn. There were 40–45 in each class. I was in the A stream (4I) with the boffins but half my heart was still in the playground. I was fascinated by all the different types and made a point of befriending them all, not because I had to but because I wanted to. Us Pisceans have always wanted to be loved and admired.

When we feel adored we can take on anything, literally anything in the world; funny that this insecurity should lead to security. I made the villains laugh. I have always been drawn to danger, finding infamy as interesting as fame.

Later, at the age of thirty whilst appearing in Sir Richard Attenborough's *A Bridge Too Far*, I confronted a nutter who had stolen a Bren gun from the armourer and had gone bonkers in the town. We were on location in the Dutch town of Deventer, and this psycho had positioned himself behind the fountain, letting off rounds at will. I was immediately drawn to him and walked slowly across the cobbled square to confront him and ask him 'why?' All I did was to look into his eyes with a steady stare.

'Give it to me,' I said. 'Come on, it's alright, just give it to me!' My eyes never left his. The bloke, a 19-year-old tearaway, slowly rose to his feet and gave me the weapon. All was calm. It was over in a minute. Funny; I didn't feel brave, just sad for this man. I had been drawn to him. Does it take one nutter to know another one? What is madness? Define it. Try and understand the other person's mental state, his or her hurt or sadness, their background and the long road from home.

Back at school, every playtime I would entertain the troops. Magic tricks, impressions and jokes before playing 500-a-side football with an old tennis ball. My Elvis Presley seemed to be favourite. Every day I performed 'Love Me Tender' for the gangsters who begrudgingly applauded me, pulling on their Wills Woodbines or Five Dominos: 'You know what, English, you're alright, mate.'

On the sports field, my cricket was progressing thanks to Mr Dodd's enthusiasm and after-school coaching. At the age of 15, I was made Captain of the school's First X1, won the *Evening News* Star Bat Competition for taking 6 for 18 and scoring 32 (proudly presented with a Denis Compton signed Gradidge Bat by the Editor of the *Evening News*), and won a place in the NW London Schools Team. But my sporting prowess was to be mightily overshadowed by several others of Whitefield's favourite sons.

As I said, every morning before the bell we would play 500-a-side football with an old tennis ball, anoraks down as goal posts. It was mainly kick and rush stuff, until one morning a golden light streamed down on to our Theatre of Dreams. In the middle of the fray stood a little fat boy, balancing the ball on his head, and then flicking it from one foot to the other, displaying sublime skills. It was as though Moses had arrived. The 500-a-side parted to watch this maestro perform his craft.

'Mr Hill, you'd better come and see this!' I said excitedly. Les Hill tapped his pipe out on the bottom of his brogue, thrust his hands deep into his sports jacket pockets and followed me to the playground. It seemed as though the whole school was entranced by this roly-poly lad.

'You boy, come here,' called Mr Hill.

The boy flicked the ball finally into his hand and walked past the sea of faces to the football master.

'Here son, what's your name?'

'Currie, sir, Tony Currie,' came the reply.

'Well, Currie, you come and see me after school. Football training at 4.30,' smiled Mr Hill.

Tony Currie went on to play for Watford, Sheffield United, Leeds United, QPR and England. Without question, one of the most naturally talented footballers this country's ever produced. On today's market, Currie would be worth £20 million. Brought up in the same era as Hudson, Bowles, Charlie Cooke and Georgie Best, his artistry would influence any game in which he played. And we had seen him first at the age of 12.

Even then I noticed his greatest virtue, to slow down the game to his own pace, and then look up and see the opening and accurately chip a forty yards pass. Tony Currie was born with great vision; the only other player I've seen like this was Glenn Hoddle. Les Hill discovered other fine footballers from our playground. Bob Turpie and Martin Quittenden went on to QPR. I was quite good at soccer but nowhere near Currie & Co.'s class. However, Mr Hill put me on the right wing in the First X1 and told me my job was simply to control the ball, look up and cross it. No need to worry, the boys would find me on the wing.

This they did with uncanny accuracy. I just stood at outside right and marvelled at my team-mates' skills. It must have been like playing in the back streets of Rio. Dave Beddell would score from the halfway line, starting with his back to the goal, flicking the ball over his shoulder before volleying it goalwards like a thunderbolt. Turpie mesmerised the opposition on his left wing, Quittenden dominated at centre half, Tony Norman performed like a big cat in goal and as for Currie – well, he just ruled the midfield, beating his man and coming back to beat him again just for fun. During my three years at Whitefields we never lost a game.

Mr King, proud owner of a shining Hillman California, was the cocky PT master, surly and self-assured. He would have us hanging off wall bars heading medicine balls, straddling the horse and generally putting us through the non-stop running-on-the-spot torture of press-ups, star jumps, flic-flacs and ... 'Wait for it, wait for it, when the whistle goes'. Mr Edmundson, his partner, came from another world. A gentle New Zealander, ever so dapper and ever so bloody brilliant! But we weren't his best pupils; just because he had represented New Zealand in the Olympic games didn't mean that we could 'Olga Korbut' it around the gym in his ever-so-simple winning style.

'Watch me,' he'd command, performing ten somersaults on the trot, in immaculate fashion. 'Now you try, Butler.'

Dave 'Bomber' Butler didn't mind Edmundson, but took a strong dislike to Reichsmarshall Herr Haufman Heinrich King.

'Come on, Butler, move boy, move!' barked King.

'I'll move alright,' sneered the Bomber under his breath. 'So will you, my son.' Dave 'Bomber' Butler would bide his time.

Cross-country running proved to be a particularly uncomfortable experience to be avoided, if possible, at all costs. Twice around Clitterhouse Park, over the rubbish dump, circle the estate up the Hendon Way and back again, six miles in all. Several of our well-honed, finely tuned athletes had a more favoured alternative route, i.e. out of sight into the café, on with the jukebox (it was 1961 and 'Telstar' by the Tornados was Number 1), apply a bit of sweat and dirt to the face, wait for the runners to return and slip back into the pack – hey presto, job done, race won!

One boy, a skinny youth, tall and angular, particularly loathed the cross-country run. On several occasions he was found skulking in the bushes refusing to compete. One day, Edmundson caught the conscientious objector, threw him a size 9 pair of brown plimsolls and a pair of ill-fitting shorts and told him to leg it. This he did with alarming ease, coming in one hour ahead of the rest; the idea of running five miles was too terrible to contemplate, so the boy sprinted the distance in record time. His name was David Bedford. Ten years later he became the 8000 metres champion of the world.

And as for Mr King? Well, one day while experimenting in the science lab we heard a mighty explosion from down below. Quickly running to the window we could see a smouldering wreck in the staff car park. If you looked carefully, you could just make out the shell of a Hillman California. Apparently, Dave Butler was nowhere to be seen. Busy, miles away on a cross-country run . . . 'Wait for it, wait for it, when the whistle goes!'

Every day, enthusiastically, I arose to take on another Whitefields day. I had swiftly fitted into the fabric of secondary modern life, absorbing the strands of academia, sport, girls, and self-survival with zest and a deeply genuine love and concern for the mixture of human life in all its forms. With great relish I strolled from Shirehall Park along the North Circular Road with its arterial decay, past the National Cash Register building and left into Claremont Road. In the distance, I could see the seagulls hovering over the dump and the workers from Tintown busily cobbling together a living from their Ford Transit and 'Delboy' dealing.

I had barely turned 16 when headmaster Haley called me into his study.

'Good morning, English,' he growled.

'Good morning, sir,' I replied.

Haley stood staring out of his window, his nicotined fingers clenched behind his back.

'You know, English. I've been watching you and thinking,' he said slowly. 'And I've decided that you are the one.'

'The one, sir?'

'Yes, English, you're the one.'

Haley wheeled around and looked at me from over the top of his glasses. 'I've decided to make you Head Boy, Captain of my school.'

A combination of genuine surprise and pride surged through my body. Up till then my only taste of officialdom had been as a sixer in the wolf cubs, a patrol leader of the Pee Wits in the 22nd Hendon Sea Scout Group and Captain of the school cricket team. True, I had always been a ringleader but now Mr Haley was making me Head of his school.

'Thank you, sir. It would be an honour.' My acceptance speech didn't take long.

That morning my appointment was announced at assembly. Mr Haley from his rostrum hoarsely heralded me to the stage to receive my badge. As I left the elite ranks of the sixth form, there was a murmur in the hall, which gradually heightened to a crescendo of cheering, clapping, laughing, and spontaneous renderings of 'Love Me Tender' from the lads at the back. I loved them all. To this day, I have never felt so proud.

On the domestic front, things were ticking along famously. My grandfather had pretended to be blind in order to secure a special pension from the government. The fact that he painted brilliant pictures in great detail and spotted a scratch on my dad's Humber from a full fifty feet seemed neither to prick his conscience, nor impede his progress in dipping his wick into Mrs Flossie Carty next door.

Flossie Carty was a large hearty woman with a big chest and a Rubens smile. Her ruddy features and ample charms had lured my grandfather away from my nana who unknowingly was happy to stay at home to embroider and serve the white-sticked lothario.

My grandma personified kindness in every way. Petite, and as delicate as bone china, she worshipped 'old Noël Coward'. Until one day he told her to go and visit her relations in Greatford, a little village in Lincolnshire.

'Rose, you look a little off-colour, my dear. A few days in the country will do you the world of good'. Two days after my nana had arrived in Greatford, her furniture and worldly belongings arrived at her cottage.

Back in Hampstead Garden Suburb my grandfather, seduced by the lusty pleasures of Flossie Carty, had moved in next door.

My grandmother, devastated at the news, never got over the shock and died of a broken heart several months later.

My grandfather's behaviour may have seemed like a passage from Errol Flynn's autobiography but the loss of my grandma and the whole sordid scenario saddened me. The idea of boy-meets-girl, falls in love, has children and lives happily ever after, for me, still seems the best plan: although a bachelor will always scupper this theory by insisting 'Why buy a book when you can join a library?'

I still cherish the fading memory of my family sitting in the kitchen at breakfast time around the blue Formica table, sharing daily desires, boiled eggs and soldiers, eager to encourage each other through the day, till we reconvened for that warm embrace at dinnertime. Far better than a family at war, sitting in silence eating their Cornflakes at Colditz, eager to make the Great Escape to their own comfort zone. My own tunnel was firmly built to Hendon Park. My sister would often come with me to join in our endless test matches; Anne Elizabeth at the age of nine was a fair old bowler.

Curiously, although my heart was firmly set in Hendon and still is to this day, my spiritual and fantasyland remains in Mill Hill. It was at Whitefields that I found myself, once again, captivated by the magic of Mill Hill. Mr Stacey, our music master, was to cricket as Les Hill was to football. John Stacey was one of the foremost left-arm quickish bowlers in Middlesex. He was also captain of Mill Hill Village CC. As captain of the school team, he quickly snaffled me up to play for Mill Hill Village Cricket Club.

I had started my club cricket career at the age of 13 playing for Teddington Town in far off Bushey Park. My uncle, Lt. Col. Tom Goodland, MC Rtd, had invited me to play and somehow every weekend I travelled on the green train to Richmond, Twickenham, Teddington via Gunnersbury Park and Kew. It gave me a great thrill to cross the Thames at Richmond. I remember clutching my cricket bag and gazing down at the fine old Georgian buildings which lined the river; with its cluster of art shops, pubs and bohemian residents it reminded me of Hampstead. Then it was on to the club, to exhibit my cover drives among the deer and the finery of the Royal Park of Bushey.

Later, Mill Hill Village CC would become my cricketing home for 18 years. Every Saturday and Sunday I took the 240 bus to the Ridgeway, alighting at the Medical Research Building. I would then walk down Burton Hole Lane, past the tramp who lived in the woods, before turning the corner to see one of the most breathtaking views in the world, the beautiful Totteridge Valley. 'How green is your valley?' I answer, very green for London NW7. I'm sure that my great pal Jack Russell, the Gloucester and England wicket keeper finds the same solace in Laurie Lee's 'Cider with Rosie' country. The moment I turned that corner in Burton Hole Lane, I was in paradise.

At 15 I was playing in the Mill Hill Village CC First X1. 'You must score 20 or more runs in each game,' said John Stacey, 'otherwise you're for the high jump, my lad!'

He meant what he said. Our first two lessons at school on a Monday morning were music. If I hadn't scored my 20 or over, he would ask some obscure musical question like 'Where did Mozart buy his underpants?' or 'What was Wagner's favourite f***in' pet?'

'You, English.'

Of course I hadn't got a f***in' clue.

'Come up here.'

Stacey gave me six of the best, muttering all the time, 'Keep your bat straight next week. No slogging over mid wicket!'

Beyond the hallowed acres of Hendon Park lay Whittaker's Sports Shop, situated on the corner of Hendon Central, opposite the Gaumont Cinema.

Every weekend, on the way to the Saturday morning pictures, I would stop and stare at this shrine to sport. Marvelling at the mighty range of football boots, signed by Johnny Haynes, and tennis rackets, I was always captivated by one particular treasure which stood gleaming in the middle of the shop window. The Gray Nicolls Superlite Five Star reinforced steel spring shock-absorbent handled cricket bat, 'signed and used by Ted Dexter', the Captain of England. There it stood proudly on a podium, rotating slowly under its own spotlight. This Excalibat cost £5, far beyond the dreams of a 16-year-old who received the princely sum of 2s 6d pocket money a week. Of course I had shown the bat to my dad on one of our trips. As a little boy my dad had taken me on a tram from the Embankment to the Kingsway. There we stepped down and walked to Slingsby's engineering shop, where I could stretch out and press my hand against a pad in the window, making a globe light up and turn slowly in the showroom. After that, he took me for an ice cream across the road.

This became a much-loved regular ritual, and I looked forward to our Saturday morning excursions with glee.

I still feel the same and think it particularly important that everyone works towards and looks forward to that 'ice cream' at the end of the day. Set yourself daily targets, however simple. A satisfied head sleeps well on the pillow. A sense of fulfilment and contentment, the ultimate Night Nurse.

Back to Saturday Morning Fever inside the Gaumont, Hendon. The lovely velvet amphitheatre was packed to the gills with escapees from the Monday to Friday incarceration of school.

As usual we had bought our Jamboree bags from the harassed confectioner next door. The contents of each bag consisted of a couple of sherbet flying saucers, a liquorice roll, a box of sweet cigarettes, a bag of aniseed balls and the ultimate prize, the dreaded 'Genghis Khan Mark One' catapult. I say 'dreaded' not by us but by Reginald Dixon, the cinema's resident organist. He would rise from the orchestra pit, playing 'Oh I do like to be beside the seaside' with incredible gusto; as Reggie reached his crescendo, he was met by wild whooping from the cinemagoers and a fearsome rain of aniseed balls propelled from their Mark One catapults. Hundreds of balls rained down on to the back of Reggie's bald head, prompting the seriously wounded keyboard wizard to descend *très rapido*, all stops blazing to the safety of his pit, screaming 'you 'orrible load of little bastards!'

Reggie, traumatised in his dressing room, would be replaced by a cleaner-than-clean shining MC character, who invited us on stage to perform miracles with our yoyos, such as Walking the Dog, Around the Moon, and the Full Monty. Finally we'd participate in the singing competition, having been invited to sing along to the record of our choice. We loved Saturday morning pictures. I always went with my special pal from school, Peter Mellor. There we would sit watching *Batman*, *Tales of Zorro*, *Flash Gordon* and *Woody Woodpecker* – that's all, Folks.

One morning, the bloke next to us set fire to Eddie Ezekiel Solomon's hair. Eddie, sitting in the front row, promptly leapt to his feet, his head in flames, howling. He ran around the auditorium met by whoops of derision and another thousand aniseed balls from the catapult brigade. The usherettes leapt on the human fireball and doused his flames with the cinema's extinguisher. For the next three months Eddie's constant companion was a woolly hat, his ardour for the Technicolor Dream seriously dampened.

The Beach Boys and the Motown bands brought us the beautiful people and the soft rock sounds of the Sixties from America's West Coast. Freedom of the spirit, unshackled pleasures, King's Road, and Biba's Boutique took us on magical trips of mellow yellow and sunshine supermen; love was in the air and it was free. A love affair can last for ten minutes, ten days or a lifetime. Making love is only the physical extension of loving thoughts and in the summer of 1962 I was ready! Although conversant in the art of five-knuckle shuffle appreciation, courtesy of the girls at Whitefields, I had never experienced the act of penetration.

Then my eyes fell on Christine Jenkins, a Welsh rarebit from Forres Gardens, Golders Green. It would be wrong to say our eyes met because although hers were deep and blue they didn't work very well. 'Christobelle', gorgeous with blonde straight hair, and always dressed in black chiffon, was terribly short-sighted. She also couldn't say her 'B's, so my nickname of 'Ingleby' became 'Ingledee'. A cross between Pattie Boyd in 'A Hard Day's Night' and Stevie Nicks from Fleetwood Mac, she was right up my street.

It was a case of falling for the girl of my best friend. She had been Peter Mellor's girl, but I had fallen head over heels for her and I had to tell him. A somewhat uncomfortable confrontation ensued, but you have to hold on to love because that feeling will never go away. Christine, wherever you are now, give me a call!

So I went to her house to take her out on a hot date. Her dad, a dapper Daffodil Cruncher from Swansea, loved his sport and talked to me enthusiastically about the 'Wizards of Wales' Rugby team. Mr and Mrs Jenkins went to the White City every Thursday to watch the dog racing. Christobelle and I planned to have a banquet the following Thursday. In our hearts we both knew it was crunch time . . . the golden path to Nirvana beckoned.

Thursday arrived. My beating heart took me to behind Christobelle's garage. I was wearing my black leather jacket, bell-bottoms and Cuban heels, and a vivid purple shirt. I was neither a mod nor a rocker, more a 'mocker'.

I waited and looked up at her bedroom window. There she was. 'Come on, Ingledee,' she cried. Swiftly I nipped around to the front door where she stood wearing her mother's baby doll nightie. I have never felt so aroused, a combination of nerves and adrenaline. Christobelle had prepared some sandwiches and grapes. We lay on the couch, Marilyn Monroe and her 'mocker'. It was like a Roman orgy. We kissed and I held her close before exploring the dark corridors to her soul. I had bought my first packet of Durex, and for an eternity I fumbled to pull the sheath on to my love pump. I wasn't sure which side should go on first, the dry or the lubricated. My darling was lying there on the couch ever so decadent, unaware of my technical hitch.

It was the first time for both of us. No sooner had I entered her, the mixture of emotion and desire drove my love juices home, lifting me to an unexplored land of milk and honey. Our foray into the unknown had only lasted a few seconds, and, with her Hampstead cavalier coming and going so fast, Christobelle was left to muse on just what was that all about?

Nevertheless, things got better. From that day on we practised in every position and in every place. Together the two virgins learned the way, crazy for each other and joined at the soul. It was Top of the Pops: – 'How Do You Do What You Do To Me?', 'I Like It', 'Try A Little Tenderness' and 'Love Me Do'.

At about this time another phoenix arose from the Raiders of Tintown. John Edward Cousins hailed from the west coast of Ireland, where as a youngster he had appeared in Sir David Lean's film Ryan's Daughter. From Hollywood to Cricklewood, the tousle-haired boy settled in with his parents before joining another institution of correction, St James's School at Burnt Oak.

Quickly, he had found his feet on the football field, learning his skills on the windswept wastes of Clitterhouse Park. The tenacious terrier in the tackle had caught the eye of Wilby, coach of Claremont United, later to become The Mighty Rapide FC. Already Currie, Beddell, Turpie & Co. starred for Claremont, and Johnny Cousins was soon installed at right back. On their day, Rapide could have beaten any amateur team in England. They were the pride of the Borough of Hendon.

I first met John at the Top Rank Suite in Golders Green. It was Saturday night, and he was celebrating another Rapide triumph along with his mates and his glamorous girlfriend, Dallas. Christobelle and I were strutting our stuff on the dance floor to Little Eva's 'Locomotion', much to the amusement of the Rapide lads. I had just got to the point of swinging Christobelle around my head when the Irishman and his girl joined me.

'Hello,' he said in a soft brogue. 'Mind if we join in? My name is Johnny.'

'Sure thing, pal!' I shouted above the din. 'So go, Johnny, go!' That night at the Top Rank with our girls we started a lifelong friendship, which has already lasted forty years – together, we have shared adventures throughout the world. 'Johnny Boy' still has the same youthful features as the day I met him. He tells me the secret of his eternal youth is to rub his face in the early morning dew and then to sink six pints of Guinness every night. Touch of the old Blarney if you ask me! But for Johnny it sure works.

Crazily in love with Christobelle, I was swept away in the boogie wonderland of the Sixties. Elvis sang 'Return to Sender', the Beatles pleaded 'Love Me Do'. Johnny Cousins, Peter Mellor, the lads and I used to go to Saturday night dances at University College London in Gower Street. There we could see Billy Fury for 5s and Lonnie Donegan followed by Joe Brown And His Bruvvers. Live music was in the air, no backing tracks, no miming. No Posh 'f***in'' Spice, just live music. The bands fascinated me. When things got too hot in the buttery we would slip away to the Gustav Tuck Lecture Theatre and make illicit love in the dark. Then the long road home clinging on for dear life in Peter's three-wheeler Reliant Robin. Perhaps a dodgy kebab in Camden Town on the way home, or a coffee in the all-night Jewish café down the Finchley Road, to chew the fat and put the world to rights.

Some Saturday nights me and the lads would meet at Golders Green Station. Over the road was the Refectory Club where once again for the price of 5s you could watch John Mayall And His Blues Breakers, or Chuck Berry, Little Richard and Jerry Lee Lewis from the USA. We danced and sweated till we dropped, except we never dropped because we were still 'Sweet Little Sixteen'. There were so many girls, we were spoilt for choice, and made no commitments. Swedish au pairs were our favourites – I remember them all with great fondness. Christina Anderson from Stockholm, blonde, all hot pants and clogs. Petronella from Helsinki, who smoked a pipe, washed her hair in urine (really!) and looked like a goddess. We always ended up with the Scandinavians because they were natural, loved to laugh and were always up for an adventure. They were so pretty. If they liked you, you were in – you didn't have to chat them up too much or spin them a line, they would tell you if it was on. Often enough, it was. The scented path all the way home.

Of course they 'went all the way' because it was natural and they wanted you. I still loved Christobelle but love was all around and we were on the road to discovery. Klooks Kleek in West Hampstead, the Witches Cauldron in Belsize Park, girls and more girls. Girls with pale Biba faces and dark lips, girls with long, long hair and reputations to be broken; we never stopped. The music, the innocence and feeling of supreme good will urged us all into a land of perfumed pleasure. I must have danced all night with a thousand girls, slinky, busty, short, fat, blonde, red heads, hippies, girls with diamonds in their ears, emeralds in their teeth, debs and dropouts . . . and I loved them all. The music took us on magic carpet rides.

I had learnt a little guitar and drums but never buckled down to the practice, too busy moving to the melodies. Others devoted their time to working at the music. Barry Gibb at the age of nine recorded some songs he had written on a cassette, and walked over the road to Col. Joye's house, to ask him to listen to them. The place was Surfers Paradise, Queensland, Australia. Col. Joye was the Australian Elvis Presley. He listened to Barry's songs and was intrigued at his gift to write those heartfelt hooks, harmonies and melodies. He contacted Fred Marks, Head of Festival Records, who immediately signed Barry, Robin and Maurice. Barry was nine, his brothers just six years old. Back in Ripley, Surrey, Eric Patrick Clapton, aged 12, was so fascinated by the American blues players, he'd practise diligently on his guitar for hours on end. A labour of love indeed. All these boys were born with music in their blood, pumping through their veins, day and night. Later in their lives their ability to write tunes like 'Too Much Heaven,' 'How Deep Is Your Love', 'Layla' and 'Wonderful Tonight' took the world by storm, filling body and soul with romance and blues-filled passion, creating musical 'leg openers' from Hendon to Helsinki – thank you lads!

We were dancing in the dark. Parliament Hill, Hampstead was a favourite location. Peter always wore a long Dr Who Scarf. He was handsome and looked like Jean Paul Belmondo. Me, I just relied on making them laugh and taking them on romantic rides to the star-filled skies.

School days were great. I was running Whitefields, keeping all the pots boiling while cooking with gas. I sailed through my six O-Levels with high grades, needless to say the Piscean way, all the arts, English Language, English Literature, Geography, History, French and Art . . . but Mathematics I failed three times, much to the chagrin of Mr Vincent. I just had a mental block with algebra, geometry and arithmetic . . . what good would logarithms, equations or Pythagoras' theorem be when I went to Oxford or Cambridge?

Then life took on a cruel twist.

You're only as good as the cards you're dealt and, boy, did I draw a bad hand. One day I looked out of my classroom window and saw Mr 'Baldy' Lewis canoodling with Miss Price the red-haired Biology mistress in the sands of the long jump pit. My impersonations of the staff were now finely honed, especially our illustrious head Mr Haley. I opened the window and boomed in my best Haley-like voice, 'Oy, Lewis Boyo, what are you up to?' The class was in hysterics. I continued my Haley full blast to the couple below but withdrew from the window when they looked up to see who was shouting. I had sat down just in time. The classroom door burst open and in walked Miss Crump from next door.

'Who made that hooting noise?' she demanded.

Nobody said a word. One by one she went around the class, each pupil declining to grass up the culprit. It was nearly my turn.

I stood to my feet and confessed. 'It was I, Miss Crump.'

'You, English? Come with me.' I was taken to Haley's study where she outlined my crime to the bemused Beak.

'Really, English? So you "do me", do you boy? Show me.'

So I did. It was surreal; my Haley to the real Haley. My first audition!

'Thank you, Miss Crump,' said the head dolefully, 'please leave us alone.' Haley closed the door and told me to sit down.

'Look, English, this saddens me because you were the one for me. You had the ability to put your foot in the door and unite all the factions in the play-ground. You have the rare gift to bring brothers to arms, to make the team work hard and to have fun. An example to the others, and, as such, I have no alternative but to take your badge away.'

Slowly I unfastened my cherished Head Boy's badge from my lapel and passed it to Mr Haley. I was defrocked.

'Now go, boy.' I turned for the door. 'And English . . . I quite enjoyed your impersonation. Not bad at all.'

Slowly and sadly, I returned home along Shirehall Park in a state of shock. When I arrived home, my mother opened the door. I walked past her, sat on the blue Formica table in the kitchen and told her everything. My head was bowed to the floor to avoid her gaze.

'David,' she said, 'one thing you must promise me. Do not tell your father. He must never know.'

A week later my mother was summoned to Mr Haley's study. I was made to wait outside his door. After an hour my mother came out, looked at me, smiled and left the school.

'Come in, English,' said Mr Haley, standing in precisely the same position I had first seen him on my first day of school three years earlier. Looking out of the window, hands firmly clenched behind his back, he spoke. 'I've decided to send you to Hendon County Grammar School. You will start there next term.' Mr Haley turned and shook my hand. 'Good luck, English.'

My mind was racing – I couldn't believe it. I was getting kicked *upwards* from Whitefield Secondary Modern School to the premier grammar school in the borough. Why? I never found out how Mr Haley and my mother had contrived their plan, but I was on my way to join the boffins at Hendon County Grammar School and their feared headmaster, Mr E.W. Maynard Potts.

I shook Mr Haley's hand. I remember there was a tear in both our eyes. I felt I had let him down badly. I turned and left his study. I was never to see him or Whitefields again.

Of course my dad was proud that I had got to Hendon County. He would never know the circumstances but he had always been there for me and he was proud.

I was still not 17 when my dad left us.

He just found it all too much. He had never fulfilled his promise but he had always done his best as a father and to me he was a great dad and I loved and admired him very much. It was very early one morning when I was awoken by the sound of someone in my bedroom. '*Ssssh!* Stinker it's me.' (My dad had always called me Stinker because as a baby in the Great West Middlesex Hospital, Isleworth, I had blown off a lot in my cot.) 'Listen, son, I'm off. I'll be in touch with you soon. Look after your mother. She's a good mum and she loves you, you know that. Take care of Annie; you're the man of the house now. I'll contact you soon.'

And with that my dad lifted himself on to the windowsill clutching a single suitcase, opened the window, and was gone.

From the stillness of my room I walked slowly to the kitchen. It was still dark and the moonlight streamed through the window, falling on to the blue Formica table. There in the middle lay the Gray Nicolls Superlite five-star reinforced steel spring shock-absorbent handled cricket bat with a little note.

To Stinker
I tried
Love Always
Dad xxxxx

Dad, wherever you are, I hope you found your silver lining.

LORDS AND LADIES

Easter came and crimson skies caught the yellow in the daffodil's eye. It was time to spring northwards to the frozen wastes of *Wuthering Heights* on our A-level Geography field trip. Overwhelmed with the exciting prospect of leave from academia we piled into our school bus (a 12-seater transit van) and made for the M1. Past the Blue Boar café and Milton Keynes, through Northampton and the Midlands with its Brummie burr and onwards to Yorkshire, proud land of the White Rose.

Packed into our transit van with our packed lunches we went potty with excitement. Me and Archdeacon and Geraldine Harris with the fulsome figure and captivating perfume. The fragrant flower of youth, full bodied and inviting. I marvelled at the breathtaking views of the valleys with their tapering chimneys and whole communities of terraced houses clinging on to hillsides. Hard graft and toil for a pint on Saturday after the match and a few bob put away for another rainy day.

We left the monotony of the M1 at Leeds to thread our way along the magical B19426421 with its higgledy-piggledy Yorkshire stonewalls. High across the moors through Airton and Gargrave, just our van of adventurers silhouetted against a star-filled sky.

2 LORDS AND LADIES

I am a strong believer that our destinies are determined by the cards we are dealt. The balance of life hangs by the luck of the game. And so there we stood in the kitchen. The depleted English family, mum, son, sis, the Gray Nicolls bat and the blue Formica table. On it, the cards lay face upwards. The King and Jack of Hearts were missing. My dad had legged it, just like my grandpa. We were a family of runners. Maybe Nike should have sponsored us.

My mother was not altogether surprised by my dad's exit. It certainly affected my little sister, whose gentle spirit required the security of a father figure. I now assumed that role and have done so ever since. How fragile life is. Every minute that ticks by is touch and go. This realisation came to me then and perhaps it's what drives me to help with the charities I work with – that we've all got so little time, really.

Hendon County Grammar School was not sheltered from the outside world, like Eton with its playing fields and Prince Harry of England. It was where the intelligentsia went to school, having earned their right to be educated by the best at no cost, just picked on merit.

In my class, the sixth form, was Geoffrey Tobias, now the world's number one brain surgeon, Stephen Solley, currently a High Court judge, Robert Earl, who went on to make millions with his Planet Hollywood restaurant chains, Grant Kriteman, a financial wizard, and Stephen 'Stodge' Kaye, a lovely 18 stone bloke with a lethal left foot and a heart of gold.

Once again I was quickly put on the right wing of the First X1 football team. Every Saturday morning we used to pile into Mickey Linn's massive Vauxhall and descend upon our pitch at Pursley Road to take on Orange Hill and the other elite grammar schools of the borough. One of Orange Hill's stars was a boy called Douglas Mark Arthur Strachan, half Jamaican, half English, who was quick as lightning. Our formidable back four of Johnny Garrard, Ken Sheringham, Dick 'Cobblers' Coldwell and Tommy Jones tried to close the wizard down but invariably he was too fast. Mark and I became firm friends; I introduced him to Mill Hill Village CC where he quickly excelled in the first eleven. He was a phenomenon, representing England Schools at athletics, cricket, soccer and table tennis. If that wasn't enough, the 'C.B. Fry of our times' became the youngest student to earn an exhibition place to St. Catherine's College, Oxford, at the age of 18. There he won a blue in athletics, along with another speed merchant, one Jeffrey Archer. Mark was the most gifted all-round sporting genius any of us had ever met, but all

I cared then was that Mark and I never stopped laughing together. An admirable foundation for adventures to come!

The Red Devils of Manchester United regard Old Trafford as their Theatre of Dreams – well, for me Lords Cricket Ground was, and always will be, Nirvana. Feel the desire building inside. Take this restless heart and let me contest my skills naked without the safety net of the coach's guiding hand. Sense the rhythm of my soul and let me loose on the Nursery End.

For 17 years I had learnt my cricketing skills in the playground, Hendon Park and Mill Hill Village's Pork Chop Hill. But in 1963 I saw Ted Dexter, Captain of Sussex and England, take the West Indies to the cleaners, scoring 85 imperiously with his Gray Nicolls Superlite five-star steel-springed bat. That was it for me. The quicker Wes Hall and Charlie Griffith bowled at Lord Ted, the harder he hit 'em, gloriously, all around the wicket with impeccable timing. There he stood, upright, elegant, unhelmeted, unshackled, Dexter of England, the Dominator.

Swept away by the euphoria I immediately approached Len Muncer, the MCC Head Coach, for a trial. I wanted to play at Lords and I wanted it bad. Len stuck me in the nets at the Nursery End and said, 'Right son, let's see what you're made of!'

I walked slowly to the end of the net and took my guard, ready to take on some of the best young bowlers in England, the young professionals of the MCC. I looked around and absorbed the atmosphere. Was this to be my second 11-Plus examination?

I have since grown up with these boys and I understand and love their ways. They are seriously good players. They can make the ball talk, nip backers, in duckers, outswingers, off the seam, googlies, offers, leggers and Chinamen, the full bowler's armoury. But I was fired up. Once again in the face of danger, I felt calm and fully focused. In they ran. I hooked and drove, glanced and swept, pulled and cut, determined to win. There was probably one delivery that really tested my mettle and decided my fate. I still wake up to this delivery in my dreams.

A tall Derbyshire lad let me have a very quick bouncer that reared up to my face. I instinctively rocked on to my back foot and hit it out of the net, clearing the Indoor Cricket School, a true carry of 90 yards. Of course my arse hit my ankles, and the butterflies flew around my stomach, but the secret was to play every ball on its merit, one missile after another.

After about 45 minutes of 'a right going over, and let him smell the leather', Len Muncer took me up the steps of the young pros room over groundsman Jim Fairbrother's garage.

I sat down still wearing my pads; my heart was leaping out of my chest. The young pros were getting changed with their backs to me, by their personal lockers.

'Right son, you hit the ball in the air too much, but to win without risk is to triumph without glory. Dave English, you're in, you've got yourself a summer contract,' announced a beaming Len Muncer. One by one, the young pros turned, cheered and shook my hand: 'Well played, Dave!'

So that summer of '63, I played for the MCC young pros on the Lords Ground Staff; my duties ranged from selling scorecards on match days, to bowling and batting to MCC Members in the nets. The pay was 3s 6d an hour. The collective team spirit was wonderful. The sacred harmony of the dressing room, exchanging ideas with team-mates who had arrived from Welshpool to Antigua to learn how to blend their individual skills for the benefit of the team, and the desire to win in the face of adversity. Ten years later a certain Ian Terrence Botham would arrive to join the staff and to stamp his swashbuckling style on to the Lords stage.

The golden summer of '63 soon passed through our hands. Sad September arrived and we all wished each other well as we left for our homes to all parts of the globe. We would miss the laughs, the pranks, the great cricket, but above all, the camaraderie. Unbeknown to me it would be 20 years before I returned to that small green square in NW8. An oasis to millions of Londoners. By then the corporate claws of the City had reduced the Nursery End, but on 16 September 1982 I strolled to the wicket to score my century and dislodge some of the tiles on Jim Fairbrother's roof, which I'm glad to say have never been replaced to this day. Of course my innings wasn't in Ted Dexter's class, but to score a hundred at Lords is still very special and remains proudly in my memory.

So for me it was back to Hendon County to pursue my A-Levels. But not before I had taken my mum through Hendon Park, past Whittakers Sports to Stead & Simpsons shoe shop. I knew she had set her heart on a pair of brown and white high-heeled buckskin brogues. I had saved my money from Lords and it gave me a special sparkle to buy them for her. I love to give and see the pleasure in the recipient's eye. . . I have always found it easier to give and be in control than to take and be beholden. And this was for my mum, and I loved her.

Days at Hendon County flew by. I fell in love with Jackie Bass, the blonde hockey captain. The perfect girl, a combination of sexy and sporty, a titillating tomboy. I immersed myself in my studies, stimulated by the brains and wit of my classmates. My sister Annie attended St. Joseph's Convent and my mum, wearing her new shoes, got a job as a beauty consultant with Elizabeth Arden. The rhythm of English life was in tune and our hearts were beating as one.

Easter came and crimson skies caught the yellow in the daffodil's eye. It was time to spring northwards to the frozen wastes of *Wuthering Heights* on our A-level Geography field trip. Overwhelmed with the exciting prospect of leave from academia we piled into our school bus (a 12-seater transit van) and made for the M1. Past the Blue Boar café and Milton Keynes, through Northampton and the Midlands with its Brummie burr and onwards to Yorkshire, proud land of the White Rose.

Packed into our transit van with our packed lunches we went potty with excitement. Me and Archdeacon and Geraldine Harris with the fulsome figure and captivating perfume. The fragrant flower of youth, full bodied and inviting. I marvelled at the breathtaking views of the valleys with their tapering chimneys and whole communities of terraced houses clinging on to hillsides. Hard graft and toil for a pint on Saturday after the match and a few bob put away for another rainy day.

We left the monotony of the M1 at Leeds to thread our way along the magical B19426421 with its higgledy-piggledy Yorkshire stonewalls. High across the moors through Airton and Gargrave, just our van of adventurers silhouetted against a star-filled sky.

It was approaching the midnight hour when we finally swept up the Gargoyle drive of Newfield Hall. The moonlight picked out the wrought iron gates, and the badger's smile. Tired and tousled we tumbled out of our van and straight into our sleeping bags in the Newfield dormitory. Journey's end and the wonderful welcome of sleep.

6 a.m. and the excitement of the early morning call. Off we marched across country to Malham Tarn and Gordale Scar to study limestone pavement with its Clints and Grykes. Our Geography master, 'pixie' Chappell (ears like Dr Spock) took the keen geographers to the hills. 'English, we'll meet you and your group back in the café at tea time,' ordered Mr Chappell.

So there we were, left to our own devices, me, Archdeacon, Ronnie Simmler, Peter Thomas, Grant Kriteman and Geraldine Harris: free as the wind under a cloudless sky.

After a sizzling bacon sandwich with HP Sauce, washed down by a large tea out of a giant beaker, we left the café, very relaxed, to amble upwards to the top of the scar. There, deep in the valley we could see the steam train chugging on its way from York to Settle. It was a halcyon spring day, as we lay on our backs looking up at the sky, touched by the warm caress of youth and the unbridled joy of just being away.

The lads sensed strongly that I was on a promise with Geraldine and, with a gesture of great charity, left us alone to our own devices.

'See you later, Dave, back at the café. Give her one for me,' whispered Kriteman. What a f***in' charmer he was.

So there we were alone, Geraldine and I consumed with the thrilling tingle of romance. I've never confused lust with love, for me it is one and the same. Every sinew, every fibre, every nerve in your body heightened by the sense of desire and the surging sensation of expectancy. Down in the valley the train disappeared, leaving flecks of white smoke and the sight of Giggleswick and its farming folk.

Standing on the crest of the scarp I took Geraldine in my arms and hugged her. Slowly we sank to our knees, kissing all the way. With moistening palms, I pulled up her sweater and explored her full white bosoms with large brown nipples. Filled with excitement, my hand went downwards and inwards, exploring the warmth of her womanhood. She in turn fumbled with my fly and took me to her and inside her. There we were, rolling and humping, thrusting and pumping, oblivious to the rest of the world. Then, as climax beckoned, I was aware of a movement behind a clump of grass. Slowly a pair of pixie ears appeared, worn by our f***in' Geography master. You could see his eyes watering behind his glasses in disbelief.

He couldn't believe it! Nor could I! Yorkshire, with its hundreds of miles of naturally rugged bleakness, and I had been caught red-handed, royally putting my Gryke into Geraldine's Clint. Still deep inside Geraldine, strangely I didn't stop. That calm feeling in the face of adversity returned. We had taken that trip to paradise together and as an officer and a gentleman I respected her virtues and wasn't about to abandon her now.

Needless to say, all hell was let loose. I was taken to Newfield Hall where Pixie Chappell phoned headmaster E.W. Maynard Potts back at HQ. My Geography adventure was curtailed and I was sent home in disgrace on the train.

'Bollocks!' I thought. I had enjoyed my short trip to Yorkshire. It had been Heathcliffe, Cathy, Billy Liar, Kes and D.H. Lawrence all rolled into a couple of days.

I went straight to school from Kings Cross Station. My mum was waiting for me in Potts' study. The old Beak with the hawk face and cloaked wingspan laid into me. Ever so eruditely he accused me of 'conduct extremely unbecoming etc.'.

'Scandalous, English! What have you got to say?'

'One of those things, sir. It just felt right at the time.' (*Perhaps you should try it, you f***in' old birdman*, I thought to myself.)

All this time my poor old mum sat there while I was berated by the Beak.

Trial concluded, sentence: a severe warning. Apparently the sports department gave Potts a glowing report on my cricketing abilities: 'couldn't afford to lose the school cricket captain.'

It was almost 1964 when God decided my life should end. The final innings, D.S. English bowled by the fickle finger of fate for 17. As usual I had dropped Jackie Bass off at Hendon Central Station and was running back to school along Queens Road. In the park, across the way a game of cricket was in progress. Without thinking, I darted out to cross the road and bang! I was flattened by a lorry driven by a West Indian gentleman called Ghose. End of life. End of story. Enter the Gates of Heaven to discover all these men with bonces like boiled eggs.

For when I came round I found myself sitting in bed facing rows and rows of blokes with baldheads. Welcome to the Neurosurgery Ward of the Whittington Hospital, Highgate – second innings – D.S. English fractured skull 0 not out.

I was now a full-blooded member of 'One Flew Over the Cuckoo's Nest'. Back at Hendon County some people, including E.W. Maynard Potts, had thought I had got run over on purpose in order to escape taking my A-Levels. Just imagine such cynicism. Anyway my tussle with Mr Ghose's lorry had terminated my education. Eight schools in all. For me it had been eight wonderful wonders of the world and now I was banged up in hospital. Bald and fractured but the spirit hadn't flown, it still burned inside, ready to take me into the wide, wild wacky world and beyond.

JE M'APPELLE DAVID ANGLAIS

There were large Moroccan-style cushions scattered about the floor. In the corner was a striking blond man, Gunther Sachs, stroking a panther in a diamante collar. 'Monsieur Bardot' was holding court, surrounded by all the bright young things, while next to him sat Brigitte, wearing a tight pair of leopard skin slacks and an angora sweater. She was barefoot and looked a little bored.

'Watch this, Pete!' I approached 'BB' and boldly went into my best O-Level French.

'*Excusez moi, Brigitte. Tu veux danser?*' She looked up at me and smiled.

'*Mais oui, monsieur. Tu es anglais?*'

'*Oui,*' I replied. '*Je m'appelle David Anglais.*'

I took Brigitte on to the floor and began to jive. Gunther hadn't noticed, he was far too busy stroking the panther and the egos of the 'It' people. 'BB' and I were getting on like a house on fire. She was so sexy, *avec les levres sensuelles*. I saw Peter in the shadows and gave him a surreptitious wink and thumbs up.

Living for the moment, I asked her outside. It was a beautiful starry Mediterranean night, the moon shining brightly and the warm breezes whispering through the masts of the tall ships in the harbour. Even Frank Sinatra was there, a crooner on a schooner.

I kissed her and held her close. Time stood still. What was next, a 'job de blow?'

3 JE M'APPELLE DAVID ANGLAIS

I had to escape the nest. Already I had given the doctors deep concern after making the boiled eggs laugh so much, their stitches had come undone. The last thing the hospital needed was a load of exploding Easter eggs so it was a case of 'Turn again, Whittington Hospital'.

Late one night I stood, dressing-gowned, in the dimly lit Victorian corridor, beneath the hot water pipes, and telephoned Mark Strachan.

'Mark, it's me, Dave. I've got to get out of here. Meet me at the Bull and Bush tomorrow morning at 6 a.m. Bring your passport. I'll explain later.'

The next call was to my mother. 'Pud,' (her nickname) 'I'm leaving hospital. I'm going away with Mark Strachan for a while. Are you and Annie alright?' My mum was concerned by my condition but realised that in my mind I was already on my way.

'Take care, David. We love you. Keep in touch.'

Early the following morning with clinical efficiency I slipped the medical noose and made for the Bull and Bush. As I was tiptoeing out of the ward, a soft voice stopped me in my tracks.

'Dave – over here.' It was my pal Danny Rogers. 'Good luck, son, wherever you're going. Send me a card. Thanks for the laughs.'

I shook Danny's hand and silently went on my way.

6 a.m. and there was a breathless hush down at the old Bull and Bush. Everything lay silent except for the old Express Dairy milk cart that wearily wended its way up the hill to the Whitestone pond and beyond.

Mark Strachan stood in the doorway of the pub looking somewhat bemused. 'What's this all about, Dave?'

'Mark, I had to get out of "the cuckoo's nest". Have you got your passport?'

'I have, but only with a visa for France.' Jamaica was no longer a member of the British Commonwealth, following independence; but this meant Mark needed a visa for every country he entered.

'We'll get round that somehow – right, we're off to Africa!' I announced.

So off we set, hardly Cecil Rhodes and Stanley Livingstone, just the boiled egg and the boffin. We hitchhiked through Blackheath and on to the A2, arriving in Dover to embark upon the lunchtime ferry.

Fair stood the wind for France. It was fantastic; to stand on the deck and to taste the salt in the air, to watch the gulls swooping in and out of the white caps, to experience the supreme feeling of escape, the breeze in our hair – Mark's, that is. For me, just the briny breath on a shaven head.

Disembarking at Calais, we made our way through customs and red tape, past the Gothic town hall, Le Place De La Ville, and on to the open road. Then plodding through northern France with its identical-looking villages, and boulevards once marched upon by the German Wehrmacht, and before that the legions from Rome. Nothing had changed, just those long poplar-lined roads with an occasional broken-down farmhouse bearing a poster of Yves Montand or Delaspaul Carambar or *La Vache qui Rit – Fromage de France*. We passed through Deauville and its Monsieur Hulot's Beach Huts before turning left into the interior.

By day we stopped at roadside cafés to watch Frenchmen in berets play table football, feverishly smoking Boyards Maize cigarettes and drinking Anis and Ricard. Pretty barmaids with red lips and olive skins served us crusty bread and boiled eggs in vinegar while we listened to the sounds of Richard Anthony's 'J'entends Siffler le Train', Johnny Hallyday's 'L'idole des Jeunes' and Françoise Hardy's 'Tous Les Garçons et les Filles de Mon Age'.

At night we stayed in towns with wonderful-sounding names, Poitiers, Angoulème, Tours and Bordeaux. We actually stayed in monasteries, telling the monks we were going to northern Africa to study in the mosques. The fact that Mark was an atheist made this story even more shameful. One night, while laying in bed, a crucifix fell from the wall above, landing on Mark's head and prompting him to leap up blaspheming in full voice. What the monks must have thought about 'the missionary's emission' I don't know, but I can tell you I had to make good the following morning at breakfast with our brothers in arms. The ecclesiastical fathers indeed stretched their arms for us right across France and Spain to Gibraltar. We knew that our first major hurdle would be to cross the Spanish border because of Mark's 'No Visa, No Entry' dilemma.

It was about 7 a.m. and the height of summer when fortune joined us on that dusty trail. Mark and I were standing on the route N10 just south of Bordeaux, a road which stretched the length of Les Landes coast to Bayonne and on to Spain. As we waited by the side of the pine forest we could see the massive Atlantic breakers crashing down on to the lonely beach. As far as the eye could see, just the mighty ocean and the shimmering sand and then . . .

I think it was I who first spotted the dot on the horizon. It grew closer, a mirage on wheels, a highly chromed smile, a large car hurtling towards us – in a flash it roared past. The pink Cadillac must have been doing 120 mph, all alone on that road to nowhere. I saw the driver quite clearly as he zoomed past us, windows open, his shirtsleeve flapping in the rush of air. Then, with a great sound of brakes locking and wheels screeching, the pink machine skidded to a halt. It reversed at high speed to where we were standing, ruck-sacks by our side, open-mouthed in amazement. As the last three things to pass us had been a tractor, a school bus and a herd of goats, the pink Cadillac did seem a shade incongruous. After all, this was the road to Bayonne, not the Route 66 across Arizona. The driver got out of the car; incredibly, he *was*

Johnny B Goode. Very good-looking, tall, blond haired with sideburns, shirt open-necked to the navel, tight jeans and cowboy boots.

'*Bonjour, mes amis. Vous allez où?*' asked the Adonis, with a gold-toothed smile.

'*Bonjour, monsieur. Nous sommes anglais*,' I replied politely.

'Ah! The Engleeeshmen. *C'est magnifique*. My name is Jean Lefèvre. People in these parts call me Johnny Cadillac – get in. I am going to Biarritz.'

Mark and I got into the pink panther and we were off. As Johnny told us his tale, he drove with one hand on the steering wheel. On his arm was a tattoo of a bleeding heart with a dagger through it and the word 'Sylvie'. He was a nightclub singer in Biarritz. He had learned his English by listening to the songs of Elvis Presley whom he resembled – a blond version of the King. The conversation was lively, with Mark and I trying out our best French, while Johnny 'C', a true showman, showed off his pigeon English. We told Johnny about Mark's visa problem.

'*Pas de problème, mes amis*,' smiled Johnny. 'I think we can have some fun here!'

Bayonne and the Spanish border beckoned. 'Just a little further down the road, the Spanish police will stop us. They will want to see your papers. Mark, I will put you in the boot. I am well known in these parts. Don't worry, *mon ami*, Johnny Cadillac will get you through!'

About five kilometres from the border, Johnny pulled over and stopped the car. 'Come, Mark, now is the time.' Into the boot climbed D.M.A Strachan. When we arrived at the frontier the Guardia Civile came out of their office.

'Hey Johnny – great show last Saturday. My wife is a big fan.'

Johnny Cadillac got out of the car to meet his fans, the police. They were more interested in talking to him about his singing than taking him through customs. After a while, they stamped the passports and we were off.

A little way down the road, Johnny stopped. We got Mark out of the boot. He had found it all rather exciting. Several hours later we reached San Sebastian, where it had begun to rain.

'*Mes amis*, the sky is crying, look at the tears rolling down the street. I must leave you here. You must make for Algeciras in the south. When you get there ask for Smokey Joe. Now go, God speed. For the eagle flies on Friday.' We clambered out of the Cadillac. Johnny got out and embraced us . . . and then gloom. With a swirl of dust and smell of burning rubber Johnny Cadillac had disappeared, a pink blur, red taillights punctuating the Spanish night.

It took us several days to cross the arid plains of Central Spain, skirting Madrid and dropping south through the Costa del Sol to the port of Algeciras. Across the water was Tangier and Africa.

It was Wednesday when we patrolled the docks looking for Smokey Joe. '*Ah señor*, you will find him over there on the waterfront.'

Wending our way along the quayside, stepping over coils of ropes and containers, we came across a café, steam coming from its windows. The red letter 'H' had fallen off the neon sign over the door – 'SMOKEY JOE'S EATING OUSE'; inside, sailors of every description lazed around eating massive fry-ups, playing pool and drinking beer.

'Where is Smokey Joe?' I enquired.

'Over there, *señor*,' and we turned to see, standing behind a huge pot of paella, this massive man, sleeves rolled up tattooed arms, unshaven.

'Smokey Joe?' I enquired.

'Who wants to know?' came the gruff reply.

'Johnny Cadillac sends his best wishes. Apparently the eagle flies on Friday,' said Mark.

Smokey's face tightened. His eyes narrowed, darting left and right like black peas. 'Come with me, *señores*,' he growled.

Smokey took us into a back room where we explained our story.

'Give me your passports, *señores*.'

This we duly did. He stamped the documents and returned them.

Friday morning Mark and I made our way to the ship that would take us to Tangier, confident in the knowledge that we had two genuine visas to get us into Africa. I say 'ship' with a certain reticence. The SS *Black Eagle* was a tramp steamer with the emphasis on the tramp. It flew with equal pride the Panama colours, and the captain's washing, strung from the funnel to the mast.

We went to the 'office of disembarkation' where we showed our passports to a surly authoritarian figure smoking a foul-smelling cigar. Talk about 'los property office,' this bloke was a real throwback from the Franco regime. A fan whirled above his head, keeping the flies off his bald patch. He studied the passports and then looked at us as though we were Basque terrorists.

'What ees this?' he enquired, screwing his eyes up for a closer look at our passports.

Mark and I studied the pages marked 'visa'. There were the stamps, clearly saying 'Come to Smokey Joe's Eating House, Algeciras'.

We stood there stunned; Smokey Joe the dirty dago had stitched us up. We were thrown into the street by two burly guards.

'Never mind, Marko,' I said to my pal. 'Out of every tragedy comes a victory; let's go and have a closer look at the SS *Black Eagle*.'

It was evening time down at the quayside. There was a flurry of activity as sailors were loading up the ship.

Then, the next moment was destiny. Earlier in my tale, I said you must have an eye for the chance. Well our chance came in the shape of a large basket marked 'Laundry SS. *Black Eagle*'. Quick as a flash, Mark and I climbed into the basket, and were unceremoniously loaded on to the ship.

Dreams of reaching Africa, Zanzibar and the markets of Marrakesh now lay among the sheets and pillow cases of a tramp steamer; it had hardly been our plan, but we reached Tangier and we had made it into Africa for £10.

Years later when I saw that episode of *Fawlty Towers* where Manuel was deposited into a laundry basket, I had a private laugh . . . maybe there was something about Spaniards in baskets!

In Tangier we ran to the beach; I remember all the women dressed from head to toe in black, bathing their children and doing their washing in the sea. All the poor people from the streets of Tangier, the ragamuffins and pickpockets trying to cleanse themselves in the Mediterranean like water babies.

I was beginning to feel ill. The hot sun beating down on my fractured head felt like a pebble crashing around the inside of a red-hot dustbin, sending me into a state of delirium. We had to get back. Like a scene from *Midnight Cowboy*, Mark took control and helped me. I remember lying in a room with whitewashed walls. There was a large pink porcelain jug in a bowl; the white-laced curtains billowed gently in the sea breeze. I felt weak and drifted off into a deep sleep. To this day, the dream sequence, which got us back to England, remains vivid and arresting.

We were literally brothers in arms. We returned to southern Spain working on a fishing trawler. We made our way to Italy, climbing the mountains to the Alpine towns of Ivrea and Aosta. Then we took a train to Brig in southern Switzerland. I sat in the compartment with Mark under a blanket and my rucksack. When the ticket collector arrived he looked suspiciously at '*les baggages*'. I knew we had been twigged. When the train rolled slowly over the border Mark and I leapt out of the window, rolling down the embankment and running over a cornfield. We slept in a church just outside Brig for the night. We were awoken in the morning, lying unshaven on the pews, much to the consternation of the churchgoers attending early morning communion.

From Switzerland to Belgium, where the police opened fire, shooting above our heads as Mark was found to be concealed in the back of a BMW. The driver, quite mad but resourceful, put his foot down and roared away from the checkpoint. I wonder what happened to him? Then France, up to Calais and back home, six weeks in all. I was 18 years old. Back bronzed and bald with a bump.

The *Daily Telegraph* actually printed the story of my accident and our adventure to Africa on £10. It was only a column but we had hit the papers!

Eighteen, Civvy Street, out of Africa, welcome to the real world! What would be my first job? Professional cricketer, comedian, actor? But these were avenues of pleasure, which I pursued every day. It didn't really occur to me that I could make a living out of what came naturally. Strange really; had I had the mentality and single-minded determination of a Barry Gibb, Ian Botham, Eric Clapton, Billy Connolly, Anthony Hopkins or Nigel Mansell, I would have been literally driven and focused on becoming very good at one career. In truth, I'm sure that their single gifts far surpassed mine. Most of us spend our lives trying to find out what we're best at – the search for excellence is an onerous task. When the career officers visit our schools they encourage us to be accountants, draughtsmen, bankers or surveyors, but if we followed that line of thinking, there would be no lead guitar players, England cricketers or conquerors of Everest. I suppose my aim at the age of 18 was to have a crack at everything – and everybody – I took a fancy to. To this day nothing has changed! So what should I do? My dad was in advertising selling space; so why not give the newspapers a go?

The first person I wrote to was Mr R.M.A. 'Mickey' Shields, Advertisement Director of Associated Newspapers, Northcliffe House, Bouverie Street, London EC4.

A letter returned bearing the insignia of the *Daily Mail*: 'Mr Shields will see you on Friday, September 14th 1964.' I tubed it to Charing Cross, strolled down the Strand, past the Law Courts before entering the fairytale world of Fleet Street.

Fleet Street, alive with the sounds of typewriters and reporters sweating on their deadlines, editorial, advertising, the smell of newsprint, putting together a chronicle of world news each day. Just think, all that work and today's newspaper would hold tomorrow's fish and chips. Wearing my first and only suit I turned right into Bouverie Street, past the *Daily Herald* and *News of the World;* the rhythm of machines, oiled and hungry, printing the broadsheets. Bouverie Street was a grand prix of bright yellow Dormobile vans bearing the names of *Evening News, Star* and *Standard.*

Left at the bottom into Tudor Street, Harmsworth House on the corner, home of the *Daily Sketch*, past the drivers loading up their vans to take the world's largest-selling evening papers to far off Romford and Gidea Park, Bushey and even Hove (a mighty circulation area for a London evening paper!): 1,200,000 copies of the *Evening News*, 600,000 *Evening Standard* daily sales. On the next corner, Tudor Street and Whitefriars Street, stood the highly polished portals of Northcliffe House, gates to the fabulous fortunes of the press barons Lord Northcliffe and Viscount Harmsworth.

I asked the commissionaire in his highly polished uniform where I could find Mr Shields.

'And your name, sir?'

'David English.'

'Ah! That's interesting,' said the commissionaire. 'We already have two David English's here – one is the foreign editor of the *Daily Mail* and the other is the head boilerman! Wait here, please, I'll tell Mr Shields's secretary you have arrived.'

He telephoned upstairs. 'Mr English, Mr Shields will see you now. Up the stairs, first office on the left.'

My heart was beating as I climbed the marble stairs, gripping the deep mahogany handrails. At the top of the stairs, I entered the advertising department of the *Daily Mail*. My feet sank in the deep pile of the lush maroon carpet. Men in pinstriped trousers suspended from red velvet braces barked their demands into telephones. Secretaries clattered away on typewriters behind glass-partitioned offices. And boys ran about clutching copy. I entered Mr Shields's office, where a very impressive man, distinguished, greying at the temples, well-dressed and wearing shiny black brogue shoes, was sitting behind a large oak desk.

'Now sit down, David, and tell me why you want to join Associated Newspapers.' I told Mickey Shields everything. When I had stopped he smiled.

'Yes, I read about your adventure in the *Daily Telegraph*, very interesting. Come here a minute.'

I walked around his desk and stood by his side.

'Now feel the back of my head.'

I did so. There was a hard back to it.

'That's a plate, they inserted it after I fractured my skull in an accident,' said Mr Shields. 'So, David, I know all about fractured skulls.'

He smiled and picked up the internal telephone. 'George, come over here, there's someone I want you to meet.'

George Cooper was tall and elegant, a real newspaperman through and through. He wore a pinstriped suit, blue shirt with a detachable white starch collar and a flamboyant red and white spotted silk tie.

'David, this is Mr George Cooper, the Classified Advertisement Director of Associated Newspapers. George, I want him to start Monday. The pay is eight pounds ten shillings a week. Good luck, David.' Mickey Shields shook my hand and sat down. Just think, putting our heads together had led to my second big break in six months!

I launched myself into the world of newspapers with great enthusiasm and energy. The fabric of Fleet Street was fascinating to behold. I started off flogging advertising space on the *Daily Sketch*; Ted Hawes, my manager, under the auspices of George Cooper, immediately put me on a bonus incentive scheme. Although my basic pay was £8 10s a week, if I sold 20 times this sum in advertising space I would receive a healthy cash bonus. We were all on this scheme, me and the other members of the *Daily Sketch* team; Lawrie Dunn, Gordon Collier, Keith De Groot, Clive Richardson, two ladies, Margaret and Maureen, Ted Hawes and his sexy secretary, June.

Incentives in life are great allies, competition is healthy. The more I sold, the more I made, and soon I was taking home £300 a month. I bought a highly polished British Racing Green Morgan sports car with a yellow grill and a brown leather belt around the bonnet – £325 of British sporting prowess. Along with Peter Mellor, and as many Swedish girls as we could fit in the 'cockpit', we conducted speed trials up and down Golders Green High Road. I wore a John Stephens of Carnaby Street brown velvet suit with bell-bottom trousers, shirts with button-down collars from Harry Fenton, and large floral kipper ties. My hair was long, life was brilliant, my mum and Annie were fine.

The power of selling was seductive; as long as you believe in the product, you can portray it in as colourful and charming a way as possible. I loved the *Daily Sketch*; we may have been the poor relation to the *Daily Mirror* and the *Herald* but I believed in it and thrived on the daily challenge of selling its advertising space. Yes, I could sell sand to the Arabs. So could the legendary Jack Reeves, Display Ad Director on the *Daily Mail*. Every afternoon at three o'clock he would sit in his office playing his trombone with great gusto. Earlier he might have accepted gold bars from Abyssinians who had come to pay for their front-page ads. No point in invoices and cheques, Jack would flog space for any denomination.

There was a wonderful selection of girls working in the Classified Ad Departments. I fell for one particularly lovely brown-eyed girl called Meriel Somerton. We used to meet and canoodle when the tea trolley came round, pushed by old Mavis.

I used the tea breaks to try out my repertoire of new jokes; I enjoyed holding court in the corridors. The managers and directors would even come out at the sound of my stand-up routines. 'Boofy', the Earl of Arran, particularly liked the risqué material, 'Marvellous, dear boy, quite incorrigible . . .'

My show business career was also flourishing, early morning, on the London Underground. Everyday I'd meet Johnny Cousins at Brent Station on the Northern Line. From Brent to Charing Cross, I would appear as the 'Great Orsini' from 'the Irresistible Novelty Company', performing my tricks, using whoopee cushions, disappearing silk handkerchiefs, doing impressions, and ending in a medley of greatest hits on the duck whistle. It was great to entertain the captive audience on the tube and try to brighten up those glum faces.

My first summer's holiday from work, 1965, and I returned to *La Belle France*, this time with Pete Mellor in my trusty blue VW Beetle 'Sid'. From Calais to the Côte d'Azur, it was all downhill, whizzing along National Highway Seven, borne on the Mistral, which blew us into St Tropez harbour.

The fishing port of St Tropez might have been the summer rendezvous of

Continental sophisticates but for Peter and me it was the perfect enclave to pull a couple of froggy birds. I was besotted with France and the French girls – they may not have been the most naturally beautiful but they knew how to make the very best of what they had. And then there was Brigitte Bardot, the most beautiful woman in the entire world and St Tropez's most famous resident. We discovered that she frequented the Voom Voom club. Set away from the harbour, up a cobbled street, the Voom Voom was the hottest spot in town.

At the door I told the concierge we were working for the *Daily Mail* in London, that we'd been sent to write a report on Europe's best nightlife, and the Voom Voom must be featured. '*Entrée messieurs, c'est mon plaisir,*' smiled the frog, waving us inside with a flamboyant gesture.

There were large Moroccan-style cushions scattered about the floor. In the corner was a striking blond man, Gunther Sachs, stroking a panther in a diamante collar. 'Monsieur Bardot' was holding court, surrounded by all the bright young things, while next to him sat Brigitte, wearing a tight pair of leopard skin slacks and an angora sweater. She was barefoot and looked a little bored.

'Watch this, Pete!' I approached 'BB' and boldly went into my best O-Level French.

'*Excusez moi, Brigitte. Tu veux danser?*' She looked up at me and smiled.

'*Mais oui, monsieur. Tu es anglais?*'

'*Oui,*' I replied. '*Je m'appelle David Anglais.*'

I took Brigitte on to the floor and began to jive. Gunther hadn't noticed, he was far too busy stroking the panther and the egos of the 'It' people. 'BB' and I were getting on like a house on fire. She was so sexy, *avec les levres sensuelles*. I saw Peter in the shadows and gave him a surreptitious wink and thumbs up.

Living for the moment, I asked her outside. It was a beautiful starry Mediterranean night, the moon shining brightly and the warm breezes whispering through the masts of the tall ships in the harbour. Even Frank Sinatra was there, a crooner on a schooner.

I kissed her and held her close. Time stood still. What was next, a 'job de blow?' '*Arrête, arrête,*' said Brigitte. '*Fais attention, c'est dangereux. Vas y! Vas y!. . .* you must go. I will meet you at the Madrague later.' She kissed me once more and was gone. There was a commotion at the door. Gunther had appeared with his entourage, and the panther.

'Over here!' It was Peter. 'Quick, Dave, get behind these dustbins.'

Together we watched the beautiful people disappear at great speed in their Ferraris and Lamborghinis. 'Blimey, Dave, that was a close one,' said Peter. 'Old Gunther was going loopy in there when he couldn't find his missis.' We clambered into Sid and made a rapid exit.

We never went to Brigitte's villa, 'La Madrague', and to this day I wonder what might have happened ... but at least we had lived our *liaison dangereux*.

Incidentally, the French for 'job de blow' is *pompier* which also means fireman. So on asking, you could either end up with her gums around your plums or a bloke carrying a hose clutching his helmet.

Thirty-five years later, I met David Ginola at a reception. I told him briefly about my encounter with Brigitte.

'*Tu fait l'amour?*' enquired the wing wizard.

'*Presque*, er, job de blow.'

'*Où, sur le plage?*' (Where, on the beach?)

'*Non Davide, sur les* dustbins.'

He pissed himself!

Two years passed and I had sold my heart out for the *Daily Sketch*. I loved the early morning ritual of badgering Bill in the executive garage for a space to park my Morgan. Then into Harmsworth House, first floor, along the corridor to my office. Open plan, linoleum floors, plywood furniture, fluorescent lighting, tea on tap, a battery of telephones and the air, thick with salesmen's spiel.

One day, Ted Hawes called me into his office. 'David, you're to be promoted, you will be the film rep on the London *Evening News*.'

I was rapidly dispatched over the road to Northcliffe House where Mickey Shields had first interviewed me. Mr Shields greeted me with a smile. 'I'm letting you loose on Wardour Street as our film man,' said Mickey. 'It is the highest grossing category on the paper and with your personality you can double its advertising revenue. I'll pay you £50 per week plus expenses and a free rein to conduct your business in your own irrepressible style!'

Sidney Torlot, the Display Advertisement Manager of the *Evening News*, called me into his office along with the former film rep, Peter Thomas. Together, they told me the key names of the publicity directors from each film company. It was 1966 and the cost of a full-page advertisement was £1,200 based on the rate of £20 per single column inch of space.

'A lot of advertising comes directly to us anyway. People buy the *Evening News* to see what's on in London. Your job is to get to know the film boys personally, see how they tick. You will be left to your own devices,' said Sidney.

Peter Thomas told me the favourite pubs of each film and agency man. Where to find them, when, their favourite tipple. It was an exciting adventure in prospect. Little did I know that the next five years would once again point my life in a different direction.

I would start my day on the breakfast run to 'Fabulous Franco's' restaurant for a farmhouse fry-up, and chat about last night's game between Inter Milan and Juventus. Then from a cappuccino to Al Pacino and the early morning vigil to Wardour Street and its Panavision Pictures and Technicolor dreams. To see Richard Harris holding court in the Intrepid Fox with its gilt-edged mirrors and endless flow of Guinness, that Dark Stranger. Into the Wellington, Al Shute of Warner Brothers and his gin and tonic circle of pals talking in circles and the deal by lunchtime. On to the Ship where Charlie Young and Tom Richards banged the gong for J. Arthur Rank, Charles with his white tache and detached dignity standing straight-backed and stiff-upper-lipped in his blue Crombie, and Tom who humped his secretaries over the bonnet of his shiny Jaguar with its wire wheels, leather upholstery and well-tested suspension. Dennis Michael was there; so was dapper David Kemp, to discuss full-page ads for the Carry On films and *The Railway Children*.

Donald Murray, Director of Columbia Pictures, along with 'Bobby' Bierman, preferred to discuss business at lunch at the Gay Hussar in Frith Street. I told them stories and gags and made them laugh. In return they gave me a large part of the *A Man For All Seasons* budget for the *Evening News*. Douglas Eames of Twentieth Century Fox did the same. So did Charles Berman, Director of Publicity at United Artists, for the James Bond films and *The Graduate*. Tony Love of UA and his ring of rogues would get the performance in the Cambridge, Mortimer Street, then down to the Blue Posts, tucked between the meat and two veg traders of Berwick Street to find Rafferty, Sid Beck and Bert Styles of UK Advertising. Then on to Leslie Pound, Director of Paramount, in his plush offices to sell him space for *Paint Your Wagon*.

Back to the Ship, with landlord Sid and his sallow complexion and wife Delilah, delicious and glittering, to have a brandy with George Skinner of Avco Embassy and Jack Elvin, The Blockmaker. Record pluggers on their way to Radio One mingled with roadies, swilling back pints before setting off for the evening's gig in the Marquee Club. In tune, Feel the Groove, Feel the Force, R&B, E.C., Santana, Mañana, Bacardi and lime, in time, smooth-skinned, Latino, Groovin' in a pink Cadillac . . .

I would have set out from Fleet Street by 10 a.m. By the time I returned, stumbling back through Soho, past the Elite Video Shop, girls in doorways, a Very Well Jeffrey Bernard and the Kingdom of Paul Raymond, it would be 5 p.m.

Every day was the same. I quickly got to know the Film Boys. I knew their haunts, what time they would be there, their favourite drinks. I was doing twenty performances a day. They loved the stories and in return they gave me their advertising. By the time I left the *Evening News* in 1971, I had increased the paper's film advertising revenue by over £1 million a year.

In the pubs and bars I was hailed as the new king of Fleet Street, having taken the crown from Jack Reeves, which was very flattering to behold. I had never met Jack but apparently we had the same penchant for camel coats and suede boots and possessed a similar gift of the gab, stimulated by a dexterity of imagination, humour and nimbleness of mind. I was constantly told that we were both 'larger than life'.

Twenty-nine years later, I returned to Fleet Street, another trip down memory lane.

Northcliffe House had been boarded up for seven years and was now about to be demolished. Just think, all that mahogany and memory reduced to rubble. But for me, the smell of newsprint, hot off the press on a hot summer's night, still hung in the air. Gone was the sound of Vincent Mulchrone and his *Daily Mail* cronies celebrating throughout the day in the back room of 'Aunties', where the champagne flowed from 11 a.m. right up till 'the Rag' had been put to bed, and then later into the night and the bleary walk home past Blackfriars and Ludgate Circus. No longer did Tudor Street flow with its galaxy of yellow vans and copyboys, mods on their vespas, ducking and diving, stopping off at Tubby Isaac's jellied eels shop at The Cut or for a swift half of lager down at the Elephant.

It's funny how tears are never far from the surface. There I was, the sad old bastard moving on my romantic wave of nostalgia. I entered the automatic doors of Harmsworth House, still in operation but now as a patents office. Ever so bland and clinical. No sign of a typewriter, just Dot Com and her sinister web. In the offices I saw people looking at blank screens, totally mesmerised. Enter Dot; exit the art of conversation, and to think I thought Laptop was a Norwegian hat! I approached the commissionaire in his ordinary uniform. No epaulettes with highly polished brass and white blancoed cord. Excitedly, I told him that this is where I had my first job, 36 years ago. 'Really,' he said, totally uninterested. I absorbed the surliness of this sixty-year-old prat standing in front of me and continued ever so cheerfully to patronise.

'Just think, thirty-six years ago you were probably still at school.' Without a flicker of humour he replied, 'You must be joking, mate. I've been f***in' married for 36 years. Now if you'll excuse me, I'm busy.'

So much for romance. I understand why old war heroes shine their medals and return to Flanders Field, clinging on to the past. Give me Shelley and Byron conjuring up magic lines over a bottle of wine or Renoir and the French Impressionists painting their canvas of life in the cafés beside the Seine – f*** Dot Com and her characterless money-making mentality on a momentum to nowhere. Build me a castle in the air where my thoughts can flow through the blue ink of a fountain pen on to parchment paper high above the e-mails, forms in triplicate and those blank screens.

DECCA'S DELIGHT

The combination of six salad sandwiches, eight chicken legs with Branston Pickle and a large dollop of Black Forest cake washed down with a bottle and a half of South Australian Chardonnay was about to take its toll, with volcanic proportions. My bottom wanted to explode.

In a state of controlled panic, I tried to listen to Sir Edward going on about the long-lost merits of Compton's batting. With a bit of luck, I could open my cheeks and slowly let out a long silent fart – cast my fate to the wind, so to speak.

Alas, all hell let loose in my nether regions as the fart turned into a landslide of solids roaring out of my arse.

I coughed loudly to try and hide the explosion which was clearly audible on the other side of the room, even making record-plugger Don Dive's hairpiece visibly tremble. Worse was to follow. As I stood in front of the Chairman in my grey and white pinstriped Lord John suit, I could feel a hot and spicy sensation fill up my underpants and start to trickle down my leg.

I had shit myself good and proper in front of the First Lord of the Recording Industry.

Fortunately, the fluctuation had occurred during a particularly noisy passage of Mick Jagger singing 'I Can't Get No Satisfaction' blaring out of our office sound system, so Sir Edward was oblivious to my rumble in the jungle.

4 DECCA'S DELIGHT

I've always known, even at the time, that I was extremely lucky to be operating during the Sixties, an age of innocence laced with a delightful decadence.

From a moment of inspiration when Mary Quant, the Pop Art Queen of Kensington, had designed the miniskirt, skinny girls in minis and patent leather knee high boots were whisked along the Kings Road in open-topped E-Type Jags past boutiques bearing the names of Biba and Granny Takes a Trip.

Beyond World's End you could hear the roar of the crowd as Peter Osgood and his artisans took on the might of Manchester United behind the closed doors of a sold-out Stamford Bridge. Osgood to Cooke, out to Houseman, back to Hutchinson, to Hudson . . . he's lost it . . . and there, inside his own half is Georgie Best, the Fred Astaire of football. Dancing past Ron 'Chopper' Harris, thrilling us with his trickery and twinkling feet, doing an Irish jig, long hair with flair, that's our Georgie! Ouch! Chopper's tried to kick him into the stands . . . Thank gawd, Georgie's back on his feet, putting on his top hat, red tie and tails, smiling and waving to the crowd who adore his every shimmy and swerve.

We were consumed with a sense of love and good feeling. The advent of the birth pill, meaning love could be made without the fear of bringing little sprogs into the world, opened up legs and all sorts of possibilities. True, you could catch NSU, which up till then we'd thought was a motorbike. But unsociable diseases were not going to stop the exhilarating art of horizontal jogging.

In this paradise of youth bursting forth, I had my own seven-year itch. I wanted to leave Fleet Street. But to what? Once again the natural progression to acting and comedy was brushed aside. Too busy acting in real life.

Then one evening at the Royal Albert Hall, I met Mike O'Mahoney, the Press Officer of CBS Records. We were watching Creedence Clearwater Revival, dressed in our velvet suits. During the interval I told Mike I was looking to move on.

'Dave, Decca are looking for a Press Officer. Why not try them?'

I phoned the Head of PR at Decca first thing the next morning. I was told that Sir Edward Lewis, the Chairman, was currently interviewing potential candidates. There had been over 2,000 applications. I knew through my cricket connections that Sir Edward was a keen follower of the game. That's all it took. I phoned his secretary on the Wednesday. He saw me on the Thursday and I was offered the job on the Friday.

High above the Thames in his office on the Albert Embankment, Sir Edward talked to me about cricket, the Rolling Stones, Mantovani, Tom Jones and many more of his recording artists.

'Ah! The Rolling Stones, naughty lads, that Mick and Keith, what can I do with them?' sighed Sir Edward with a large grin.

He showed me some album artwork that Mick Jagger had sent him: *Beggar's Banquet*, featuring Sir Edward, the Chairman, sitting on the toilet.

Sir Edward told me that EMI had turned down the Rolling Stones and Decca had snubbed The Beatles. Years later, George Harrison told me that after auditioning for Decca in 1961, the band had heard nothing for ages. Their manager, Brian Epstein, kept calling and harassing Tony Meehan, the former Shadows drummer, who had become an A&R (artist and repertoire) man for Decca.

'Do you like the band, Mr Meehan? Have we got a job or not?' enquired Epstein.

'Sorry, I can't help you, Mr Epstein, now if you'll excuse me, I'm a busy man,' came the reply. Head of Decca Records, Dick Rowe, signed Brian Poole and the Tremeloes instead. 'Guitar groups are on their way out, Mr Epstein,' predicted Dick Rowe.

Five hundred million albums and 27 Number 1 records later, The Beatles had reached more people of more nationalities with their music than any other band in history. In fact most of the really good popular music thirty years later has been pinched from The Beatles. Most of the good licks and riffs, ideas and titles have been derived from the Fab Four. Just listen to Oasis for a start.

'Dick Rowe must be kicking himself,' said Paul McCartney a few years later. 'I hope he kicks himself to death,' said John Lennon.

The Beatles themselves had kicked down all the doors and barriers playing their own brand of blues and R&B. Honed in Liverpool's Cavern and the Star Club in Hamburg they had become real trendsetters. Up till then all there had been were acts like Roy Orbison and The Shadows, before that Bill Haley, Guy Mitchell and the great Elvis Presley. The Beatles wore black turtleneck sweaters under smart collarless suits. Anello & Davide in the Charing Cross Road made their boots. The Hollies from Manchester followed their example of including a harmonica in the band. Then there was Freddy & The Dreamers, and the Swinging Blue Jeans with 'Hippy Hippy Shake'.

Lennon and McCartney wrote wonderful little four-minute stories. So vivid, so tuneful. In the words of Barry Gibb, they were *Technicolor Dreams*. Their lyrics made us sit up and think. The nation used to wait with baited breath for the new Beatles single. Would it be a fast one or a slow one? A 'Paperback Writer' or a 'Yesterday'?

But I had inherited the Rolling Stones. A spectacular rock 'n' roll circus; warm-hearted, quick-fire gags, endless chicks and no sleep. The thing about the Stones was that they were very visual, and the quality of their music was mind-blowing. So accomplished, they could play in small clubs as easily as in a big stadium. As they entertained the crazies in some Blonde Ambition lounge, I would conduct my business more sedately from the offices of Number 18 Great Marlborough Street, where I had a secretary and a staff of 15. We were situated next to the Magistrates Court where many a pop star capitulated to the ravages of fortune. Further on was the London Palladium, home of variety, Frankie Vaughan, Tommy Steele, Ken Dodd and Morecambe and Wise, all treading the boards, enthralling the coachloads of punters who streamed in on a perfumed wave from Woking and Ribblesdale.

The Beatles had ruled the North from their Cavern. London and the South East had their own music scene and ten years earlier rock bands had taken over the trad jazz clubs. But at that time they were called rhythm and blues bands: you could not call it a rock band if you were going to play in a traditional jazz club, it was a kind of musical snobbery.

Strongly influenced by the Chicago blues and the music of Muddy Waters, Jimmy Reed and Chuck Berry, the Stones had originally had a residency at the Crawdaddy Club, which was in fact Richmond Station Hotel. They then went on to Kingston and Eel Pie Island and eventually hit the West End scene playing in the Marquee Club.

Any child of the Sixties and early Seventies will tell you that if they went to a party and there wasn't a Beatles and a Rolling Stones album you might as well go straight home.

The rhythm of life at Decca was different, more personalised than Fleet Street. I was responsible for all Decca's recording artists who performed on our many different labels.

For example, Dionne Warwick was on the London label; Neil Diamond on MCA; Al Green on Hi; The Marmalade with Decca and the Moody Blues on their own label, Threshold, for which they produced and released one album a year. Gordon Mills had discovered his three artists, Tom Jones, Engelbert Humperdinck and Gilbert O'Sullivan, and managed and recorded them on Gordon's MAM label. Different labels, all distributed under the Decca umbrella.

I became good friends with Tom Jones. Every time I went to his hotel, even early in the morning, he always appeared in his suite wearing a white dressing gown, holding a glass of champagne and smoking a big cigar.

Gilbert's real name was Ray. He came from Swindon and Engelbert was actually Gerry Dorsey from Lancashire.

I enjoyed working with the American artists. Neil Diamond, totally professional, a master performer. Dionne Warwick, the same; and then there was Al Green.

One night, the famous R&B musician (writer) producer Willie Mitchell was in Texas on a scouting mission for Hi Records and caught a live gig by Al. Willie persuaded him to move to Memphis and sign for the Hi label. Following in the footsteps of the great Otis Redding, Al recorded in a variety of styles from gospel-inflected blues to deep soul ballads, based on a Baptist choir heritage. In the summer of 1971 Al returned to his gospel roots with the stunning, spine-tingling 'Tired Of Being Alone'. Released on Hi, distributed on our Decca label, the record went to Number 1 worldwide.

We arranged a big concert at London's Rainbow Theatre, plus *Top of the Pops* and the usual promotional TV appearances.

I went to meet the Love Man Supreme at Heathrow Airport. When he appeared he was wearing a full-length Technicolor leather coat holding an ivory-topped cane. The high-priest of Southern Soul swept through the 'Al Green' area of customs, charming everybody with 'It's my pleasure'. 'Nice to meet you, Al,' I greeted him with a warm handshake which quickly turned into a deeply searching soulful hug.

'It's my pleasure, Dave, now what's happening?'

'Well, I'll get you settled into your hotel and then how about some lunch?'

Midday in Bond Street, I took Al for a stroll. Dressed in even more extravagant clothes, he brought London's traffic to a halt. We had lunch in the Old Vienna restaurant, where autograph hunters engulfed Al.

'It's my pleasure,' beamed Al; and with an exotic flourish he suddenly stood on the table, gingerly moving between the freshly served sea bass and spinach, and sung the complete version of his world Number 1, 'Tired Of Being Alone', much to the open-mouthed astonishment and delight of the diners.

Singing, unaccompanied, is the true test of any vocalist. Frank Sinatra was famous for it, singing to the girl croupiers in the Vegas casinos in the early hours. So are the Bee Gees and the Beach Boys. Al's impromptu a cappella performances in public places became legendary. He would sing in shops, down Oxford Street, patting girls' bottoms as he went. Any excuse to perform his sexually enhanced lyrics.

We became firm friends. Every time he visited Britain he would come and see my mum in her small but cosy West Hampstead flat. He loved to sing to her; there we were, just me, my mum, Benny the Yorkshire terrier, three ducks on the wall and Al Green. Believe me, if he had been accompanied by the entire choir of the Church of Memphis full Gospel Tabernacle he couldn't have sung with more feeling. Try a little tenderness was always Al's way.

Mind you, he once nearly came a cropper. His next release was 'Let's Stay Together', which once again rocketed up the US R&B Billboard Chart, hitting the UK Top Ten in February 1972. Over came Al to promote the single. It all looked so warm and smooth when it appeared on *Top of the Pops*. I arranged for a BBC film crew to follow amiable Al wandering along Regent Street, awhistlin' and a-smilin', with the local girls responding well to the strains of 'Let's Stay Together'.

So I told Al, 'There's a couple of girls with the right shaped backsides, just pat 'em, smile a bit – they'll know who you are.'

Al said his thousandth 'It's my pleasure' of the day and patted. One of the girls turned, glared, glowered and yelped, 'Eee, just 'oo do yer fink you are?', which was unintelligible to the amiable Al. Worse was to come. A passing taxi-driver, noting the apparent familiarity of the visiting star, roared: 'Why don't you push off back to Pakistan, you black layabout!'

This too was unintelligible to Al, though the driver's face was explicit enough.

'What did that gentleman say?' asked Al.

'Er, um . . . well, he said that you can't park here, Al,' I said.

'My pleasure, sir,' said Al.

Later, when I left Decca I lost touch with Al. But in 1974, tragedy befell my soul-mate. A former girlfriend, Mary Woodson, totally obsessed by Al, had burst into his apartment while he was taking a bath. After throwing a pan full of boiling grits down his back she shot herself dead with his gun. The effect on Al was shattering. The pull he had always felt between his music and the gospel intensified and he was drawn further back into the sacred fold, eventually taking over the church in Memphis where he became minister.

To this day he can be heard preaching the word – that is when he's not making a guest appearance on *Ally McBeal,* or on the road, sharing his gentle romantic conversations with us and seducing us in an entirely winning way.

How great a singer was and still is Al Green? Well, I say his name is right up there alongside the other soul greats such as Sam Cooke, Otis Redding, Smokey Robinson and Marvin Gaye. His is a sermon of love. Just listen to his extraordinary reading of the Bee Gees' 'How Can You Mend A Broken Heart?'. So tender, wistful and, one feels, autobiographical.

Life at Decca was busy and successful and I came to the notice of the Chairman, Sir Edward, who sent over a memo. 'The improvement of your Department has exceeded beyond our most optimistic expectations . . . the record side of the business remains our largest single profit earner – congratulations, keep it going!'

The Moody Blues albums were selling over a million copies per album. Tom, Engelbert and Gilbert were singing their hearts out, swelling the coffers, and the Rolling Stones were and still are the best live rock 'n' roll band in the world.

Directly opposite our offices stood the valley of snappy dressers, Carnaby Street. The silks, velvets and incense of the Sixties had been replaced slowly by flash-fitting suits, floral shirts with big collars and towering stack-heeled shoes. Lord John Stephen presided over this peacock's parade. Lord John, Irvine Sellers, Take Six, Harry Fenton and Toppers shoes sold their wares via the silver tongues of salesmen from Barking and Hoxton. Pop stars converged on 'the Street' to have their stage clothes made to measure. The buzz and excitement of rock 'n' roll's outrageous glitterati would heighten as the gleaming white Rolls-Royce convertible purred past the pavements of precocious pleasure.

Afghan dog in the back, radiant wife by his side, the King of Carnaby Street was paying his courtiers a visit. Even the tick-a-tape parades on Wall Street could not surpass these moments of pop majesty.

The King? His name was Barry Alan Crompton Gibb.

The Bee Gees had arrived after The Beatles, landing in England from Australia in 1966. Already their songwriting talents were being compared to Lennon and McCartney.

My first personal encounter happened on a late afternoon in 1971. There was a bit of a commotion in the street below. I nipped downstairs to find Barry and his wife Linda standing next to a Rover Saloon. 'What happened here?' I enquired.

'I'm not sure,' said Barry. 'It could be the battery.'

'Let me see what I can do. By the way, my name is David English.'

'Barry Gibb, nice to meet you,' came the exchange. Hands were shaken, banter and laughter ensued. The battery was forgotten.

Little did we know what adventures had just begun!

My job description had become broadened under the leadership of Head of Promotions, Don Wardell. I was responsible not only for the Press and PR of Decca, but also given a free reign to work with the artists in all aspects, recording, touring and management.

I loved my job, music moved me to special heights and I revelled in promoting the talents of the talented, very often for 24 hours a day. I worked closely with the Rolling Stones, the Moody Blues and The Marmalade, especially in the recording studio. I learned how they wrote their songs, the tricks that made a hit record, the chord changes, bridges and harmonies, the little flaws in the vocals, what would touch a nerve and send millions into the shops to buy their records. I got to know all the top producers and the programme directors at the BBC and Radio Luxembourg, and what they looked for in a hit record. I'd learn how they chose records for the crucial Radio One playlists, where the DJs' producers would sit down every Monday morning to decide which records would be played throughout the week. If the pluggers couldn't get your record on that list, you were doomed.

I studied the industry throughout, saw how it worked, and understood how hits were made, the importance of presentation, the movers and shakers. Believe me, from the start to the finish, from the idea for a song to the record racks of HMV, or from the cradle to *Top of the Pops* was a long and tricky journey. A fascinating and exhilarating adventure, full of devilry and wheeler-dealing, which could lead you to the podium of the Brit Awards, or abandon you, in despair, upside-down in the Speakeasy Club in Margaret Street at 3.05 a.m. looking for the new Jimi Hendrix. But above all it was fun!

Decca's records continued to soar. The Rolling Stones' 'Tumbling Dice', the Moody Blues' 'Isn't Life Strange', 'Radancer' by The Marmalade, the 1972 reissue of The Chiffons' 1966 hit 'Sweet Talking Guy', 'Oh Girl' by The Chilites and Gilbert O'Sullivan's 'Himself' were all well up the charts.

It was June 1972. High above the Thames in his executive office, Sir Edward, our Chairman, was delighted, and told Don Wardell when he called him on the phone. 'Donald, I want you to put on a party to congratulate your Department. Make it next Wednesday at 7 p.m. I'll be there. I will announce great results for the first six months of this year. Marvellous stuff, keep it going.'

My love stakes were booming as well. I had met Miss World, Eva Rueber-Staier in the street below, and we'd clicked immediately. After whipping her up to my office for a quick aperitif, I arranged to take her to see Neil Diamond at the Royal Albert Hall the following Saturday. I will always remember my first date with Eva for the amount of chocolate and sweets she consumed. By the time Neil had launched himself into a rousing rendition of Cracklin' Rosie, Miss World was tucking into her fourth Crunchie bar.

'What about your figure, Eva?' I enquired.

'Bugger the figure,' she said in her strong Austrian accent, 'just pass me the Maltesers!'

Our party with the Chairman was a heady night; a mix of background music and a wonderful buffet of scampi in the basket, chicken legs and all those other Seventies delicacies, stretched out on an endless trestle table, lovingly prepared by Sir Edward's personal caterers.

Back-slapping, beaming and brown-nosing were in full cry. We all had our special moment with the Chairman, 'an audience with Sir Edward', who met us with an engaging smile, fuelled by the knowledge of record profits and our promotional success.

'Congratulations, David, you've done a fine job,' enthused the Guvnor. 'Now tell me what's the latest score from Lords.' It was then that my tummy started to rumble. I could feel the gases building up inside. The combination of six salad sandwiches, eight chicken legs with Branston Pickle and a large dollop of Black Forest cake washed down with a bottle and a half of South Australian Chardonnay was about to take its toll, with volcanic proportions. My bottom wanted to explode.

In a state of controlled panic, I tried to listen to Sir Edward going on about the long-lost merits of Compton's batting. With a bit of luck, I could open my cheeks and slowly let out a long silent fart – cast my fate to the wind, so to speak.

Alas, all hell let loose in my nether regions as the fart turned into a land-slide of solids roaring out of my arse.

I coughed loudly to try and hide the explosion which was clearly audible on the other side of the room, even making record-plugger Don Dive's hair-piece visibly tremble. Worse was to follow. As I stood in front of the Chairman in my grey and white pinstriped Lord John suit, I could feel a hot and spicy sensation fill up my underpants and start to trickle down my leg.

I had shit myself good and proper in front of the First Lord of the Recording Industry.

Fortunately, the fluctuation had occurred during a particularly noisy passage of Mick Jagger singing 'I Can't Get No Satisfaction' blaring out of our office sound system, so Sir Edward was oblivious to my rumble in the jungle.

'Did you ever see Edrich actually sweep Miller over the Mound Stand?' he continued. By now the aroma was particularly pungent. Sir Edward actually stopped and looked at the bottom of his shoe.

'Phew,' said Don Wardell, standing close by. 'What is that!' With great restraint, I politely excused myself from the presence of my boss and gingerly backed away from the partygoers, cheeks firmly clenched, into the toilet outside on the landing. With great difficulty, I removed my brown Y-fronts, opened the window in the loo and lobbed them out into the undeserving night.

When I finally left the building three traffic wardens had actually cordoned off the part of infected pavement from the public who were queuing up to see Tommy Cooper at the London Palladium.

ALL THE PRESIDENT'S MEN

Chaos ensued. Burly bouncers appeared from every angle to apprehend the 'Golden Rainmaker'. The stripper was jumping up and down like a dervish and when the curtains were pulled back, Dicky Sims was rogering Miss Denmark, giving her a huge portion of his pink trombone.

All hell let loose. A full-blown punch up was quickly followed by Eric Clapton and his band in various stages of undress fleeing for the waiting limos.

'Arfur, you better go back for Carl, he's still strapped down in the dungeon of love!'

Eddie had started a real tremor in Europe with his Earth Quakes. The boy was back in fine form and continued to devastate audiences in Warsaw, Amsterdam, Paris, Milan and beyond to Madrid. I kept leaving and joining the tour as it blazed a trail across Europe, while Eric revelled in high jinx, masterminding pranks and practical jokes on and off the stage.

5 ALL THE PRESIDENT'S MEN

The summer of '72 slipped by. I was 25. I had Miss World on my arm, Decca were top of the charts; *The Virginian, Sgt. Bilko* and *Happy Days* filled our screens. My mum and I had moved to Golders Green, where we lived in an airy top floor flat above a rabbi and his family.

Alas, my sister had followed in my father's footsteps and fled the coop. She had struck up a friendship with the boy next door, who was a shirt salesman at Take Six in the West End; he had promised her sunshine, happiness and a new start beyond the bagels and buses of Golders Green.

One Saturday morning, Anne Elizabeth had told my mum she was off to the launderette to do the weekly wash. She never returned. Six weeks later we received a postcard from Fiji. She had legged it good and proper with the shirt salesman. An open-necked escape of daring and cunning. Too young to be buttoned down. Hot under the collar, in pursuit, were Interpol and the police in Asia.

My mum was distraught. Her marriage had failed, and now her daughter had done a runner. After my father's exit, she had probably over-possessed Annie a little, just the deep love of a mother for her daughter. We had been a close threesome, there being nothing quite like the bonding of a family. Encouraging each other at breakfast, then tackling the day as individuals, safe in the knowledge that you can return to the warmth of the home and be together in your own special world.

We were a great team: I contributed to the housekeeping from my Decca salary, Annie was about to take her A-Levels at my old seat of learning, Hendon County Grammar School, and mum, who suffered terribly from varicose veins, went to work in all weathers as a beauty consultant for Elizabeth Arden.

But now it was just the two of us, plus Benny the Yorkshire terrier.

Things were to change again some months later. Approaching Christmas time, I was on my way to the office, 8.30 a.m., a ham roll from the café, and then a swift exchange of the latest gags with my pal Tony, the news vendor on the corner. 'West Ham Tony', sharp in his full-length leather coat and Doc Martens boots, had the ability to listen to gags and tell me about Bobby Moore's 'blinding game against Spurs' while flogging his papers at a rapid rate. What a pro! While we chatted, his eyes never left mine. Moving his weight from one foot to the other to keep warm. Both his hands working in a blur, the left palm outstretched, he could tell if it was the right money by the feel of the coins while the right hand folded and delivered the punter's daily rag. If you want to know what's on in London, speak to a newspaper seller or a London taxi driver. That's what I learned in business.

When I arrived in my office, my secretary had a message for me. 'David, Gini Smythe, Robert Stigwood's secretary called you – she wants you to phone her back.'

'Hello, Gini. This is David English.'

'Hi, David, Robert would like to see you.'

'When?'

'As soon as possible.'

'How about lunchtime?'

'Fine.'

67 Brook Street stood elegantly in a row of gleaming white Edwardian buildings. On the door was a shiny brass plate: 'The Robert Stigwood Organisation'. I entered the portals of the man who was a legend in show business. Already, he managed the Bee Gees, Eric Clapton, Tim Rice, Andrew Lloyd Webber, writers Johnny Speight, Galton and Simpson, actors Frankie Howard and Derek Jacobi. His productions of *Hair* and *Jesus Christ Superstar* had been major successes, both in England and on Broadway. Robert had been Brian Epstein's partner at NEMS. When Brian had died, The Beatles went on to form Apple and Robert took the Bee Gees and Eric Clapton to set up RSO. His organisation covered all the facets of show business. Music, TV, film, theatre, publishing, artist management and agency and record production.

He was known to be a visionary with exceptional intuition for a hit. Above all he gave the young a chance to fulfil their talents in the business, riding a fine line between the controversial (*Jesus Christ Superstar, Oh! Calcutta, Hair, The Dirtiest Show in Town, Till Death Do Us Part* and *Up the Chastity Belt*) and the more conventional and brilliant household favourites of *Hancock's Half Hour* and *Steptoe and Son*.

He loved to surround himself with young, vibrant, radical and restless talent and would take enormous risks on their behalf to promote their energy and their hunger to succeed. If Robert Stigwood believed in you, you really were on to a winner – from the wilderness, to a big star of stage and screen.

'Go straight up,' said the immaculately turned out commissionaire.

From the hall to the golden discs lining the stairway, the place was heavy with the trappings of success.

Gini Smythe, a lovely looker, met me with a warm smile. 'Go straight in David, Robert is expecting you.'

From that moment my life was to take a massive step upwards.

The room was long, softly lit, heavily carpeted, tastefully decorated. Pride of place was given to a large oil painting of Ray Galton and Alan Simpson over the John Adam fireplace. Later I was to learn that while writing *Hancock* and *Steptoe and Son*, Ray and Alan would sit opposite each other from nine till five. At lunchtime they strolled around the streets chatting and observing. At 5.01 p.m. they left the office, never phoning each other in the evenings or at weekends with any ideas. Writing for the two giants of comedy was strictly 9–5.

And there, at the end of the room, sitting behind a huge glass table supported by four stone lions, was Robert Stigwood. Well dressed, a nice face, slightly florid with gold wavy hair. He beckoned me in a slow soft Aussie drawl, and shook my hand.

Then, after a seemingly endless thirty seconds of silence, from his end of the table, his face bathed in a pool of light, he looked across at me and announced: 'You're the one.'

I looked behind me thinking there must be someone else in the room. 'Me?' I asked.

'Yes, you're the one,' repeated Robert. 'I've decided to start my own record company, and *you* are going to make it the greatest in the world.'

Steady, Dave boy, I thought to myself. *This bloke doesn't take no for an answer – keep your cool.*

'Now, how much do you want?' continued Robert. 'What car? When can you start?'

My mind was racing. To Robert it was already a foregone conclusion, I'd join him. But what of Decca? What money could I ask for? Well, Johnny Haynes was the first £100 per week footballer so, '£100 per week and a BMW,' I said.

'A BMW? Isn't that a motorbike?'

'No, Robert, it's a car. £100 per week and I'll start on January 1st.'

'Fine,' came the reply, across the four stone lions. 'Now RSO Records – what logo would you suggest?' Talk about hitting the road running! My mind raced. I had read in Tony's *Evening Standard* that it was the year of the 'Red Cow' in Japan. 'Tell you what, Robert, The Beatles formed an Apple. How about a Red Cow? It's lucky in Japan.'

'Fine,' came the reply. 'You can have whatever staff you require. You will build your own team, press officers, pluggers, and secretaries . . . anything you wish. Thank you, David.' And with that Robert sat down to pore over some contract or other. I stood up and turned to leave the room. As I approached the door once again I heard that soft Aussie drawl.

'And, David, remember . . . *you're* the one.'

On 1 January 1973, high above Brook Street at Number 46, and right opposite Claridges Hotel, I started RSO Records. Just me and the Red Cow. I was 27 years old. On my door it said:

D.S. English
President

Outside sat two secretaries. My office was palatial, vast. Chandeliered, elegant, top-of-the-range sound system to listen to new talent, big comfy sofas in trendy designs and a whopping great walnut drinks cabinet to entertain my artistes. Robert Stigwood certainly believed in doing things in style!

My entrée into the Big Time as a record mogul, earning £100 per week, made me think of investment possibilities. There was no way I would pay someone rent, I was still living with my mum in Golders Green. Rather invest in my own bricks and mortar. But where?

West End Lane was the long and winding road which took my pals and me from the top of the Finchley Road, through to St John's Wood and on to the West End. It was the land of the bedsit.

One Sunday morning, I drove down the lane exploring the side roads. There was an old board outside Number 26 Kingdon Road. I knocked on the door and was met by an Indian gentleman who took me up to his flat. On one side of the room, a lady was breastfeeding her baby in the corner. On the other side were live chickens in a run made of wire. I couldn't pull up a chair to talk terms because there wasn't one.

'How much do you want?' I said.

'£4,500,' replied a chicken.

Watcha cock! Only joking.

'I'll give you £4,250.' The deal was done.

Three weeks later, I moved in, and set up my palace with utmost speed. Big leather chair where the chickens had roosted, another in the breast-feeding corner and my drum kit in the alcove. The bed was an all-purpose adventure playground, strong and springy. Now I needed to audition some horizontal joggers to try out my furniture and fittings. West Hampstead. You couldn't go wrong. Between Shamrock, the dry cleaners, and Pronto Print, was the Golden Mile. Swedish, French, West Indian, Japanese, birds of every denomination would pound the pavements on the way to the tube station. There was Dominique's Bistro where poseurs would sit outside for hours, reading the papers over one cappuccino. Regardless of the weather they'd sit and crunch away at their croissants; you could have been in St Tropez.

The transport situation to get the girls home had to be addressed. True, I had my shining green BMW outside, but somehow when you'd consumed some of that Portuguese Chianti rocket fuel from the Bohemian Shop on the corner and your body was spent through wrestling with the opposition, a minicab from the door was a salvation.

This is how I met Mr Patel. Delta 1 Cabs was situated in a mews behind the Nautilus Fish and Chip Shop.

I had spent a riotous evening with Joanna Van Den Eyden, part deb, part dancer. 'Jo, I'll phone for a cab,' I said, pulling up my Y-fronts.

'Delta 1 OK, be ten minutes,' came the voice. My intercom buzzed. The cab had arrived and off went Jo dressed in a fur coat over very little else.

The next day I called to see if she had got home safely.

'Yes, if you like Billericay.'

'Billericay? But you live—'

'That's right,' interrupted Jo, '555 Park Lane. Your driver took me off to Billericay and tried to get fruity.'

I put on my coat and nipped up to Delta 1 to investigate.

'Oh you'll be wanting Mr Patel,' said the controller. 'He'll be asleep round the back.' Sure enough, spark out in the back of a Golden Granada lay Mr Patel. He resembled an Indian Chuck Berry. Black quiff, Teddy Boy draped coat and suede shoes. The upholstery was covered in stained leopard skin. A half-finished Prawn Korma lay on the passenger seat.

'Mr Patel . . .?'

'Yes sir?'

'You were meant to take my young lady to 555 Park Lane not Billericay.'

'I know, sir, but I had to make a couple of stops on the way.'

Priceless, I thought. For the next twenty years Mr Patel would be my driver, grateful for my sloppy seconds. Just think, my girls got two dates for the price of one. Me, Chuck and 'No particular place to go!'

Extravagance and style are all very reassuring, but without the product you might as well have a Fabergé Egg without a centre. My artist and repertoire department certainly looked a bit on the bleak side: the Bee Gees weren't talking to each other, out of harmony in the middle of a sibling spat; Eric Clapton was lying low deep in the Surrey Hills; and Tim Rice and Andrew Lloyd Webber were resting after their highly successful production of *Joseph and His Amazing Technicolor Dreamcoat*.

I decided to launch RSO with three pre-recorded albums. *Derek and the Dominos In Concert*, a live double album, the Bee Gees' *Life in a Tin Can* and the live album of *Joseph*. But I needed a single to set our Red Cow loose on the charts.

I called up Tim Rice and after a brief and highly creative meeting of minds we decided to release Rover's 'How Much Is That Doggie In The Window' – backwards.

I sent a promotional copy, with dog bowl bearing the title of the song next to a couple of paw marks and our Red Cow logo, to the top radio producers.

'Window The In Doggie That Is Much How' by Rover sold eight copies.

It certainly caught my Chairman's ear. My internal phone rang. It was Robert. Was I in the dog house?

'Interesting first release,' came the entrepreneurial drawl. 'Remember, David. You're the one.'

I first met Eric Clapton on the stage at the Royal Albert Hall. I remember it clearly. He remembers it vaguely. It was Cream's Farewell Concert, 26 November 1968. For years I had bunked into 'the Albert' and actually gone on stage with the band. All I did was stroll through the artist's entrance (door 1), dressed in a tracksuit and holding a towel. I got to know the doormen and security. Straight in, down the stairs into the bar, mingling with the real 'road staff' and at show time following the act on to the stage and sitting down, towel at the ready, behind the amps. For years, for Bob Dylan, Buddy Guy, The Who, Rolling Stones, Stevie Winwood, Delaney and Bonnie, Creedence Clearwater Revival and George Harrison, I'd been the 'roadie with no name'.

I vividly remember passing Eric the towel at Cream's farewell concert. They had played encores of their favourites 'White Room', 'I'm So Glad', 'Sitting On Top of the World', 'Crossroads' and 'Sunshine Of Your Love'. As usual the three of them played with intense power and as far apart from each other as possible. Eric had lifted the roof off with another flowing solo, prompting the fans to climb on the stage and shower him with confetti.

'Towel, El!' I cried.

'Thanks,' replied Eric politely, exhausted but smiling.

In 1966, when Frank Sinatra was top of the charts with 'Strangers In The Night', and the pop world was still gripped by The Beatles and the Stones, Robert Stigwood had formed Cream.

Eric, 'the musician's musician' and hottest guitar player in Britain, was joined by Jack Bruce, a brilliant bassist, harmonica player, pianist and singer with Manfred Mann, and Peter 'Ginger' Baker, the incredible drummer with the Graham Bond Organisation.

They were called Cream because they were simply the best. Jack and Ginger's background was jazz; Eric had meticulously followed American blues. Ginger Baker had virtually run the Graham Bond Organisation, in which he and Jack Bruce were key members. The communication between them was musically compatible; but in human terms disastrous. One night Ginger fired Jack from the Bond Band telling him he didn't fit. Jack defied him and simply kept turning up to each gig, this going on for weeks.

I remember seeing Ginger and Jack on stage at the Golders Green Refectory. Jack – technically fired – commented that Ginger's drums were too loud. This prompted the percussionist to throw drumsticks at Jack, hitting him on the head. The next thing the audience saw was Jack lifting his double bass and hurling it at Ginger, followed by the two of them rolling around the stage fighting. The audience loved it, Jack and Ginger punching the hell out of each other.

The trio became the catalyst to a rock revolution and the most powerful live band in the world. But Eric was faced with an unsolvable dilemma; while the music was brilliantly pulsating, he was sandwiched between two men who fundamentally loathed each other. On stage you could feel the fire burning, the very pain of their relationship creating the hottest rhythm section, inspiring amazing solos from Eric's guitar.

Eric, Ginger and Jack wanted to turn each other on – they weren't playing for the audience, they were playing for themselves. If the punters wanted to come, they were quite welcome to listen.

Robert toured them coast to coast in America, where they made a fortune. Cream broke all barriers, marking a historical change in popular music records from singles to albums, and were a vital backbone to Robert's show business empire. He needed the money they were generating to subsidise his investment in other long-term properties, like the Bee Gees.

On Christmas Eve, 1967, Eric, Jack and Ginger trailed wearily back into Heathrow after another tiring American tour. So dismal had become their relationship, exhausted and needing privacy and independence from each other, they were hardly talking to each other. Eric wanted to go back to playing contemporary blues. With Cream, solos had been the driving force, and he felt over-exposed. They had become a moneymaking machine selling millions of records and catapulting the three men into legendary global rock status, and they had died the death from playing too much.

And there I was passing 'Slowhand' his towel on his highly emotional farewell.

Little did I know that the next thing I'd pass to Eric Clapton would be a pair of cream trousers, high up above the Rainbow Theatre at his comeback concert in January 1973. No longer the phoney roadie but the First President of his record company, RSO Records.

My 'Doggie' single had not set the music business alight. I had to get my artists working.

The Bee Gees had enjoyed enormous success after signing a management agreement with Robert in 1967. 'New York Mining Disaster', 'To Love Somebody' and 'Words' had been big hits throughout the world. In September 1967, 'Massachusetts' went to Number 1 in the UK followed by another Number 1, 'I've Gotta Get A Message To You' (August 1968). In June 1971 they had registered their first US Number 1, 'How Do You Mend A Broken Heart?', a beautiful song lyrically highlighting the brothers' wonderful three-part harmonies. Of course artists like Al Green had covered it because it was essentially a singer's song, and the brothers Gibb were master writers of a popular tune.

Currently, they weren't talking to each other. Nothing serious, just a bit of brotherly friction.

In 1972 after touring America, performing with a 40-piece orchestra, the brothers Gibb had begun work on their next project at the Record Plant in Los Angeles.

Life in a Tin Can was to be one of my first releases, officially launching the RSO Label.

I rang each one of the boys and asked them to come to my office to do an interview with Penny Valentine from the music paper *Sounds*. I was desperate to meet them.

First in the door was Maurice, laughing and joking. Robin arrived with his wife Molly and personal assistant Ray Washbourne. Ten minutes later in walked Barry, wearing a fur coat with Linda by his side. I had been waiting for this reunion with great excitement. 'Don't tell me,' he said, 'the broken down Rover in Great Marlborough Street!' (Not another Rover, I thought to myself, I've just released one.)

'Tell you what lads, why don't we release "How Do You Mend A Broken Rover?"' Everyone in the room collapsed about laughing. The three brothers performed the new version straight off the cuff and a lifelong friendship was born there under the chandeliers of 46 Brook Street. We've been working and laughing ever since.

I released 'Saw A New Morning' off the *Life in a Tin Can* album and the boys played a big concert at the Royal Festival Hall with the London Symphony Orchestra. At the end of February 1973, they went on another tour of North America, kicking off in Canada. They were masters of the live gig, having been brought up on the fairgrounds and speedway circuits in Australia from the age of nine. The Bee Gees' empathy with the audience, however big or small, is unique in its warmth and sense of goodwill. This is based on the importance of their family values, which have always been the foundation of their success. A Bee Gees tour party consists of their mums, dads, grannies, kids, even the dogs.

One of the strangest 'family outings' had been a concert in Jakarta in Indonesia. They had toured Australia and the promoter had suggested that they do a gig on the way home to break up the flight. As usual manager Dick Ashby and road manager Tom Kennedy drove to the venue to check out the facilities. They had been told there were 10,000 seats under cover, but when they arrived there they discovered they were playing at a Wembley-sized stadium outdoors.

The promoter greeted them with, 'Don't worry. I'm a Catholic and I've prayed for eight days – it's not going to rain.'

Eighty thousand punters arrived and it pissed down!

'The band can't go on,' said Dick Ashby. 'If a guitar touches something, someone could be electrocuted.'

The promoter's wife burst into tears. 'You must go on, the Prime Minister and the Royal Family have arrived!' The promoter added, desperately, 'If the support group go on and aren't killed will you go on?'

The warm-up set went potty, throwing microphone stands up in the air, rubbing guitars up against mike stands. Believe me, Mick Jagger had nothing on this bunch!

The band didn't get blown up and the incredulous Bee Gees performed in monsoon conditions, water lapping against the amplifiers. They decided an acoustic set was the safest way forward, but the punters wouldn't have it and went crazy. Sukarno ordered that his soldiers should go in front of the stage to stop the audience attacking the group. But that wasn't all. 'If you don't go on, there will be 80,000 people rioting,' screamed some five-star general.

At this point the soldiers turned to face the Bee Gees with machine guns to prevent them leaving the stage. The general had driven the group around Jakarta the day before to show the people they really were the Bee Gees. In the past, the promoters had advertised Tom Jones and there's a little speck on the stage pretending to be Tom Jones, who in fact turned out to be a local lad. The crowd got him and 'Tom' was lynched while the promoter had f***ed off to the airport with the money.

So the boys played and 80,000 people went berserk, screaming and shouting. You couldn't hear a word. The Bee Gees were in the spotlight and that was all that mattered. It was reminiscent of the early days of Beatlemania. The performance was immaterial to the event: the crowd wanted the Bee Gees and the fact that 'they' were there was all-important.

But what of our other main act, Derek and the Dominos? The great success of Cream had brought Eric money and freedom and he'd bought a beautiful 20-roomed mansion deep in the Surrey Hills and moved in with Lord Harlech's daughter, Alice Ormsby-Gore. Hurtwood Edge has a magical character, misty and mysterious, with ornamental ponds, donkeys grazing in the fields and even an observatory. On a clear day you can see three counties from the bedroom window. It cost Eric £40,000 in 1969. Away from the relentless touring with Cream, he enjoyed his freedom, happy to immerse himself as a sideman. He guested with John and Yoko's Plastic Ono Band in New York and Toronto. In lieu of payment for the Toronto Show, Lennon gave Eric five drawings on Apple Records writing paper. They were typically witty. Years later I found them framed on Eric's wall.

Eric played with Stevie Winwood in Blind Faith and jammed with Delaney and Bonnie. He was enjoying his solitude and in 1970 decided to go on tour incognito as Derek and the Dominos, playing at small clubs throughout Britain. He wanted to get away from being the famous front man, much preferring to play alongside Carl Radle on bass, Bobby Whitlock on keyboards and Jim Gordon on drums.

The disguise was a failure. Everybody knew it was Eric. When I released our double album three years later, I had to get maximum publicity, so I showered the music industry with 'Derek is Eric' badges.

One autumn afternoon in 1970, Eric was strolling around the West End and went into a music shop where, on the wall, hung a left-handed Fender Stratocaster guitar. He bought it immediately for his good friend Jimi Hendrix. Eric had loved the raw fiery energy and originality of Jimi Hendrix, and admired his gimmickry, like playing with his teeth. That same night Eric had gone to the Lyceum Ballroom to see Sly and the Family Stone. He took along the Fender Stratocaster for Jimi as they had arranged to meet in one of the boxes, but Hendrix was not at the concert. Next day, Eric learned that Jimi had died that night.

Eric was deeply affected by the loss of his friend. The whole world mourned the death of the shining star who, like Eric, was rooted to the blues. Six weeks after Jimi's death, Derek and the Dominos were on tour in America when Robert Stigwood phoned Eric to tell him that his grandpa had been taken to a clinic in Guildford with cancer. Eric cancelled a press reception for his new group and flew home. Jack Clapp died shortly afterwards, aged 60.

Eric was traumatised. Jack and his grandma Rose had brought him up in Ripley. He loved them both very deeply, particularly Rose, and knew what the tragic loss would mean to her. It would be too simple to say that Eric plunged into his long silent reclusive period after those two deaths. But it is certain that they contributed to the deep-seated soul-searching that affected him. At the age of 25, with the world at his feet, he went home and closed the door. I don't want to delve into the dark road he took into drugs and despair, because I always like to think of him as I've known him. A crystal-clear mind, full of love, emotion, mischief, adventure, deep feeling and light-ning humour. Believe me, to hear Eric laugh is something else.

But he had fallen into that silent and lonely vacuum, lost to the world. From the end of December 1970 to the beginning of 1973, the only time he appeared with his guitar was for the All-Star Concert for Bangladesh organ-ised by George Harrison at New York's Madison Square Garden on 1 August 1971. The attraction of playing with old friends, including Bob Dylan, was a contributory factor in forcing Eric out of hibernation. It was a miracle he could stand on stage at all. He had achieved what he wanted, to become a sideman in a Band of Stars. The New York audience's applause for him was loud and clear.

So you can guess how I felt when I took a call from the Chairman. 'Eric's making a comeback,' came the Chairman's voice crackling down the car phone of his white Rolls-Royce convertible. 'Alert the press!' After two years of hibernation, Eric had been persuaded to make a comeback by Pete Townshend.

The rock world was gripped with curiosity. What shape was he in? Could he still play?

Pete had assembled an all-star band: Clapton, Townshend and Ronnie Wood, all on guitar, Rick Grech on bass, Steve Winwood playing keyboards, and Jim Capaldi on drums. They would play at the Rainbow Theatre, Finsbury Park.

In the audience sat George Harrison and Ringo Starr, Klaus Voorman, Elton John, Joe Cocker, Jimmy Page, Rory Gallagher and Ahmet Ertegun, President of Atlantic Records, who distributed Eric's material on RSO records in North America.

Would he show? The tension backstage was palpable. Robert, Pete and I prayed on the back stairway. One minute before the start of the concert Eric arrived with Alice. An extremely agitated Robert asked him why he was so late. 'His cream suit, which he hasn't worn for two years, needed letting out,' said Alice.

He had to wait for Alice to get out her sewing machine and let out the waist of his trousers.

Eric's bodyguard took Eric's suit and hung it in a little room high above the Rainbow Theatre. Eric quickly exchanged hellos with the band and went up to the little room on his own.

I had nipped in there first. For the second time in my life, I came face to face with Slowhand.

'Here we are, "El",' I said, 'try your strides on.' I passed Eric his suit.

'Thanks, man,' came the reply.

'By the way, I'm David English, President of your record company.'

'No you're not,' laughed Eric. 'You're Arfur and Robert tells me that "you're the one".'

From that day on he's always called me Arfur, after Arthur English (no relation) the comedian.

A mighty roar went up as Eric took the stage and played the first bars of 'Layla'.

Eric played his hits one by one. The whole evening, which I recorded for RSO as *Eric Clapton Live at the Rainbow*, was packed with emotion.

It was a triumph, but inwardly Eric hated it because it was the type of 'showbiz occasion' that he shunned.

The Rainbow Theatre did not cure Eric; he was still addicted to drugs when he went on and came off the stage. But it was a powerful axis on which he could think about reshaping his life.

He owed Pete Townshend a great deal; in 'Give Me Strength', Eric wrote about his need for the Lord to help him out on the highway, to give him the strength to carry on.

After a seemingly endless period in the wilderness, Eric finally kicked his habit, helped by the Harley Street doctor, Dr Meg Patterson. She gradually cured him through acupuncture, inserting little needles into the contours of his ears.

He called Robert and asked him to contact Tom Dowd, one of Atlantic Records finest producers. Tom Dowd assembled just the right musicians to suit Eric's mood. Carl Radle (bass), drummer Jamie Oldaker, singer Yvonne Elliman, Dicky Sims on keyboards and local guitar player George Terry.

Tommy booked Criteria Studio in Miami. Eric was on the plane to Florida to make a clean start. I was with him during that month. He wrote, played and sang with a new, clear, inner consciousness. He recorded his album in just two and a half weeks. For me, it stands out as one of his finest: *461*

Ocean Boulevard, named after the address of the house he and the musicians lived in.

Cindy Lee Johnson and Jeri Jenkins's company, 'Home At Last', had an arrangement with Criteria Studios to accommodate the musicians there during their recording. She had found Eric 461 Ocean Boulevard, and created a warm and loving atmosphere for him to work and play in.

The music sparkled and was a mixture of melancholy and drive from the raunchy 'Mainline Florida' and Bob Marley's 'I Shot The Sheriff' through to the plaintive 'Please Be With Me'.

Following the incredible commercial success of the album, Eric embarked on a 26 week, coast-to-coast tour of America. The Americans loved him and had followed his progress through Cream and Blind Faith. Eric Clapton and His Band, as it was officially named for the first time, played to sell-out sports stadiums, with between 60,000 and 70,000 at most venues. And then on to Europe: 'Arfur, I want you to find me a venue, low key where we can start our tour. Go incognito.'

Together with tour manager Roger Forrester, I contacted the Swedish promoter, Per Johannson. I told him it was Eric, but to the rest of Sweden, we would be presenting 'Eddie Earth Quake And The Tremors'.

Picture the Scene. Grona Lund, or Green Valley, Amusement Park, with all the trimmings: a Big Wheel, Tunnel of Love, the Dodgems, all the fun of the fair. At the far end of the fairground, next to the Crazy Golf, was a gypsy caravan and a little stage. Perfect, I thought.

I met El and the band at a private airport. They had flown in from the States and were well weary. As the black limos snaked through the cobbled streets of Stockholm, he asked me how big the hall was.

'Not exactly a hall, El.'

'What do you mean?'

'Well, it's more like a funfair . . .'

Eric nearly choked on the bottle of Remy Martin he was swigging.

'Funfair! Leave it out, Arfur!'

He wanted to turn back to the airport.

'Come on, El,' I pleaded. 'It's low key. You're Eddie Earth Quake And The Tremors; you can have a gentle run through. Try out a few numbers. No pressure, believe me.'

At 3 p.m., 'Eddie Earth Quake', wearing a plastic mac with a doll's head broach, took to the stage for a sound check. Just a few bars of 'I Shot The Sheriff'. Bobby Pridden, the soundman we had nicked from The Who, was up the tree setting up his PA.

Young kids in bobble hats, holding their dad's hands and eating candy floss bigger than their heads, looked up in idle fascination as the Legend went through his paces.

7.30 p.m. Showtime. Mickey Turner, strong arm and confidante, put his head around the door of the gypsy caravan where El and the band were enjoying a few beakers more.

'Arfur, I think you better come out here,' said Mickey.

Most of the funfair had come to a halt. Just the Big Wheel and Tunnel of Love were still in operation. There must have been 25,000 punters out there holding lighters and gently swaying in the flickering light. Word had got out, and they knew Eddie was Eric.

Gawd, here we go again, I thought. El was now tucking into his second bottle of Remy; with a bit of luck he'll only see the first ten rows.

'How many out their, Arfur?' he enquired.

'A couple of thousand at the most.' I lied to my pal through clenched teeth.

Out went Eddie and his Earth Quakes to a massive ovation from the sea of light.

Eric gave me what can best be described as a strained look, followed by a creased smile. My ears were in trouble later, big time. Whenever he got excited with me he became the Artful Dodger and pulled at my ears mercilessly.

What happened next was a scene that could only have come from Hans Christian Anderson's Fairy Tales. 'Willie And The Hand Jive', 'Crossroads', 'Let It Rain', 'Presence Of The Lord'. Hit after hit, followed by a sensitive rendition of Jimi Hendrix's song 'Little Wing'. For this Eric decided to kneel down and do a full Hendrix impersonation, including at one point playing with his teeth. The trouble was he couldn't get up again. Still playing with his teeth, he looked over to us and nodded his head urgently in an upward and downwards motion implying he had had enough.

Mickey and I misunderstood this sudden jerking of the head as we gave El the thumbs up – 'Great! Keep it going!'

The band was in great form. Yvonne sang like a bird and Eric and George Terry's guitar playing soared into the Swedish night.

However, when Eric had started to play, all the electricity from the funfair was channelled into the equipment on the stage. We didn't know this until we heard a plaintive cry from the top of the Big Wheel. A family was marooned in one of the carts. It turned out that a number of the clogs-and-hot-pants brigade were stuck up on the wheel and in the Tunnel of Love. They remained there for a good five hours; Eric had got the taste and wouldn't stop playing.

Meanwhile, Per Johannson, busy counting the loss of revenue from his stationary funfair, attempted to pull the plug. We in turn kept feeding him more kronas. . . it was like a scene from a viking man's club!

The surreal Swedish experience had put us in good shape for Copenhagen. The gig there was indeed 'Wonderful, Wonderful'. We had encountered Miss Denmark, who was spread all over the current edition of

Penthouse. Instantly recruited as our tour mascot, Miss Denmark took us to this country club. Four stretch limos, nightclubs on wheels, full of us drinking and laughing, crunched up the gravel drive of 'Le Club de Paradise'.

The entrance hall was delightfully decadent in deep maroon velvet. Sat about the bar were sexy ladies on high stools provocatively pouting over their Martinis. El was in fine form, sporting a pair of denim dungarees, and soon we were ushered through to the 'Live Show'.

Whether it was the sprightly performance of the nubile peroxide blonde writhing on a pink bri-nylon rug to the strains of 'You Really Got Me' which prompted a band member (who shall remain nameless) to explode into a freestyle version of 'Flashdance', I'm not sure. All I know is it brought the audience quickly to their feet.

Not as quick as the stripper. For our 'Nureyev' decided to end his performance by standing over her and peeing like a horse!

Chaos ensued. Burly bouncers appeared from every angle to apprehend the 'Golden Rainmaker'. The stripper was jumping up and down like a dervish and when the curtains were pulled back, Dicky Sims was rogering Miss Denmark, giving her a huge portion of his pink trombone.

All hell let loose. A full-blown punch up was quickly followed by Eric Clapton and his band in various stages of undress fleeing for the waiting limos.

'Arfur, you better go back for Carl, he's still strapped down in the dungeon of love!'

Eddie had started a real tremor in Europe with his Earth Quakes. The boy was back in fine form and continued to devastate audiences in Warsaw, Amsterdam, Paris, Milan and beyond to Madrid. I kept leaving and joining the tour as it blazed a trail across Europe, while Eric revelled in high jinx, masterminding pranks and practical jokes on and off the stage.

THE RED COW RULES THE WORLD

There was a knock on the door. I went to open it, wearing just a Holiday Inn towel around my midriff. When I opened the door, I was confronted by a giant wearing a ten-gallon hat with his arm in plaster, holding a shotgun. By the time Big Tex had looked over my shoulder to see his 'gal' lying on my bed, I had legged it, *très pronto*.

Tex swung into action, firing his shotgun, which seriously disturbed the brickwork above my head as I swerved around the corner. He let off another round as I fled for my life down the stairs. I circled the swimming pool and made for the fire escape at the back of the hotel.

By now lights were coming on as people ventured outside on their balconies to follow the commotion.

Completely stark naked, I stood on the hotel roof behind the neon Delta sign. Every time the air hostess winked, I ducked. I was up there all night.

6 THE RED COW RULES THE WORLD

As a record boss, my number one priority was to know and work intimately with the artists. To get inside their heads, know how they tick, judge their moods, to explore and maximise all of their creative potential. To get up close and personal, work as a team and make it happen. Luckily, for me, to be able to communicate and see the possibilities in people quickly is the key to life.

I returned to London. Robert was delighted; *461 Ocean Boulevard*, *Derek and the Dominos* and *Joseph* were big hit albums, and I had Eric's comeback concert *Eric Clapton Live at the Rainbow* up my sleeve. Robert's belief that 'I was the one' rang in my ears incessantly and made me work with a devoted passion. He allowed me to make all the decisions, and I had complete freedom to record, sign, hire and fire. He had given me the chance to pioneer and innovate, to put my dreams into schemes and above all to project the careers of his supremely talented artists.

I never did discover how he had found me. But that lunchtime sitting in front of the glass table on the four stone lions had given me the chance to conquer the world!

I decided to release three more albums, 'The Best Of' series, packaging the best work of Eric, Jack and Ginger.

Ginger was a great drummer. His background was jazz and his ability to extemporise with a demonic intensity put him right up there with the very best. He was on a par with Phil Seaman and the giants of American jazz drumming, Buddy Rich, Art Blakey and Elvin Jones.

After the dissolution of Cream, Ginger had helped to form Blind Faith before going to Nigeria in search of different drum sounds. Unfortunately, he had got busted, but the charges were dropped when he agreed to produce the Nigerian Police Band: I still have the album sleeve showing a team photo of the Nigerian Police Department with Ginger sitting proudly in the middle.

One day he came and saw me at the office, unannounced. In strolled the tall, lean and bony 'Gypo' with an angular smile and shock of ginger hair.

'Dave, I've got these tapes. You'll love 'em,' he smiled.

We played them on my Revox. They were the sounds of distant drums.

'Ginger, I do love them, but they won't play it on Radio One. Look at the charts, it's all Slade and the New Seekers.'

The great man gave me a quizzical look. 'Give 'em another listen. I'm going over the road to see Stiggy. I'll get some money and I'll take you to lunch.'

Off went Ginger to Number 67. Robert was in the middle of a high-powered meeting with shareholders and potential investors for a new musical. Ginger entered Gini's office and announced, 'I want some money. Where's Robert?'

'He's in an important meeting. He can't be disturbed.'

'Bollocks to that!'

In stormed Ginger and, to the amazement of the assembled top brass, in a fit of Anglo-Irish pique lifted the green baize table, covered in glasses of water and jugs, clean off its legs, throwing it high in the air.

'Come on, Stiggy, I want some money. Take it out of me f***in' Cream royalties!'

Meanwhile Jack had been busy forming another supergroup, joining forces with the legendary guitarist Leslie West and drummer Corky Laing. But more of 'West Bruce and Laing' later!

'Arfur, we know you play cricket, how about football?' asked Roger 'Bilko' Forrester. I told him about my pedigree from Whitefields, playing alongside Tony Currie.

'Fine, we need a right winger for this Sunday's battle against the Warner Bros Music XI. Come and have a run out with the "Stiggy Kickers".'

'What kind of standard is it?' I enquired.

'Well, put it this way, Arfur, we don't lose many games,' laughed Roger. 'See you at Stanmore, kick-off three o'clock sharp.'

Robert lived at The Old Barn, a Tudor mansion in Stanmore, on the outskirts of London. He had discovered the beautiful old house somewhere in Worcestershire and had it moved brick-by-brick to Stanmore.

Robert had his own football team, the Stiggy Kickers, who were unbeaten in 144 games. The very name of the 'SK's' sent a chill through the industry. Played 144, won 127, drawn 13, abandoned 4 (through massive punch-ups, brawling with the referees and on one occasion threatening to strangle one of the linesmen).

Sounds a charming bunch, I thought as I drove up the long drive to the spectacular Stigwood Home.

Robert's assistant welcomed me in and showed me through to the lounge where the Chairman was sitting by a roaring fire surrounded by his six dogs.

I swear to this day that one of them, Mickey, a Staffordshire bull terrier, actually talked.

'Tell me what kind of day have you had?' asked Robert, rubbing Mickey's tummy.

'Ruff! Ruff!' replied the terrier, lying on his back grinning. There was Melissa the Red Setter, a golden Labrador, a Dobermann, a German sheepdog called Fritz and a smaller hound that fussed around the others. Robert loved his dogs.

I could hear a bit of a commotion outside and strolled over to the stained-glass window to investigate. A procession of vehicles of all descriptions were arriving, including a DER Rentals van, a ready-mixed concrete lorry actually still mixing, a couple of Ferraris, and a Harley Davidson with a mad-looking bloke sat astride it.

'Ah! Here comes my team. Lovely lads,' purred Robert. 'You'd better go and get changed.'

Bilko introduced me to the team. Ginger Baker was in goal, Rod Stewart at centre forward, Harry Reynolds, a decorator/songwriter, at inside left, the DER Rentals salesman at left half, and the mad bloke they called King Charles playing at left back. Patrolling the midfield was Errol Brown from Hot Chocolate, and on our right flank was Bilko at right back, Laurie O'Leary at right half and yours truly on the right wing.

'Just stay on the wing, Arfur, we'll get it to you and then bang it straight across to Rod who'll do the business.'

Rod, with a mane of blonde spiky hair, acknowledged me from the centre spot. Already with a trial for Brentford FC under his belt, he would be our target man.

When the whistle went I quickly found myself witnessing a remake of the Battle of Pork Chop Hill.

Scything tackles, flying left-handers, squeezing of the bollocks were rife. One particularly fearsome challenge from 'Lol' O'Leary sent their number 9 headlong into the rhododendrons. Ginger sprang about his goal, at one point actually hanging off his crossbar like an orangutan while tipping over a searing drive; Harry Reynolds had the ref in his pocket, charming him with a look of pure innocence after poleaxing their number 7 with a crisp right-hander.

The Kickers played like clockwork, mesmerising the 'oppo' with nifty footwork and endless banter. No wonder they were unbeaten – they were a well-oiled killing machine. Half-time we were five up. 'I told you we don't take prisoners, Arfur,' laughed Roger, chewing on a bit of orange.

We finally flattened Warner Brothers 10–1.

Off trooped the Kickers to the pavilion, no shower, plenty of piss-taking, 'See you next week, lads', and off we went.

Up in the Old Barn Robert was entertaining Huw Weldon, the Director General of the BBC, and others, including the local MP for Stanmore.

Huw Weldon took a leisurely glance out of the window. He visibly blinked, rubbed his eyes, stared again and looked blankly into his glass.

'Are you alright, Huw?' enquired Robert.

'What? Oh yes. It's just that I thought I saw a ready-mixed concrete lorry and a DER . . .'

'You better have another drink,' smiled Robert.

'Don't mind if I do,' barked Mickey.

* * *

My number one priority now was to get the Bee Gees back to where their talents richly deserved, the Number 1 spot. 'Saw A New Morning' and *Life in a Tin Can* had not done that well in America, and so it was time for a new direction.

We talked to Ahmet Ertegun in New York for ideas on a possible producer. After discussing it with Jerry Wexler, Ahmet suggested their own house producer, Arif Mardin, famous for his work with Atlantic artists such as Aretha Franklin and Roberta Flack. Arif was also a fine arranger. Robert rated him as a terrific producer and knew him well because of our Atlantic connections.

We asked him if he would come in and start recording the Bee Gees and he did. Barry, Robin and Maurice were delighted, they knew he'd add another ear to their production. So off went the gang to Miami to record at Criteria Studios.

Never change a winning formula. It had worked with great success for Eric, so we followed the same path, accommodating the Bee Gees, band and family, in Cindy and Geri's *461 Ocean Boulevard*. The problem was that everybody who had bought the *461* album used to start coming into the grounds because there was access off the beach. So all Eric's fans would come by the house and ask if Eric was in.

Typically the Bee Gees made their 'live in' band feel very much part of the family. Alan Kendall (guitar), Dennis Bryon (drums), Derek (Blue) Weaver (keyboards) and Geoff Westley (keyboards and flute) formed a tight unit. Together with the band they were spending 18 hours a day for two months in the studio. Under Arif's production, everybody had an input. It was a highly creative and dynamic time.

As usual the brothers wrote together. Melody first, lyrics second. Barry started on guitar, Maurice played chords on the piano and Robin came in with his soulful voice.

And the falsetto? The first time I heard Barry going for that really high note was in the back of a car coming from a radio interview we had done in Pittsburgh. The Stylistics were singing, 'You Make Me Feel Brand New' on the radio, and Barry sang along with the falsetto, supported by Robin and Maurice on harmonics. Back in the studio Barry displayed his new direction to Arif. He was delighted and encouraged it, likening the falsetto to Brian Wilson of the Beach Boys and Frankie Valli of the Four Seasons.

That day, the brothers wrote 'Nights On Broadway' featuring Barry's falsetto throughout the song for the first time. In the next studio The Eagles from California were recording their album. Clearly musicians are influenced by each other's music. The Bee Gees vibe on 'Nights on Broadway' was heard by Don Henley and Glenn Frey who went next door and wrote 'One Of These Nights'.

Robert and Ahmet visited the studios and were delighted to discover the

Bee Gees' newfound energy and enthusiasm. We were having a great time and when we played 'Nights On Broadway' to Robert he was bowled over by the power. 'This is dance music. It has a great tempo for dancing in a club.' Once again his intuition was spot on but he couldn't have realised just how spot on his prediction would be.

By recording the *Main Course* album the Bee Gees sound had changed dramatically from an orchestra and a piano to synthesisers and technology. Once again they had reinvented themselves. The creative writing juices were flowing.

One night on the way back from Criteria Studios to 461 Ocean Boulevard we were crossing the Sunny Isles bridge. As the car crossed the bridge the wheels went 'tickety, tickety, tickety tick' . . . It gave Barry a thought. He started to sing along with the rhythm, 'just your jive talkin'.

'That's a great groove,' said Barry. 'We must remember it.'

The next day when we crossed the bridge again, we all started to sing along with it. That night the brothers put the lyrics to the groove and played it to Arif the next day. Arif asked if they knew what 'Jive Talkin' meant in America, and Maurice told him they were thinking of the dance, a rock 'n' roll jive.

'No,' said Arif. 'In the States it's a black expression for bullshitting somebody.' The boys had written the lyrics 'Jive talkin', you dance with your eyes' but now changed them to 'Jive talkin', you're telling me lies'.

Arif helped them with the groove. 'Jive Talkin' opened up the creative gates even wider, spurring the Bee Gees and the band on with incredible energy.

Our cook at 461 was a lovely big black lady called Fanny. She had an incredible capacity to love and care for us all. Like a beautiful mamma she took us under her apron strings and looked after us, home from home. 'Fanny Be Tender With My Love' would become the third single off the *Main Course* album. It was written with great feeling and compassion by the boys, dedicated to Fanny and, along with 'Too Much Heaven', remains my all-time favourite Bee Gees Song.

The secret to their songwriting? Everybody asks me this question. Melody, bridge, chorus, harmony, lyrics and those special hooks, which touch a nerve throughout the world. You can learn most of these things but, believe me, the ability to know when to touch a nerve, this is a talent you're born with.

Seeing the possibilities in life drives me to distraction, with a sense of excitement just knowing what can be achieved. Before I discovered the Dictaphone, I had a pad by my bed and a magic pen which lit up on writing the ideas that flowed through my head in slumber's subconscious. From a clear vision to final glory can leave you breathless, but if you are driven by an idea and can 'give it your best shot', believe me, everything is possible.

You are left spent but fulfilled. Occasionally my passion has had to be curbed, but more of that later!

I knew that 'Jive Talkin' was extra special and I was determined to make it our first Number 1 in America. Let me explain: to have worldwide success with a record, the USA is your number one priority. If you take the global record sales cake it is approximately cut up in the following proportions: USA 44%, Japan 31%, Germany 16% and the UK 9%. However, the actual talent, i.e. the artists, are roughly split 50/50, USA and UK.

'Jive Talkin' was a departure from the Bee Gees powerful ballads. It was funky. It had made us dance on the Sunny Isles bridge and Robert and I knew it could get the whole world dancing. It was happy; it had a universal appeal and would get the punters bopping in the discos.

Because there was a certain prejudice against the Bee Gees on radio, Robert and I decided to send out blank white labels to all the DJs, radio producers and media critics. That way, if they liked the song, they would come back to us with an affirmative without knowing it was the Bee Gees. Then having said they'd liked 'Jive Talkin' it would be very hard for them not to play it! A cheeky ruse but at least the new direction would be judged on merit.

To promote 'Jive Talkin' and the new album *Main Course* we decided to take the Bee Gees on a 40-date tour of the USA, starting in Dayton, Ohio.

After rehearsals in New York we finally started our Bee Gees Holiday Inn Tour, opening at the Arena in Dayton, Ohio, 30 May 1975. We stayed at the Holiday Inns for budgetary reasons – cheap and cheerful service for our massive family-on-the-road entourage. For me it was to be a hard-working, glamorous and dangerous tour.

To keep the spirits up I had Air Force outfits made for the brothers and the band. At every concert the boys would go on stage dressed as RAF flyers. During the performance I would appear somewhere in the auditorium and salute, wearing a bow tie which would light up and revolve at the same time. At this point in whatever song they were performing they'd stop and return the salute. St Louis, Kansas City, Oklahoma City, Fort Worth, Texas, the crowds got bigger and bigger as 'Jive Talkin' raced up the charts.

After travelling through the tumbleweed towns of the Wild West we finally hit the mission trail into San Antonio, Texas. San Antonio is most famous for the legendary Battle of the Alamo in 1836. 139 years after Davy Crockett had been buried, I faced my own battle with the rodeo-riding boyfriend of one Billy Jo.

When we pulled into the Holiday Inn, I noticed the big neon sign on the roof showing an air hostess winking next to 'Fly Delta Airlines'.

I met Billy Jo at the gig. She looked great. Blonde hair, hot pants and boots, a real Lone Star Texas Rose. I took her backstage to meet the lads. The stage was elevated with a walkway underneath. As Dennis Bryon was drumming, Billy Jo and I were vertical jogging below him to the beat of 'Jive Talkin'. Dennis knew we were there and could see us through the cracks in the stage.

Previously, I had asked her about her marital status. 'Yea, I gotta boyfriend. He's a rodeo rider. Broke his arm last week. Fell off his horse.'

After a great concert we returned to my room at the Holiday Inn. An hour must have elapsed, when I heard a voice sharp and clear piercing the night.

'Billy Jo! Billy Jo!'

'Who's that?'

'That's my man. You'd better get outta here.'

There was a knock on the door. I went to open it, wearing just a Holiday Inn towel around my midriff. When I opened the door, I was confronted by a giant wearing a ten-gallon hat with his arm in plaster, holding a shotgun. By the time Big Tex had looked over my shoulder to see his 'gal' lying on my bed, I had legged it, *très pronto*.

Tex swung into action, firing his shotgun, which seriously disturbed the brickwork above my head as I swerved around the corner. He let off another round as I fled for my life down the stairs. I circled the swimming pool and made for the fire escape at the back of the hotel.

By now lights were coming on as people ventured outside on their balconies to follow the commotion.

Completely stark naked, I stood on the hotel roof behind the neon Delta sign. Every time the air hostess winked, I ducked. I was up there all night.

One night in Tampa Alan Kendall, my pal and the lead guitarist, got lively in a bar, resulting in an altercation with two large locals. 'Pongo' was finally arrested up a tree and taken to the downtown jail.

After bailing him out I took him to a club to drown his sorrows and have a bit of a laugh. It was one of those warm Florida nights; the moon was out, and I fell in love with a waitress called Bobby Parker, a former Playboy bunny, and asked her to marry me.

The next morning she arrived at the airport holding a suitcase and a letter of acceptance from her father.

We travelled to Houston, Texas, then on to Shreveport, Louisiana, me with my new 'wife'; love was in the air. It was . . . till we got to Nashville, where we stayed at Roger Miller's hotel, 'King Of The Road'. Our brief marriage ended harmoniously, and I took Bobby to the airport, gave her a few dollars more and bade her farewell. Our time would come again.

When we arrived in San Francisco, I realised all those things you hear in that song do not exist. I checked into my hotel room, opened the drawer and discovered Tony Bennett's heart. I guess he had left it there.

'Little cable cars' didn't 'climb halfway to the stars'; but when I did ride the cable car from Nob Hill to Russian Hill at the point where it turns to tumble down to the Pacific, San Francisco looked as though it had just been shampooed and then hung out to dry in the morning sun. All crisp, and blue and white. Adorned by radiant colours, firebird red, sunflower yellow, the blue ocean and orange bridge, and the grey and mysterious Alcatraz prison incongruous in the beautiful twinkling bay.

On to Chattanooga and the lady with the big policeman's helmets. We had just packed our bags and were ready to leave for the airport when this vision appeared teetering around the pool with one of those white fluffy dogs.

Maurice had just called by my room for his hairdryer. 'Mo, take a look at her!' I said. 'You go to the airport, and I'll catch you up.'

I chatted to the lady who invited me back to her room, where she took off her shirt and displayed her mighty twin peaks. 'These cost me $5,000,' she announced proudly. It was the first time I had encountered silicone.

'Come on boy, kiss my titties. Don't worry; my hubby has gone to work!'

I gave both the helmets a big kiss. Talk about 'Chattanooga Chew Chew!'

Robin had always had a fear of flying. Very often we would spot him testing the tyres of the aircraft before taking off.

One night in Pensacola he knocked on my door. There he stood holding his massive blue suitcase which I knew only contained a change of pants and a toothbrush, as Robbo believes in travelling light. 'Dave, I've seen the weather forecast for tomorrow and there are storms ahead. So I'm off to Charleston on the train.' And off went Robbo on his own to the station, and on to Carolina.

It was a great tour; we played to 72,000 at the Milwaukee Wisconsin Summer Fest down by the lake; Pittsburgh at the Stadium with the Sliding Roof; Philadelphia; Hampton, Virginia; Comack, Long Island; and the beautiful Performing Arts Centre at Saratoga.

It was a race to our final gig in Central Park, New York, between us and 'Jive Talkin'' whizzing up the charts.

We had been head to head with its progress since we left Dayton, Ohio back on 30 May.

7 July, Central Park, New York. 100,000 people watched our warm-up act, Diana Ross. When the Bee Gees walked on the stage and played the first few bars of 'Jive Talkin'', the crowd went mad.

It was Number 1 in the USA. Our RSO Red Cow had conquered America.

ᴏᴠᴇ: Head Boy of Whitefields School, aged 16
ᴛʰe playground of life.

ʟᴏᴡ: Raising funds for Save the Children Fund
ᴍeeting the Patron, Princess Anne, at the gala
ᴛner 1969, aged 23.

ᴀʙᴏᴠᴇ: First President of RSO
Records, 1973.

Robert Stigwood (left) – to this day the greatest showman on earth.

From Cricklewood to Hollywood – my first film break as Captain of the Hussar's in Ken Russell's *Lisztomania*.

A bearded Rueben in *Joseph and his Amazing Technicolour Dreamcoat*, The Grand Theatre, Leeds.

The Boys from the Bridge. Attenborough's Private Army. Notice the captain (centre) with the limp hand!

Dickie inspects the troops – *A Bridge Too Far*, Deventer, Holland, 1976, directed by Sir Richard Attenborough.

ABOVE: Trouble on the Rubble. 'Have you heard the one about … Anthony Hopkins give me his best Tommy Cooper impersonation.

LEFT: Butch Cassidy an the Sundance Men – a break in shooting on *A Bridge Too Far*. (From left to right) 'Big' Frankie Mughan, Robert Redford and David English.

LEFT: (Top right) in *Rea Column*, Everyman Theatre, Cheltenham, 1981. My greatest ordeal. Learning all those lines – two and a half hours on stage as Major Bartolott.

ABOVE: Billy Steele's Wish – living with Cindy Lee Johnson in North Miami, 1979. A golden time.

RIGHT: Arrested. Backstage at Madison Square Gardens, New York City, 1975. *Jive Talkin'* is number 1!

BELOW: Simply the best. My blood brothers, the Bee Gees.

EC on tour. The Eric Clapton XI, Northampton. (Back row) John Cousins, Alan Border, Gary Mason, Nick Cook, Mike Holding, Dennis Waterman, Godfrey Evans, Roger Forrester. (Front row) David Steele, Eric Clapton, Allan Lamb, David English (capt.), John Keeble. (Seated on ground) David Essex.

ABOVE: An ear bashing from Eric, Ripley, 1986.

RIGHT: *Let it Rain*. David English, Phil Collins and Eric Clapton, 1986.

Silly 'Benson &
Hedges' Wyman.

ABOVE: *One Love*. Meeting the Master Blaster IVA
Richards. We've been laughing non-stop ever since!

BELOW: Two Bunbury legends – Lara and Lineker.

Lamby, the Human Jukebox and the dog from HMV. Rory has enthralled crowds
with his million voices and immaculate strokeplay wherever we've played.

There's only one Ian Wright! The Pied
Piper of the Bunburys. Wrighty and a
very special young Gooner.

'Super' Sam Fox holds one of my
bouncers – Sammy is our favourite lady
Bunbury.

TECHNICOLOR DREAMS

It was time for my screen debut. 'Just follow Ringo!' shouted Ken above the din of the last scene, which had involved voodooism and sadism among the steaming caves of hell.

'Sound running, turnover, action,' cried Ken. The Pope (Ringo) burst into Liszt's cell followed by me and my soldiers. I cried, 'Stop' and started blasting away with my pistol wildly above my head, as in my audition piece.

The Pope told Liszt that his daughter Cosima had deserted her husband Hans, renounced her faith and married Satan himself – Richard Wagner. All hell let loose. Ringo was screaming for Roger to cast out the devil in Wagner – 'Only by saving his soul will Liszt redeem his music.'

Rick's organ music reached a deafening crescendo, I continued to run about firing my pistol and we all ended up dancing with 30 naked girls around a giant penis amidst the burning ruins of Hitler's Berlin. All this and we got paid for it! What a way to make a living. Lost in that Surrey dream factory, framed in the fantasy of film.

The wild and wacky world of Wagner, Wakeman and Liszt had certainly wet my whistle for further film appearances.

7 TECHNICOLOR DREAMS

We had achieved our objective in making RSO number one, and the Red Cow was now grazing happily around the world. There was still a great deal of work to be done. And yet, a big part of me remained unfulfilled. Since my earliest days at school people had continually told me I was wasting my talents, telling me I should be on the stage. True, I had spent years promoting the talents of others – maybe now was time to have a go myself.

One night back at 67 Brook Street, I had a heart to heart with Robert. It was 6 p.m., J & B time, and the Chairman, drinking his favourite whisky while seated behind the four stone lions, was in a receptive mood.

'Robert I want to be an actor,' I blurted out. The Chairman looked up from his glass and gave me a long and solitary stare. 'What for?'

'Well I've spent all these years acting in real life. I might as well have a go at creating "make believe".' Robert remained focused and silent.

'After all,' I continued, 'acting is grown-ups pretending. Salesmen are the best actors in real life turning in a performance every day. Being spontaneous, improvising, using their wits and their own lines. I feel I do that naturally. Maybe it's time to learn someone else's lines. You know me, Robert, I know how to make people laugh, break the ice . . .'

'I'm certainly not going to release you,' said Robert. 'You can do both jobs.' Typical Robert, I thought, always looking at the wider picture.

'It would be difficult to run a record company and be a film star,' I suggested, laughing.

I had worked with Ken Russell on *Tommy*. Ken had directed the film for RSO and I had watched carefully just what went into the making of a film, particularly the actors' involvement and dedication.

'Listen,' said Robert. 'Go and be an actor with my blessing. Get it out of your system; on one condition. I'll keep you on a retainer, so you can continue the great work you've started here. You created our Red Cow and there's no way you're leaving him. Come on, David, we're partners, and remember, "You're still the one!"'

We laughed, shook hands, finished our drinks and with a whiff of aftershave I had gone. The next minute, I was out in the street looking back at No. 67, but already looking forward in my mind.

The first morning of my new life, I bought a copy of *The Stage* and one or two film magazines. There were rows of pictures of stars at parties, all arriving at premieres or clutching awards and glasses of champagne.

Laughing with perfect white teeth through vacuous smiles. 'Blimey, they all seem to be preoccupied with partying. Nobody seems to be actually acting.'

As I leafed through the pages of *The Stage*, my eye caught an advertisement for *Joseph and His Amazing Technicolor Dreamcoat* auditions – National Tour – Contact: Donald Bodley at Grosvenor Entertainments. What a coincidence – I had released the album, now I could end up acting in the *Dreamcoat*.

Donald Bodley was a middle-aged man. Mild-mannered, well dressed in a sober suit. His office was not ostentatious in a theatrical agent style. There were no pictures of Tommy Steele 'Live At The Winter Gardens Clacton' or 'Norman Wisdom in Panto at Blackpool' on the walls. Just a business-like gentleman behind a large leather-topped desk.

'So, Mr English, what theatre experience have you? What have you done recently? How's your singing and dancing?'

In truth, the only stage work I had done was performing comedy in the Northern clubs. I had always told gags and the clubs were a perfect platform to try out new material, anonymously. Nobody knew me anyway. You were up there standing alone, no safety net, just your imagination and delivery, and the rapid audience response; you were either funny or not funny. Unbeknown to many, I have spent a great deal of my life performing at clubs and dinners, many lonely nights in Doncaster, making people laugh, there is no greater feeling. Funnily enough, you always remember the bad nights, like the Hallam and District Tennis Club where the older folk walked past me muttering, 'What is a meat and two veg, pink trombone, Norwegian hand pump and Fagin the one-eyed assassin?' . . . 'Disgraceful'; and there was the Wakefield Trinity Rugby League Club Awards Dinner, where my Prince Charles impersonation fell flat on cauliflower ears . . . 'Bloody Southerner'. . . 'Boy's a poofter!'

How could I answer Bodley's question? I knew that my reply would determine a new move in career, or not. I couldn't tell him that I'd been at the RSC or worked with Olivier at the National or I had just completed filming 25 episodes of *Z Cars* after three years' outstanding training at RADA. Because I hadn't.

Alright, I knew how to flog a few records, tell a couple of gags and score a century but in my mind I was starting from scratch. *Come on, boy, keep your nerve, don't bottle it*. So in a flash I leapt on to Bodley's desk and went into a full-blown version of Elvis Presley's 'Hound Dog'. This was followed by a scissor jump back to the carpet, gyrating to 'Don't Be Cruel', 'Return to Sender' and 'Love Me Tender'.

'Stop! Stop!' cried the startled impresario. 'OK, you've got the job, sit down!'

Still panting, I sat down and listened. 'You'll play the part of the eldest brother Reuben. Rehearsals start next week at Brompton Oratory, 9 a.m. sharp. Two weeks rehearsal. You'll open at the Grand Theatre, Leeds, on to the Lyceum, Edinburgh and finish at the Theatre Royal, Brighton, £30 per week plus £7 towards your digs. Thank you, David, a very interesting performance. Now will you show the next man in?'

I left feeling on top of the world but completely unsure what Donald Bodley had thought. What was great was that he had no knowledge or interest in my past, he had judged me purely as a thespian.

Weeks later I met him backstage while on tour. 'Mr Bodley, sorry about my Elvis on your desk . . .' Bodley looked up at me and smiled. 'Don't worry, David, extreme characters have always fascinated me!'

That weekend, the *Sunday Express* had run a banner headline 'Record Boss Quits Job for £30 per week'.

I even got a call from Arista Records in America to come and run their label worldwide, but my mind was made up and at 9 a.m. the following Wednesday I entered the world of fantasy, standing around the piano singing 'There's One More Angel In Heaven'.

I immediately felt at home with the actors. Nobody judged you on what you had or had not done. A tremendous sense of camaraderie prevailed. We were the cast; we would sink or swim as a team, egos would beat in private. Nothing phased the actors, they had experienced the highs and lows, the bullshit and the empty promises, the exultation of performance and the false dawns. They were peddlers of dreams, kind, fun loving, caring, receptive and accommodating. They were my new friends and I would learn from them every minute of the day. A few of them had read the *Sunday Express* article, but only one or two asked why I'd given it all up to bum around the stage. The others seemed to understand. There we were, clustered around that piano, from all walks of life, like the French Foreign Legion, with the same desire to escape from reality, to dissolve into Technicolor Dreams, to show off and get paid for it.

I loved performing in *Joseph*. What an honour to be able to walk on the stage of the Grand Theatre, Leeds with its magnificent proscenium arch and one hundred years history of great opera. Alright, I may not have been Albert Finney or Tom Courtenay, but I was deliriously happy being a sheep in the first half, especially 'Baa Baaing' past Lennie our percussionist, cocking my back leg over his drum kit and hearing him breathe the words 'you bastard' every night. As a cowboy, I sang 'One More Angel In Heaven', as a Frenchman I sang the solo in 'Those Canaan Days'. We performed the Elvis song supported by 26 pupils from the Intake High School, Bramley, Leeds and when Leonard Whiting, our Joseph (who had recently appeared in Franco Zefferelli's *Romeo and Juliet* as Romeo), burst into 'Close Every Door to Me' high above on the scaffold, there wasn't a dry eye in the house. We were a company of players on the road, having a ball.

Four of us had found digs in an old farmhouse at Sowerby Bridge. It was winter and bitterly cold. From our Wuthering Heights, I remember gazing at the old mill deep in the valley. Abandoned now, years ago it had been the heartbeat of the community, offering work and security.

During the rehearsals back in London I had found myself a great commercials agent, Joy Galloway, who had put me up for a Head & Shoulders commercial. They'd wanted a cricketer – perfect casting. I auditioned and got the job.

On the day of shooting, the director, who was a Bit Iffy, gave me my motivation. 'Sweetie, you've been playing cricket and want to shampoo your hair after the game. Be a love, I know f*** all about cricket, so improvise, extemporise, feel the part, feel it, my love.' So improvise I did.

'Well, I was batting and the sun was very bright, so I asked one of the fielders if I could borrow his cap. After the game in the dressing room he said, "Do you know you've got dandruff?" Well, I looked in the cap and it was like a snowstorm inside. "Have you tried Head & Shoulders?" he said. "No," I replied. So I used Head & Shoulders for the first time and the "barnet" has been shiny and dandruff-free ever since!'

I concocted and delivered these immortal lines in 45 seconds. We filmed it in one take, the director was elated. Little did I know that my 45-second oration would be transmitted to the nation for the next ten years. Great for the royalties. The power of television – taxi drivers used to pull up beside me at the lights and enquire, mischievously, 'How's the dandruff, my son?'

We completed our run at the Grand Theatre and moved on to the Royal Lyceum Theatre in Edinburgh where we climbed Arthur's Seat and stayed in a beautiful farmhouse at Liberton Brae.

The spirit of friendship generated by the company was brilliant. When the acting had finished we played together, particularly in a pub around the corner from the theatre called Chez Fred's. The Scottish girls reminded me of the Swedish, blonde, brave-hearted and full of fun. I fell for an East German girl who lived in Saxe-Coburg Place. Together we shared the magic of Stockbridge and the feeling of being far away from home.

On to Brighton and the last leg of our tour. The majesty of the Theatre Royal, the esplanade and the solitude of a seaside town out of season with its rows of beach huts, empty shells of summer dreams. To see the lone angler casting his line into the shimmering surf, and the silver seagull soaring northwards.

Sad and fond farewells were exchanged as the company split up after the final performance. I had absorbed my first lesson in the craft of the theatre: to be directed, the moves, projection and the playing of characters, interacting with your fellow thespians. One thing was for certain; with acting, you learnt your trade in the theatre, your exposure came on television, and the money from films. Three different techniques, three different disciplines.

Back at RSO Records, Robert had decided to leave Atlantic for Polydor, who had stepped in with a much bigger financial commitment to distribute

RSO worldwide. I had always dealt with two great characters who ran Polydor in Hamburg, Peter Sibley and Chris Youle. When I had left RSO on a day-to-day basis, I had recommended Chris Youle to Robert to take my place. Chris Youle was the king of Hamburg. He knew everybody from royalty to the down and outs. A modern day D'Artagnan, longhaired, big moustache, with a knowledge of the record business second to none.

My next ambition was to crack the movie business. I had experienced my first taste of television with Head & Shoulders, toured the theatres with *Joseph*. It was time now to enter the world of Panavision Pictures. I had worked with Ken Russell on *Tommy*, the brilliant rock opera written by Pete Townshend about a deaf, dumb and blind boy who became a new Messiah. Roger Daltrey, the lead singer of The Who, played the title role, Robert Stigwood had produced the film and we had recorded the album on RSO.

Ken's celluloid biopics on the lives of distinguished composer-musicians, including Elgar, Debussy, Delius, Strauss, Mahler and Tchaikovsky, were legendary; but these had been 'straight' biographies. As in his highly successful motion pictures *Women in Love* and *The Music Lovers*, he wanted to enrich his subjects with his own form of imaginative Russellmania.

He had decided to make *Lisztomania*, depicting Franz Liszt and Richard Wagner as the world's first two pop stars. Roger Daltrey would play Liszt and my pal and RSO recording artist Paul Nicholas would be Richard Wagner. Shooting would take place at Shepperton in its first four-walled studio. I called Ken's PA at the film's production office. 'Tell him it's David English and I want to come and see him.' It was late evening when I arrived at Shepperton. Driving past the studio lots was fascinating. A hive of make-believe, with actors in full dress scurrying from their trailers to the sound stages. Key grips, focus pullers, sound men and best boys ran about their business clutching film stock, the wardrobe masters and continuity girls spoke incessantly into two-way radios and the producers walked slowly pondering on their budgets and the director's every whim.

The production office was spartan but friendly. In the outer office, production secretaries sat behind typewriters hammering out scripts and talking furiously into telephones. Ken's door was open. He was talking animatedly to producer Roy Baird and co-producer David Puttnam.

I could see, by the way he commanded the conversation, that he could well be a producer's nightmare. He always used the slimmest of scripts merely as a guide – the rest he composed shot by shot in his head. All great directors use their heads and eyes as cameras; Steven Spielberg is the king of cerebral direction, and Ridley Scott is not far behind.

Ken's own interpretative visual genius certainly communicated and perhaps infuriated audiences in every age bracket. His screen images never failed to influence and intrigue his admirers and it's a safe bet that his dissenters would never be allowed to become bored. While making a Russell picture the producer's problems heightened day by day. If Ken suddenly wanted to introduce 200 Hell's Angels riding their motorbikes through the sets dressed as Nazis with naked nymphomaniacs clinging to their backs, the producers had to point out diplomatically the necessity of bringing the picture in on budget.

'Ah, David! Good to see you.' Ken gave me a warm welcome. He was a biggish man with a friendly florid face and a mass of white hair.

'Now tell me the story. I thought you were running Robert's record company.' I explained my story so far and my desire to act.

'Interesting,' he said, 'very interesting. You know, David, music for me is the most incredible event in the history of the human race. It comes from nowhere. You can't expect the composer to fit into the usual idea of normal behaviour patterns. My films are about some of the things I feel when I think of Liszt and Wagner and listen to their music. Perhaps if I could write great music, then I wouldn't have started making films.'

He then reached into the top drawer of his desk and took out a handgun. 'David, take this gun and stand on that chair. Fire it when I tell you.' I obediently followed Ken's direction. There was a terrific gunshot. David Puttnam and Roy Baird cowered and the hustle and bustle stopped outside the door.

'You'll be my Captain of the Hussars,' boomed Ken. 'Shooting starts in two weeks. Roger is Liszt, Paul is Wagner and Ringo Starr will be the Pope. Have you an agent?'

'No, Ken,' I replied.

'Never mind. You go and see Shirley' (Shirley Russell was Ken's wife, who had designed all the clothes and uniforms featured in his films) 'for your uniform. Wally Schneiderman will do your make-up. Leave your address with the girls outside and they will send you your script.'

'Now Roy,' Ken resumed his conversation with the slightly shell-shocked producer. 'We'll open in 1830 and conclude amidst the ruins of Hitler's Berlin where the Frankenstein figure born of Wagner's music and philosophy is destroyed and disintegrates into flames as Liszt and the Angels head off towards the infinite.'

I listened and left, excited beyond belief at the expectation of being Ken's Captain of the Hussars. Acting in my first motion picture, I couldn't wait to tell my mum, Annie, Robert and Mr Patel!

Day one of shooting. The Captain of the Hussars saddled up his green BMW and cantered through the back roads of West Hampstead before opening up the throttle into full gallop on to the A3 and the open road to Shepperton film studios in Surrey for a 7 a.m. call time.

6.30 a.m.   Bacon sandwich and *Daily Express* on arrival in the canteen.
7.00 a.m.   Make-up

7.30 a.m.   Costume
8.00 a.m.   On the set to report to the Director.

'Ah! My captain, all is well?'

'Yes, sire,' I replied, extremely excited at the prospect of entering his fantasy of the life of Franz Liszt.

Franz Liszt (Roger Daltrey) was currently in bed with the Countess Marie D'Agoult, a very tasty actress called Fiona Lewis. At 8.30 the cameras rolled and Franz and his aristocratic young beauty were surprised by the unexpected arrival of the Count D'Agoult, Marie's husband, brandishing a rapier. Clearly Franz was no match at swordplay for the Count, who had engaged the Hungarian composer to tutor his wife in the art of making music, not love.

As Roger is caught rogering the Count's missus, Marie begs her husband to spare Liszt's life, so she may share with him whatever fate he had in mind. The Count decrees that 'they who deceive by the piano shall die by the piano'. He orders Liszt and Marie to be incarcerated together inside a grand piano and carried to a railway line. An express train, puffing like the wrath of God, bears down menacingly on its impotent victims.

Bugger me, I thought, *and it's only 9.25 a.m.*

Next the film dissolved into Liszt's crowded dressing room before a Beethoven concert. He is surrounded by bodyguards and a throng of attentive groupies. Just like being backstage at a Who concert, I thought.

Suddenly, a shabby young man bursts in and demands to see Liszt. It is Richard Wagner (Paul Nicholas), a talented but penniless composer. He wants Liszt to buy the score for a new opera he has written about ancient Rome. Liszt replies that he is a musician not an impresario. Hans Von Bulow, Franz's pal and confidante, brings him a wad of notes, which he thrusts into the young man's hand, and Liszt promises to give Wagner's composition a 'free plug' that evening.

For me, making this film was like being back in the rock 'n' roll business. Roger Daltrey and Paul Nicholas were in their element playing rock stars from the past.

It was fascinating seeing how a motion picture was made and I watched every development very carefully. Make-up artist Wally and the special effects team had their talents really stretched, creating the terrifying warlike Thor/Frankenstein monster based on Wagner's Siegfried, as well as the vampire sequence when Wagner sprouts fangs and sinks them into the neck of his by-now former friend Liszt in the fantastic laboratory he has set up in the hall within his gothic castle. Another challenge was the interstellar space rocket, with organ pipes as booster tubes, to carry Liszt dressed as the god Mercury and four space-suited angels, lifted by the composer's keyboard pyrotechnics.

The entire crew was amazing, following Ken's visual genius and sense of surrealism on the hoof. Shot by shot, scene by scene, everything was achieved spontaneously and although we all learned and performed our lines, a great deal of the action was ad-libbed. The end result was like a cross between Mel Brooks's *Blazing Saddles* and Ken's own *Tommy*.

My old pal Rick Wakeman was brought in as musical arranger, composing themes based on the classical compositions of both Liszt and Wagner. It was great to see him in fine form after recording and touring with his worldwide Number 1 album *Journey to the Centre of the Earth*. All these pop stars and my boss in the film, Ringo Starr – the Pope – still to come – it was like 'Top of the Popes'! Ringo was great. He reminded me of Maurice Gibb, very alert, forever cracking gags with a keen sense of comedy timing.

It was time for my screen debut. 'Just follow Ringo!' shouted Ken above the din of the last scene, which had involved voodooism and sadism among the steaming caves of hell.

'Sound running, turnover, action,' cried Ken. The Pope (Ringo) burst into Liszt's cell followed by me and my soldiers. I cried, 'Stop' and started blasting away with my pistol wildly above my head, as in my audition piece.

The Pope told Liszt that his daughter Cosima had deserted her husband Hans, renounced her faith and married Satan himself – Richard Wagner. All hell let loose. Ringo was screaming for Roger to cast out the devil in Wagner – 'Only by saving his soul will Liszt redeem his music.'

Rick's organ music reached a deafening crescendo, I continued to run about firing my pistol and we all ended up dancing with 30 naked girls around a giant penis amidst the burning ruins of Hitler's Berlin. All this and we got paid for it! What a way to make a living. Lost in that Surrey dream factory, framed in the fantasy of film.

The wild and wacky world of Wagner, Wakeman and Liszt had certainly wet my whistle for further film appearances.

Back at RSO we had released 'Fanny Be Tender With My Love' from the Bee Gees album. It had reached Number 12 in the USA charts. But as the boys went back into the studios, sadly they had to say farewell to Arif Mardin. Arif was contracted to Atlantic and as the Bee Gees were signed to Polydor under the new RSO arrangement, he would no longer be available to produce the group's albums. So ended a great partnership.

A producer's job, like a cricket coach, is to enhance whatever natural talent is there. To influence and to guide, not to change and discourage. When the cricketers Viv Richards and Andy Roberts first came to this country, they attended trials at the Lansdowne Club in Bath, watched by a senior coach, clipboard under his arm. They went through their paces in the nets. Years later Viv showed me the coach's report.

'I.V.A. Richards from Antigua has talent and an exceptional eye but hits across the line too much.'

8,500 Test runs later, 5,000 of which were whipped by Viv from outside his off stump over the mid wicket boundary, makes one wonder about the coach's wisdom and ability to spot a true talent.

'A.M.E Roberts, Antigua, bowls quickly but with little control.'

Ask Ian Botham about this 'little control'. Facing Andy on his Somerset debut, Beefy hooked a short one for four. The next ball looked the same, Beefy shaped to repeat the shot but it was deceptively quicker, hitting him straight in the mouth on the left hand side. So powerful was the blow it dislodged his 'Hampstead Heath' in sympathy on the right.

Viv and Andy went on to be legends in the game by playing it their way.

Arif's gift as the Bee Gees fourth set of ears had been to give them confidence and self-belief in their new direction, to guide not change.

But I was also worried about my career as an actor. Having the taste for film-making, I started looking for more work. Scanning the papers, my eye caught an article: 'Sir Richard Attenborough to direct "A Bridge Too Far", the story of the Battle of Arnhem.'

In the autumn of 1944, Montgomery planned an invasion of German-occupied Holland which he hoped would bring the war to a rapid close. Lieutenant-General Sir Brian Horrocks would lead the charge through Holland to Arnhem, then regroup for the final thrust into the Ruhr that would cripple Germany's industrial heartland. British, American and Polish troops would be parachuted into Holland ahead of Horrocks's Corps to take and hold the 11 bridges that stood in the path of the main attacking force. But the plan misfired; some of the positions the paratroopers had taken at great cost were never relieved because of the unforeseen delays and setbacks the main force encountered. The Allies lost 17,000 men.

Why would Hollywood want to make a film about such a tragic and bloody battle? My Uncle Tom, a Lieutenant Colonel in the Royal Artillery, had told me that the word Arnhem was indeed a scar on British military history. 'A Bridge Too Scar?', well I suppose they had made *The Charge of the Light Brigade*, another story of failed military planning which, when filmed, had gone on to achieve box office success.

I was drawn to the story of 'Operation Market Garden' and was determined to get a part in the film. As usual, I researched the best route to reach my objective. Miriam Brickman, the legendary casting director, would be casting the film. I went to see her, on a windswept day, in her basement office in Redcliffe Gardens. Miriam Brickman was a little Jewish lady with a colossal reputation for casting some of the world's greatest films. I made her laugh. I told her about my part as the Captain in Ken's *Lisztomania*.

'Look at me, Miriam. I'm perfect officer material for *A Bridge Too Far*.'

I listened, fascinated, as she told me the story behind 'The Bridge'. Joe Levine was the producer. It was going to cost him 25 million dollars and it would feature a stellar cast, among them Robert Redford, Sean Connery, Michael Caine, Laurence Olivier, Anthony Hopkins, Ryan O'Neal, Gene Hackman, Edward Fox, Elliott Gould, Hardy Kruger, Liv Ullman, Maximilian Schell, Dirk Bogarde, James Caan – the list was amazing: 14 of the most famous names in the business.

'But 25 million dollars, how can he recoup that sum and make a profit?' I asked.

Miriam told me that Joe Levine, who had made some massive movies like *Hercules*, *The Graduate* and *The Lion In Winter,* would use his 'famous 14' as a bargaining point with which to pre-sell his yet unmade film throughout the world. He is a unique salesman. He would spend $9 million on his 14 stars, $2 million on Robert Redford alone – for just 20 days' work and probably only 15 minutes of screen time.

'You have to make two and a half times the production costs at the box office before you go into profit. So Joe will have to sell $62,500,000 worth of tickets before he goes into profit,' she explained.

In Hollywood there were then five big names that would almost certainly guarantee you success at the box office: Clint Eastwood, Charles Bronson, Steve McQueen, Paul Newman and Robert Redford. Eastwood makes his own movies, happy at 'playing the loner'; Bronson wasn't available; Paul Newman was too old to play any of the major American military characters; Steve McQueen's price for coming out of temporary retirement to act in the film was astronomical; so Joe was happy to get Redford for $2 million.

'Joe will sell different distribution rights throughout the world. Take Japan for example. They said if you can get Redford as part of your cast, instead of giving you X amount of dollars we'd give you X times two for distribution rights. So Joe will have recouped his original outlay, through selling the distribution rights before the first day of filming.' She made it sound so simple.

'And the director?' I enquired.

'He went after Richard Attenborough because he directed Joe's favourite all-time film *Oh What A Lovely War.* Joe believed that correct publicity and distribution would make the public go and see a film they would otherwise stay away from. He believed that Paramount, *Lovely War's* distributor, had not understood the picture, resulting in its poor box office returns, but he had faith in Attenborough, and after watching his second film as a director, *Young Winston,* knew he'd do justice to *Bridge.*

'To an extent *Bridge* is a Second World War version of *Lovely War* without the overt satire or the music. Attenborough would be faced with the same two problems: to illustrate the folly of the generals. And to move the audience with a genuine sense of grief at the catastrophe. Of course Dickie is bound to attract a vast audience with his galaxy of stars and the wide-screen war action but to make it a great film, his message has got to come over.'

As we drank tea in Miriam's dimly lit basement I asked her what that message was.

'He will want the picture to acknowledge all the gallantry, all the selflessness. The comradeship and the instantaneous bravery that was involved in the action.'

'And the screenplay?' I had learnt that the screenplay was massively important, telling the story and giving the actors the material to exhibit their skills. 'William Goldman has written the screenplay,' continued Miriam. 'He is currently the most successful screenwriter in the world, having written *Butch Cassidy and the Sundance Kid*, *All the President's Men* and *Marathon Man*.'

'So what about a part for me?' I asked, eagerly.

'Well, Sir Richard will be casting for a body of men who will play soldiers in his film, not just extras, but trained actors who will be in the forefront of most scenes, just behind the stars. They must be versatile – any individual must be able to play any role. One day a British Red Beret, the next an American, maybe a Polish paratrooper and even a Nazi. Moreover, they will live like soldiers and work like soldiers. David, the work will be hard and not very glamorous. You will undergo military training with a stuntman called Doug Robinson under the supervision of the film's military advisor, Colonel John Waddy, who actually fought at Arnhem. You will be taught how to march, to do arms drill, to fight hand-to-hand and learn to fire every conceivable weapon, 303s, Bren guns, German Mausers and you will learn how to die. You will collectively be called the APA – "Attenborough's Private Army". Are you still interested?'

THE BOYS FROM THE BRIDGE

Big Frank and I were selected to be two of Robert Redford's 'Dirty Dozen' that took the bridge at Nijmegen.

I had just been through the terrifying experience of crossing Waal (Rhine) in a dinghy full of US Airborne with a fair amount of trepidation, looking like a Michelin man because under my uniform I had two life-jackets, fully inflated, in case I went overboard. This safety precaution was taken for two reasons. First, the river is particularly deep with fast-moving conflicting currents and, secondly, my swimming abilities are limited to a width and a half at the Finchley outdoor pool. Undaunted by the perils of the deep we rowed back and forwards across that river with explosions sounding in our ears and six inches of water seeping into our trousers.

8 THE BOYS FROM THE BRIDGE

A lot of people still ask me, 'Well we watched *A Bridge Too Far* and we didn't see you in it . . . were you the third dead German from the right?' The answer is never as easy as that. Beginning at the beginning, it all started back in March 1976. Sir Richard Attenborough's film was based on Cornelius Ryan's book *A Bridge Too Far*, the tragic story of the battle for the Arnhem Bridge. This, the greatest of all war films, featured some of the world's foremost stars but the thing I remember best about it is the team I joined, 40 of the finest guys I have ever met, blokes of all shapes, sizes and dispositions, a motley crew who were to be called Attenborough's Private Army.

The APA was the guv's brainchild. He felt that to complement his super-stars he would need a band of young actors who at any given time could be asked to play a role or express a particular emotion, a kind of repertory company who would be taught to live and think like soldiers. To find this hallowed gathering, Sir Richard held an open audition at London's Dance Centre, Drury Lane, 26 March 1976, 9.30 a.m.

I became fascinated by the story of the Bridge or Operation Market Garden, as it was known, so, after badgering the local librarian into finding me every existing book on the subject, I made my way to the 'big one', determined to get on the picture at all costs.

On arrival I was to find out it was indeed the 'big one' for, on opening the door, I discovered the room packed to the gills. The deafening presence of 400 actors talking, laughing among themselves, expectant and hopeful. Suddenly the hubbub subsided as the door opened and in walked Sir Richard, David Tomblin, the assistant director, stunt organiser, Alf Joint, and Miriam Brickman, the casting director. Quietly we sat down and listened to the man, who, before directing, had appeared in so many war films himself. Articulately, Sir Richard outlined his intentions, telling us how we would have a crash course in military training in Holland, living like soldiers in barracks style conditions, before we even saw a film set. There would be no glamour attached. Because of the very nature of the picture a high regard for discipline would be exercised; but it would be bloody good fun and a tremendous experience as we would be working with a brilliant crew and the three times Academy Award winning cameraman Geoffrey Unsworth.

I was impressed with Richard Attenborough from the start. His dapper appearance and jocular manner won the attention of the 'cattle market' as 400 men sat listening to his every word.

'I want to take 40 of you from the beginning and others may well come later. You will all be paid £125 plus £50 per week expenses and live in an old folks' home in the town of Deventer. Incidentally, gentlemen, if any of you are against having your hair cut and beard shaved, you had better leave now.'

No one moved. Dickie then introduced David Tomblin, his assistant director, Alf and Miriam and then proceeded to outline the story and members of the unit in detail. Nobody would have a huge part in the film. There were 14 main stars including Robert Redford, James Caan, Gene Hackman etc., and from our resources some of us would be chosen to be featured and given lines as the film progressed.

At the end of the speech we had to fill in forms stating previous experiences, sports and physical pursuits. A particularly relevant clause was 'reasons for wanting to be in the picture'. This of course was where the document became purely individual and where people would outline their personal claim to a place in the company.

All the following are genuine examples in response to the question: 'Is there any other information which you feel may be relevant to this production?'

Was in the Boy's Brigade national marching team.

I have travelled all my life and am certainly very adaptable to different people of different nationalities and cultures.

Have been down in a submarine during filming of 'Warship' so jumping out of a plane would come as no shock.

Yes, hire me and it will be even better. I would love to do this production given half a chance.

Practised knowledge of 39/45 small arms [my underlining]

I have been trained as a ballet dancer and have danced for 3 years with the Royal Ballet and 2½ with Festival Ballet and this I consider is very regimental training and very disciplined.

I have read book.

Very energetic. Good actor. I know Deventer very well and could relieve your budget of the cost of my camp bed by staying with friends.

Worked as lifeguard. (Need the money badly).

Intimate knowledge of mud and bad weather.

Not a bad actor.

Willing to have hair cut.

Don't mind getting knocked about a bit.

I like to kill.

Close to death once in Turkey by a bandit's ambush.

Played a German-speaking NCO in 'Colditz' BBC-TV including submachine-gunning David McCallum.

Good at heights – last year spent mending roof of house.

Played a soldier in 'Overlord' – mind you, it was a dead soldier.

There are Irish soldiers in the book.

I have used a bow and arrow.

In response to the question: 'Do you take part or specialise in any sporting pastimes?'

Chess, walking, squatting – a man who has already fallen to earth.

We then met Dickie individually, had photographs taken and left the Dance Centre with our head in the clouds, wondering.

A couple of weeks went by and I was offered a film and theatre part. These I turned down and just waited and hoped for a call from Miriam. Ten days later it finally came. Meet at Twickenham Studios at two o'clock, along with 200 of the flock who had been recalled. In the studio 12 of us were asked to line up by the left hand wall – I was first, God knows why, I thought. Alongside me, Francis Mughan, Jason Gregory, David Auker, Dan Long, James Wardroper and Mark York. The names were read out. People sorted into different groups. English actors who could speak German, actors who had lived in America, those that could speak Polish. Well, are we in? Have we been chosen? Why had we 12 been singled out? The studio was filled with the buzz of anticipation. After a few hours we were asked to leave and told that we would hear the final selection in a couple of days. On the way out I managed to glance at the lists on the production assistant's desk, and there were our 12 names under the title 'physical types'!

On 1 May I got the call to have a short back and sides and my flight details, KLM 124, 10.50 a.m. on 4 May. The adventure had started – I was in – one of the fabulous 40!

At eight o'clock sharp the limo, one of those huge old Austin Princesses, arrived at my home. The chauffeur took my bags and off we cruised, through the streets of West Hampstead. Well, this shows a bit of style, I thought, lounging in the backseat, and all for me! My illusions of grandeur were short-lived for in the next hour we had picked up six more blokes, their suitcases, tennis rackets and other paraphernalia. We only needed Wilfred Hyde White when we finally crunched to a halt outside Terminal 2, Heathrow and we would have looked like something out of those old Ealing Studio farces. When we met the other 34 in the departure lounge, most of London Airport must have thought it a meeting of mercenaries, Angola-bound. Extraordinary the transformation a couple of hours in the barber's shop can do. I remembered a few faces from the auditions, but most were not familiar. After exchanging handshakes and smiling nods the lads 'duty freed' and boarded the DC9 flight KLM 124 to Amsterdam.

At clinically clean Schipol Airport we were met by Jack Dearlove, and a hairy individual called Rocko.

'Jacko' Dearlove, as he became known, was in charge of our everyday welfare (an unenviable task which aged him considerably). A sprightly character, Jacko, who has done almost everything in the film business from understudying, producing, to directing, looked about 40 but secretly to his chums was nearer 65. Rocko, an Amsterdamer, was also an assistant whose particular advantage was that he spoke English fluently and therefore could handle any communication difficulties between the film company and the Dutch people.

The old folks home in Deventer stood impressively as a bastion dominating the square. Once an orphanage, it had been sadly neglected. I could imagine the children running through the marbled hallways, down the winding stairway and out into the garden full of roses and pansies. The older people had probably stayed more in their rooms, solemn affairs with bare walls and high ceilings. Sir Richard Attenborough and David Tomblin, on one of their location-finding jaunts, had stumbled across the home, done it up, put in some showers, and generally made the place suitable to be our barracks. Across the square the old folk, now in their new houses, waited with interest for the arrival of the new folk in their old house. When our charabanc finally swung to a halt outside two huge green gates, the imposing factors of our new home were overlooked as 40 thespians dived in to find sanctuary. I found myself in the 'motorway', a huge room on the first floor, positioned between the bogs and another dormitory.

My early exuberance soon waned, for after a few days I realised I was trapped in the middle of the most evil-smelling latrines in eastern Holland and a room full of maniac runners who suffered from acute dysentery and insomnia in equal measure. Sharing my suite was Farell Sheridan, a dear Irish soul who spoke constantly of impending doom in a lyrical brogue, usually pissed out of his brains. Opposite Farell lay Milton Cadman, a generous Scot who complained about everything but was kindness personi-fied and who became a staunch friend. He also possessed a tremendous remedy for piles (a condition from which I sometimes suffer), which managed to relieve this anal horror and made sitting more bearable. Next to me was my buddy Francis Mughan. As well as being neighbours in West Hampstead, we had sometimes bumped into each other at interviews back in London. He didn't like to stay at home during the evening, instead prop-ping up some bar, flaunting his good looks and breaking most of the young girls' hearts. On the other side of the room, Jason Gregory, a shrewd char-acter, knowledgeable about the business, who kept himself to himself. His keen sense of humour allowed him to fit in anywhere.

On the first night we all explored the town, although the boys-own sortie in Deventer was met with mixed feelings from the locals. The thought of a mighty film company besieging their town for the next six months excited the bar and nightclub owners, while many of the Dutch people were fasci-nated by the story of the film. However, a lot of the men folk were far from happy at the idea of their women being wooed by a lascivious bunch of foreigners.

That night my particular party certainly did the town. Strolling down the little cobbled streets, we dived in and out of the bars like hungry beavers, the Brasserie, Pelican, Chez Antoinette, Nellie's Bar and then on to the clubs – St Tropez, Safari, Voodoo, drinking, chatting to the locals and sensing the feeling of excitement and expectancy in the town. We discovered where the porno shop was situated and that there were three old pros sitting in windows down by the bridge.

I got lost. So did James Snell. In a paralytic stupor on his return from a huge binge, the Dutch police apprehended him. 'Listen here, my good chap, I'm perfectly capable of getting home. Just point me in the general direction of Swiss Cottage, and I'll be fine!' James's insistence seemed to satisfy the police who stood back, open-mouthed, and watched him stagger into some doorway and apparently not come out.

The next morning at breakfast was hopeless. The babble of conversation and loud bravado of 'knee tremblers' in the Town Square and uncanny drinking displays were soon halted at the first sight of Ollie's omelettes. Ollie was our Irish cook who served up his very special recipes at very early hours each morning. Built like a whippet, his prowess as a sweeper in our football team somewhat surpassed his cooking abilities, but his work in the home and nimble sense of fun made him very special.

At 6.30 am the coach arrived to take us to Twello to be kitted out. Each chap had to be fitted with four lots of uniforms – German, American, Polish and English clobber. I think 'Wardrobe Brian' would have accepted suicide as a happy alternative rather than fit out our forty valiants but after a seemingly endless period of time we staggered back on to the coach clutching our garb, dropping helmets and battle smocks but looking comparatively military. At last we were off to war or, to be more precise, the dreaded training camp.

As the coach swung along the dyke road it was amusing to see each other decked out as paras. This frivolity came to an abrupt halt on first seeing Scherpenhof. As a training camp for the Dutch Military, Scherpenhof served two purposes, a holiday camp and an assault course, though whoever designed it must have possessed strong sadistic qualities. On entering the barbed wire gates, we were confronted by various obstacles: ropes, a sandpit (where one crawled on one's belly under street poles), pulleys suspended between two towers, a lake three miles in circumference, and, worst of all, dominating the scene, a 60-foot hill, grass on one side, a steep ski-slope on the other. For us soldiers this hill quickly became a mountain!

We lined up to meet Dougie Robinson, the stunt man who was to put us through our paces, and he set us off on a run around the lake. Those hot, clammy army uniforms sticking to your body – this was going to sort the men from the boys. The torture was made worse by the 100°F temperature, the hottest summer in Holland for 100 years.

Hilary Minster had the misfortune of putting a bolt through his head (after a rather robust forward-roll embedded the inside of his helmet in his cranium) and spent the next half an hour puking in the lake.

Most of the contingent started to lag after the first 500 yards, but towards the end there were about seven of us left, six of whom comprised of Desperate Dan Long and his Maniac Runners. Dan, in fact, managed to lap the stunt man.

The hill presented the next harrowing experience. I remember clambering to the top only to see Ollie's omelette floating across the surface of the lake, propelled from the yawning chops of Hilary who was by now prostrate, moaning unintelligible oaths. Drooping spirits were only just rejuvenated by lunchtime. Sprawled about the grass, our 40 paras got stuck into the beer and sandwiches provided, dreading the thought of the drill, hand-to-hand fighting, rope climbing and street patrolling that dear old Dougie had in store for us.

That afternoon we seemed to march everywhere in the unbearable heat. It was clear that not all of us would stay the course. Then out of the blue, the company had a stroke of fortune. It was discovered that among our ranks were three actors with previous military experience. Shaun 'Sarge' Curry, Jock 'New Pin' McKenzie and Mark Sheridan. The weight of responsibility was now reduced from the broad shoulders of stunt man Doug as the three of our lads started to drill us, teach us how to fire weapons and generally spur us on through our paces.

Fortunately for Hilary his boots started to squeak a lot, so when the noise wasn't to be heard we knew that he was probably horizontal behind some bush and desperately needed attention.

Our crash course in soldiering completed, we drove over to the first location to meet Dickie. It was an exciting and marvellous feeling as we marched across the field and came to attention, ready for the director's inspection. It was also our first glimpse of the film set and crew since arriving in Holland; James Caan and Arthur Hill were filming that day in an army medical centre sequence. We must have looked reasonably impressive because as we stood there in that field everybody on the set stopped and all eyes turned towards our ranks. Sir Richard beamed as he walked along our lines and chatted with us. Even Colonel John Waddy agreed that after another five or six haircuts we would look authentic, and coming from the ex-para chief, and former head of the SAS, that was praise indeed.

Dickie was delighted. There was a cheer from the crew and Attenborough's Private Army was finally born.

From that day things really started to move. We had a crash course from armourer Bill Aylemore, on how to fire every conceivable weapon, and in a week all of us could handle the British Sten gun, Bren gun, 303 rifle, German Schmeisser, Luger, American Garrard and M-1 Carbines, plus the heavier German Spandau and British Lewis machine gun. Although we were only firing blanks from five yards they were lethal, as Bill demonstrated by blowing the head off a rabbit tied up against a tree. We realised that, although we were only playing at war, infinite care had to be taken.

Our first professional assignment was as Frost's men. Anthony Hopkins played the part of Col. Johnny Frost, a somewhat eccentric leader who rallied his men by blowing a hunting horn and carried a dinner jacket and golf clubs into battle. During one incident, Frost had been held up on one side of the bridge with just 13 men. Under a constant barrage of gunfire from a Panzer division, the German tanks finally came to a halt on the other side. A German soldier walked slowly to the middle of the bridge, brandishing a white flag.

'What do you want?' boomed Frost

'Let us come and talk to you about surrender,' was the reply.

'Sorry, we haven't room enough to take you all prisoner,' replied Frost, completely undaunted.

That day there was a lot of street patrolling in Deventer and not much action, but at least we were in front of the camera and helping to make the film.

Being in front of the camera at once, to our amazement, became a major problem. We were instructed to keep our faces out of shot where possible because to be seen would mean the 'elbow' and the dreaded flight home! We had only come for six weeks after all, so if we were to be featured after a few days as British paras we couldn't appear later as battling Poles or dead Germans. Para-paranoia struck in the ranks. F***, I thought, all this way to become a film star and now we had the option either of avoiding being seen clearly and stay on, or being featured and it was on your bike back home! The possibility of being seen became known as the Terrible KLM shot – but it was too late for some eager beavers, their 'Bridge' days were numbered!

While filming in Deventer we quickly adjusted to a routine: waking at 6.00 a.m., Ollie's breakfast at 6.15, coach at 6.45, make-up by 7.00 and on the set at 7.30 ready for the day. We would then be immersed in the war until about nine o'clock when, regardless of how frenzied the battle may have been, it was down guns to queue up for breakfast supplied by the excellent Hobbs Catering and Giovanni, the laughing Italian. Giovanni, a rather round Roman, would serve tea or coffee while singing songs from Mario Lanza and for half an hour the war-torn paratroopers were transformed into a bunch of galloping gourmets. It was in the latter department that our pals, the Dutch extras, excelled.

After filming we would break for lunch at about one o'clock and wander off to the cheese factory taking our guns with us. Security was very tight with the weapons, the police having told Sir Richard that if any guns were left around or went missing, the film would be closed down. In charge of security was location manager Norton Natchbull, apparently a distant cousin of the Queen, who on day two was to be sorely tested. We had just staggered back into the cheese factory and settled down to roast lamb and potatoes when there was a sound of gunfire and all hell was let loose. People flying to the left and right or ducking under tables, while the culprit, a rather red-faced student from Nijmegen, just watched as his Schmeisser went berserk. In charged Norton, some would have thought a little overzealously, and slipped on a trifle, skidding on his arse across the floor of the factory. The pandemonium finally settled down and from then on all weapons had to be checked in during the lunchtime period. Nobody was hurt, only, perhaps, Norton's pride and Hans's pocket. His days as a soldier were over for he was sacked and sent on the next bus back to the safety of his studies in Nijmegen.

At the end of the afternoon's fighting, we stopped at 4.00 p.m. for cream cakes, tea and a chance to talk to the locals, who crowded behind barriers straining to get a glimpse of a superstar or two. Together with David Auker we would do an impromptu cabaret featuring jokes, tricks and a splendid display of tap dancing from Dainty Dave in his army boots.

Back in the orphanage, we played endless pranks on each other, but one seemed to be beyond a joke; the phantom turd dropper shocked us all. For several days the lads had woken in the morning to find a pile of crap positioned in some part of the home or other. Certain members of the APA were more than disgusted at these nocturnal antics and threatened to notify the production office if the culprit was not apprehended.

'No don't do that,' said Jimbo Wardroper. 'Let's some of us stay up and follow the tell-tale jobby marks and catch the fellow with his trousers down.' That night no one appeared, but the following morning there was a large roker perilously close to Desperate Dan's slippers. Dan recalled that early that morning he had stirred from a deep sleep to find a pair of huge white buttocks heaving over him, choking out a darky. Thinking he was dreaming, he ignored this anal display and went back to sleep. The mystery deepened and that evening an emergency committee positioned themselves in hiding places in each of the dormitories. Nothing seemed to be happening and about three o'clock I was just about to give it up as a bad job when the door opened slowly. Through the gloom I could make out the silhouette of a fat figure swaying from side to side, mumbling. When he got to the centre of the room he stopped and with certain difficulties undid his trousers and crouched down, his pants round his ankles.

As there was only a little light shining in from the street lamp outside it was difficult to make out who he was, but in any case he was very very close to young Sebastian's unsuspecting sleeping head. Just then I darted from behind my locker with Jimbo and grabbed the fellow by the shoulder, spinning him round. I couldn't believe it – it was – well, to avoid embarrassing the guilty party, I'll keep his name quiet.

'Oh my gawd, wake up for f***'s sake!'

'What's going on?' moaned X as we dragged him out, his trousers round his ankles. Waking him from his stupor, we realised that he had been performing his goodies in his sleep; returning from town after a good drink he would collapse on his bed, waking later to ramble around the home. Well, we have heard of sleepwalking but this was ridiculous!

Physical pursuits of a different nature started to take place in the home. As the APA began to split into different groups it was clear that in our midst we were blessed with some pretty nifty sportsmen. Apart from the dormitories and dining room there was a common room which had a TV at one end and, more importantly, table tennis at the other. True, there was a little friction at times, as the ping-pong fanatics sometimes smashed the ball and bounced it on to the heads of TV viewers. But we all had to relax from a hard day in the army somehow.

Six-a-side football in the square opposite was played with gusto, and cricket with a make-do bat and stumps soon became a firm favourite. These great events were watched with interest by the old folk who found the spectacle of 12 blokes dressed in sneakers, army trousers and other strange attire faintly amusing.

Trained to peak fitness, most of us hired bicycles and went for rides to the local lake, Busslo, where we swam or held mini Olympics of high jump, long jump, running and water polo. By now the temperature was over 100°F and wearing those hot sticky uniforms in smoke and dust was becoming unbearable so sport in the evenings and on our days off was a welcome release.

The Dutch, being a great footballing nation, watched the formation of our football team with more than a passing interest. Sure enough games with local clubs were soon arranged, the first one being against the Deventer Fire Service.

I found Big Frank a tremendous boon in forming the team. So devoted to the game, as a boy he would stand on the terraces watching his beloved Liverpool with his full football gear on under his clothes just in case some player was injured and they called on anybody in the crowd to substitute. His fanaticism still exists to this day. Surely anybody who watches BBC's *Match of the Day* dressed in full Liverpool kit with his foot on a ball at the age of 29 must be a fanatic. I suppose you've been sent off, one wag was heard to say; Frank ignored this remark – his mind was miles away on Anfield's hallowed turf.

The APA X1 were excited at the thought of representative soccer and each evening before the big day we trained hard in the park across the river. The notice board in the home was watched eagerly: who would make the exalted X1? On Friday, Big Frank and I selected the team, which read:

Sebastian 'The Cat' Abineri (in goal)
'Desperate' Dan Long
Chris 'Playboy of the Western World' Williams (defence)
'Nifty' Norman Gregory
Tony 'eeh by gum' McHale
Mike 'never a hair out of place' Stock (midfield)
'Dainty' Dave Auker (also midfield)
'Jimbo' Wardroper
Ollie Beak
Big Frank Mughan
and yours truly in the forward line.

On the Saturday we knocked off work at lunchtime and made our way to the fireman's ground on foot, some by bicycle and the rest in Tim Morand's old van, accompanied by many of the crew. Sir Richard had been alerted, and we'd also put up notices round the town and in the local paper.

The spectacle on arriving at the ground surprised us all. There was a true carnival atmosphere, people drinking, flags all over the place and in the middle of the pitch the fireman's band obviously well lubricated, and playing like mad. Pre-match tension increased at talk of their huge striker and catlike goalie. On we trooped and tried to sort ourselves out into positions. The game consisted of kick and rush tactics at first, but soon we settled down to a smoother pattern of play. The firemen, a little inebriated, found it difficult to keep their footing and quickly the well-oiled APA machine went ahead.

Half-time saw us ahead by 3–1, courtesy of a 40-yard pile-driver from myself, a glancing header from Big Frank and a hasty back pass from the ageing fire-chief, which beat his own goalie nicely. After the interval some of our boys started to sag, tempers became frayed and kicks were aimed at the opponents' legs. Just then there were explosions and mad flashes behind the opponents' goal. The special effects unit had wired the place up. Fortunately our opposition took this all in good spirit, although it's fair to say that had their goalie not been covered in smoke we wouldn't have put another five goals past him in the next 15 minutes.

By the time the final whistle blew a great proportion of the town folk had come to watch and enjoy the festivities. There followed much drinking and a good night was enjoyed by all. However, the next day disaster was to strike. Two of the most expensive houses built on the set, including Frost's house, which had cost a fortune to build with highly detailed interiors, caught fire. Sir Richard and his assistant directors were screaming for the firemen, but by the time the hoses were turned on, the houses were a blazing inferno. The aftermath of the football match had taken its toll. Helpless from the 8–2 drubbing the valiant fire-fighters moved around like zombies, trying to adjust ladders and temper the flames with dribbling hoses. This day was a sad loss for the film company for it didn't have time to rebuild the houses and many important scenes had to be rethought and restructured.

As the weeks began to slip by, each person's motives for staying became more clearly defined. Jason Gregory wanted to stay as long as possible for the money. To meet debts in the UK, each morning he swathed himself in bandages and blood and volunteered for the wounded sequences. His face hidden, Jason spent his day on obscure parts of the set playing dead on the rubble or eating Giovanni's cakes behind some burnt out tank. There were those who were weapon-crazy and plagued Bill to use the more classy guns like the Piat and Bren. These lads would listen wide-eyed and open-mouthed at Bill's stories of what damage a Sten could do to a man at 50 yards; where the few remaining Tiger Tanks from World War II could be found; or could they sign for a pistol if they cajoled 'wardrobe' into supplying an officer's uniform for the day?

While these 'killers' were volunteering for any blood and thunder that Dickie might have had going, outside the cheese factory, James, Hilary and Ben were equally as occupied making moves of a not so violent nature in a game of Scrabble. Stripped down to their underpants, trousers down to their ankles (ready to be pulled up in case they were called into action), they pored over their beloved board, the sun on their backs, their minds absorbed in word formations.

As the desperately keen types, oblivious to the dreaded KLM shot, tried to rub shoulders with Connery, Caan and Hackman, their helmets tilted on the back of their heads, faces beaming camera-wards, Big Frank was organising five-a-side football on the space between the Honey Wagon (shithouse) and catering lorries. Desperate Dan and his sun-worshippers had slipped off to a rooftop to soak in the mid-morning rays. From a good vantage point you could see Dan's kneecaps gleaming behind some chimney pot or other.

Handsome Chris Williams from Brighton, who told all the women he was Brad from Florida, was leaning on his rifle surrounded by a gaggle of young girls – all clogs and hot pants – telling them of his Miami mansion and the forthcoming parachute drop he was to do tomorrow with his pal Robert Redford. It would be fair to say that the latter prophecy was particularly pie in the sky as old Chris suffered from vertigo while standing on a top step, let alone tumbling from a Dakota at 20,000 feet.

I had a narrow shave myself, on set. One of my favourite pastimes was throwing, which my spell with Middlesex County Cricket Club had high-lighted; I could throw flat and reasonably accurately over the stumps from one hundred yards. This information had filtered through to stunt organiser Alf Joint and visualiser and fellow cricket fanatic Michael White, who quickly commandeered this talent and allowed me to execute the entire grenade throwing in the film. My first effort nearly led to my last. I was posi-tioned on a roof with Anthony Hopkins, David 'Rep' Killick and Tony 'Iron Man' McHale. As the gallant Colonel Frost, Anthony was positioned behind the chimneystack while David and Tony were manning their trusty Bren guns behind some sandbags. From the road below Dickie boomed his orders through a loud hailer:

'David dear, Grabner [some Kraut Lieutenant] will lead his charge over the bridge. He will be in a half-track followed by Jerries in other vehicles. On action I want you to watch Col. Waddy in the house next to you for a signal. He has two Bren guns which will be firing in your direction. When he nods they will stop, you run out to the edge of your roof, hurl your grenade at Grabner, then fling yourself to the ground.'

Well, that might sound simple to you, but f*** me I was glad I was wearing my brown trousers! Before running out I was pinned on a ledge between the chimneystack and edge, not more than 18 inches in width, with a 90 foot drop to the street below. I then had to dodge the Bren gun bullets before hurling my grenade from the roof's edge to the Bosch legions, killing poor old Grabner.

The scene was set. This always takes ages in the film business and from my roof top position it gave me an excellent view of the professional way the crew went about their business. The stunt men had to choreograph their falls carefully from the vehicles, Johnny 'Special Effects' Richardson had to wire up all his explosions, smoke and flames. The 'sparks' were busy setting up their 'brutes', the big searchlights used for lighting a film set, talking and laughing in a dialogue of their own. Lighting Cameraman Geoff Unsworth, an eccentric character, walked around the chaos, trilby on head, glass in his eye looking up at the sun deciding what lens the camera should use. Dave Tomblin directed his assistants to 'elbow' all members of the public – little boys in trees, barges on the river and any other obstacles that may have been in shot. The security team manned all exits and entrances making sure nobody could encroach upon the set. I could see Nifty Norton Natchbull diverting traffic way down below.

It was peaceful up there on the roof. As I looked across the river I could see the windmills. Beyond that were the fields with animals grazing by the lake. It was four o'clock and the town's children were leaving school; running through the streets in and out of the cars across the marketplace, they made their way to see us playing at war. The ice-cream vendor was making a fortune selling his wares to the onlookers jostling behind Norton's barriers. In the town's square, mothers went about their shopping as they had done for years before, crossing off their domestic chores one by one. The cathedral clock with the marzipan face struck five, the sun had lost its heat and Dickie was ready to shoot. The flares and smoke were lit as 'background action' and heralded the charge. From roofs and windows either side of the bridge the English paras opened fire on the German divisions, which started to advance over the bridge.

Then the fireworks started. Explosions, vehicles careering off the road. Stunt men 'dying' – the air was rent with bloodthirsty cries. I could see camera operator Peter McDonald up in his camera crane, while Dickie sat beside him. Back to the chimney. I didn't dare look down but just waited for Col. Waddy's cue.

In the window barely ten feet away, two Bren guns barked into action. This was it, I thought, adrenaline surging through my body – at last my big moment – a film star – I can't f*** it up now! Waddy nodded, I tore out, and helmet set firmly over my brow, clenched teeth, caught a glimpse of Grabner below and hurled my Mills bomb before hitting the deck.

It all seemed to happen very quickly. There was a huge explosion and the next thing I saw was old Grabner sinking in the turret of his armoured car, face contorted in pain, covered in 'blood'. All I know is that I must have hit the target first time because Dickie gave me the thumbs up and it was in the can. I only wish the Chairman of England's Cricket Selectors could have been there – I might have got an England place in Australia for that throw! Down below, the debris was cleared and as we weren't in the next shot we decided to stay on our roof. Off with the shirts and helmets, we stretched out across the sandbags and started to tell stories.

Well, I thought I told a good joke, but Anthony Hopkins is superb. He still has this Welsh brogue and all his stories were edged in that tuneful lilt of the valleys. We had just started to drink some orange juice we had hidden behind the sandbags, when out of the corner of my eye I saw this Tiger tank coming over the bridge. At first I didn't pay much attention, I knew it was getting closer, but . . . 'Have you heard the one about—' Tony started to say. Just then I looked down and saw the tank's long barrel pointing menacingly towards us.

The first explosion lifted Tony McHale about two feet off his arse, followed by a warm blast which rushed through my hair making it stand on end. Before we knew what was happening the second blast smashed the chimney to pieces.

'Jesus Christ,' squealed Hopkins, as we rushed over to the corner of the roof. While we huddled together I thought our number was finally up. Unknown to the crew we were still on the roof which was to be completely demolished. In desperation I ran to the middle of the roof waving and shouting. Dave Tomblin saw me just as the Terrible Tiger was about to put the final touches to its demo task. It must have looked crazy, the gallant Col. Frost and his men, 'veterans of many skirmishes', brought down the ladder of that plastic and wooden house, shaking to the bone. It certainly was a close shave.

As to be expected in the company of 40 actors the standard of 'pulling' techniques would be very high. In this company it bordered on the fantastic. The approaches and chat-up methods adopted defied belief. As our war heroes stumbled into the room back at the old orphanage, their newly found girlfriends would rise and follow their masters to comfort them in their quarters, like obedient adoring spaniels. My love nest was to be found in the linen cupboard, as I'd been driven out of the motorway by the lack of privacy. The linen cupboard, a small room full of pillows and pillowcases, with a window at one end and precious little elsewhere, was at least self-contained. I stuck up a few pictures on the wall, hung up my four uniforms and draped a sheet, which acted as a curtain, over the window.

My sexual life had settled down a little after the initial burst of *nine* women in the first week. Three in their homes, one in a cupboard, one in a shop doorway, one in the lavatory of the St Tropez Club, one in the garden of the old folks' home, one actually in Frost's house and the last under the bridge. Now I was getting used to the vertical luxury of my cupboard. Lovemaking like any sport was an important release from work for the lads and many had now earned a reputation as ace gigolos in the town.

My first conquest had been in the Safari nightclub, where I had been sitting at a table eyeing this girl across the dance floor. Admittedly after a few lagers any old tart looks like Sophia Loren, but I was convinced that she really did resemble the Italian beauty. A mass of curly hair, like a cornfield in the wind, well-defined lips, superb bust and black dress clinging tightly to her slender body. She was obviously conscious of my attention, so I went and sat down next to my 'Mrs Ponti'. She really was lovely. I asked Anna to dance, and so we sweated away a few fast numbers and finally I took my chance in both hands, as a romantic Elvis ballad boomed out through the disco system. I felt her crotch rubbing against mine, and her heart beating fast against my chest. But the news that she was married and her husband was about to arrive certainly did not overwhelm me with happiness.

'I have,' she whispered, 'always had enough love for two.' Sure enough her old man arrived, a rather flashy-looking Italian character and I returned to my seat. I waited until Anna got up and walked through the dancers to go to the toilet; outside the ladies I couldn't hear much inside so after a precautionary glance over my shoulder I nipped in. Anna was brushing her hair in the mirror. On seeing me she uttered some Dutch in astonished tones.

'Come on, we must be quick,' I said, pulling her into one of the 'traps'. The presence of her husband in the club certainly didn't enhance my chances of a long-term relationship, so in times like this one has to get the 'old meat and two veg' into action as soon as possible. I thought the knee trembler that followed may have lacked the aura of a Charles Boyer bedroom scene, but the climax reached was spiced with rich superlatives from me and quite a few ooooohs and aaaaahs from my newly found love. Thus satisfied, Anna pulled down her skirt and adjusted her curls, smiling softly at her lover who was experiencing considerable difficulty in pulling up his Y-fronts with one hand, holding the pan with the other, while hopping on one leg rather like a crazed stork. Our escape from 'trap one' was executed somewhat gingerly as we had heard certain movements in trap two. As one chain was pulled Anna flushed, kissed me and disappeared into the dancers and drinkers outside.

During my stay in Holland I was to meet my disco lady on numerous occasions, though our lovemaking was performed rather more discreetly by the lakeside or in the woods. Sometimes she'd visit me at the orphanage. We had other visitors, though; and the 'Attic Queen' was a favourite, if mysterious, one. She had been seen many times in the home. Quite tall, rather tarty, dressed in trendy clothes she was always the quiet one. I still to this day do not know her name, but some of the chaps had talked of her vaguely in amorous terms without any of that detailed descriptive banter which abounded at breakfast time. The truth was soon to rear its ugly head. One evening I was talking to Norman and Frank in the corridor when the young lady swept past us and started to climb the stairs.

'Phew, take a whiff of that perfume!' exclaimed Norman. 'Where's she going?' We decided to follow her. After the first floor in the home there was another set of stairs, which led up to the attic. Generally, not many people ventured up there as it was rather spooky and, being wooden, very hot and dusty. Objects left by the old folk covered the floor, old potties, boots, a broken television set, leather suitcases and a couple of picture frames. At the far end a shaft of light came from a little room, its door ajar. We could hear stifled voices and, our hearts beating faster, we went up to the room and looked in. There, sitting on a bed, was Harry, a junior cook, while standing over him lustfully was the girl dressed in just her bra and panties. On the bedside table stood a toilet roll and a selection of contraceptives. We couldn't believe it. This must have been her own love nest. As he sat there nervously puffing on a cigarette she started to stroke his hair and gyrate in front of him like some oriental dancer, pursuing her seductive techniques. Just then Norman stood on a potty and the sordid silence was shattered.

'What the f*** was—' came the voice from the room.

Never have eavesdroppers moved so swiftly! The next day we discovered that the young lady had entertained at least twelve of our chaps in her secret rendezvous. Apparently she was as discreet about her individual lovers as she was clinical about her appointments. She became known as the Attic Queen and I've often wondered what she might be doing now, years later. How does she feel when she walks past the haunted home? Maybe she still conducts her salacious sessions in that attic room or perhaps the dream is broken and she reverted back to the life of a shorthand typist again, with just a few beers and a bit of the old 'social finger' on Saturday nights to look forward to.

It was now August and there were just 18 of us left. We had already stayed twice as long as we had expected. Sometimes I thought I was going mad, but then I looked round at my pals and realised that they looked as crazy as myself. My mind felt like a pebble rolling round and round in a hot dustbin. But there was, as always in my life, one sure-fire method of releasing the tension: cricket.

Cricket wasn't just my saviour, either. We spent a week in Amersfoort, facing the dismal prospect of running around blowing up tanks for the second unit. As per usual we had got 'gunned up' and had tea on arrival, carried Frank off the coach and prepared a pitch for a quick game of cricket. We bowled the first over at 6.50 a.m. and all I can tell you is that when work finished at 7.00 p.m. we were still playing, completely absorbed in the same game. True, we had stopped for a new feature on our sports itinerary, a race between the explosions, but that was all.

We had been overlooked. The forgotten army! There was no point asking

Jack Galloway either. No, at that moment my ace slip fielder was miles away in the land of nod, tousled head lying on his battledress jacket, eyes closed, Jack was up to his favourite pastime knocking out the zzzs. Norman was lamenting on how he had turned down the part of holding a spear in the background for the duration of the Royal Shakespeare Company's *Henry V*. Jimbo half-listened while trying to stick his bayonet into a nearby log. The next morning having temporarily given up the idea of press-ganging my colleagues into playing the noble game, I wandered through the trees to the perimeter of the wood and looked out to the parched sandy heath lands.

In the distance the first unit were filming Sean Connery getting in and out of his glider for the umpteenth take. The sun was now up and burning the gorse and bracken, which stretched for miles.

I had decided to return to the coolness of the woods when I heard this sound. Jimbo, restless as ever, had also heard the strange noise. As I lay on my back looking up at the sun flickering through the trees, it grew louder. The drone of an engine. 'Jesus Christ!' Before Big Frank had time to leap to his feet, the Spitfire had appeared out of the trees, barely skimming the tops.

By this time we were on our feet and staring at the fleshy belly of that beautiful plane zooming in at ground level before soaring up into the azure sky. Loop the looping, and making his silent pattern far above, the pilot was going through a spectacular series of aerobatics. Next he flew upside-down, barely 40 feet off the ground, tipping his wings before rising steeply to miss the woods. He came so close at one point that we could see his head, face and white scarf. The five of us just stood there in wonderment, staring at this relic from the Second World War and imagining what the Battle of Britain must have been really like.

The Spitfire came as a pleasant relief during what had been a particularly gruelling week. Filming the parachute drop sequences, the APA had each been made section leaders of 15 Dutch extras. This appointment made us responsible for knocking them into shape, removing spectacles, adjusting uniforms and generally giving them the appearance of soldiers. Although I found the Dutch kind, peaceful, inoffensive people, this experience was a particularly uncomfortable one. Already suffering from first degree burns to my face, things were not made easier by a number of my command deserting down ditches, up trees, behind gliders, to enjoy the more leisurely task of playing cards, drinking whisky or soaking up the sun. There we were, hundreds of people spread out as far as the eye could see across that vast heath-land, ready on 'Action' to get out of our parachute, run towards different colour flares and group up into units.

I remember one morning that water was not provided for quite a while and at one stage it looked as though we had a mutiny on our hands. Because of the size of the exercise it was impossible to reach each individual promptly with refreshments and about 11.30 Dickie and his assistants were involved in a somewhat tenuous situation as Dutchmen disappeared into holes like rabbits in their burrows. Water finally arrived in the shape of a large military container and our friends' temperaments were further appeased at the sight of the excellent Phil Hobbs Marquee where they regularly performed great gastronomic feats of woofing three or four dinners in one go.

The night shots introduced a different dimension to our soldiering activities. Starting at 7 p.m. we would dine in the grounds of the International School and wait until dark.

As the story here featured General Urquart and his men moving stealthily through the forests in driving rain, to re-enact the scene Sean Connery led us through the trees with a huge fire-hose turned on us, assisted by a wind machine. This exercise backfired as the first jet from the hose smashed 007 full in his chops, lifting his moustache off in the process. The last we saw of the hose bearer was scorch marks in the forest as Mr Connery announced loudly, in a broad Scottish brogue, his intention to knock all kinds of shit out of him. We just stood there dripping in that forest as our gallant General went off to commit his own personal battle. Eventually we finished and returned to the drying-out tent to peel off our soggy uniforms.

Night and day also brought together my all-time best cricket team. As usual the 'Day/Night game' was organised off the cuff.

It was the biggest night shoot of the entire film: the parachute jump of the 82nd Airborne, where the Americans land and then make their way across country to link up with the British Grenadier Guards to take the bridges at Arnhem and Nijmegen. All the film's biggest stars would appear in this massive shoot.

Subsequently, the David English X1 was selected and put on standby for quick games in-between scenes.

DAVID ENGLISH	Captain
ROBERT REDFORD	Opening bowler
RYAN O'NEAL	Spin bowler
ANTHONY HOPKINS	Opening batsman
MICHAEL CAINE	Third man
DIRK BOGARDE	First slip
JAMES CAAN	Square leg
ELLIOTT GOULD	Silly mid-on
EDWARD FOX	Long on
LAURENCE OLIVIER	Elegant middle-order batsman
SEAN CONNERY	Long off
GENE HACKMAN	Twelfth man
LIV ULLMAN	Drinks and sandwiches

The might of Hollywood sparked into life. Hundreds of cameras captured the drop and ensuing battle. We fought the bloodiest combat throughout the night and into the dawn. Cricket commenced at 4.30 a.m. and continued in spasms throughout the battle, as we played our 'Cricket Game too Far'.

The next evening we were sitting watching the rushes in a makeshift viewing theatre outside Deventer. As this was the film's biggest scene, producer Joe Levine insisted on sitting in the middle of the actors to watch the action: 5 ft 6 in and dressed entirely in black, wearing a leather coat, the mogul waved his stick, a black cane with a replica Golden Bridge on top, at the screen.

'Roll 'em,' growled Joe. It was spectacular, the whole sky filled with para-chutists and Dakotas and the ground thick with running figures, guns blazing, Gung ho stuff! All was going well until suddenly, Joe leapt to his feet and waved his stick at the screen.

'What the f*** is that?' cried the mogul. 'Stop the film!' There was a deathly hush as we followed Joe's eye line.

'What is it, Joe?' enquired Dickie politely.

Joe was now beside himself with rage, jumping up and down on the spot. Once again we stared at the action then . . . Shock! Horror! Sure enough, in the bottom corner of the screen there were a group of paratroopers, shirts off, bare-chested, playing cricket against a tank.

I've never seen a viewing theatre empty so quickly.

August slipped by almost unnoticed. Most of the original APA had gone home. New actors had come to the old folks' home but they weren't the same. It's funny but we found it difficult to accept them, having been together from the beginning. Hackman, Gould, Fox, Caine, Caan had come and gone. Lord Olivier had arrived to contribute his own magic to the picture and also a very fine line in batting technique. Whenever he could he would slip away from the interviewers and pressmen and join us in our cricket matches. When bowling to him first I thought I had better treat the 'old boy' with a bit of respect and lobbed up a couple of full tosses. These were quickly dispatched over the wall into Kate Ter Horst's house with great gusto. Much to everybody's amazement Larry then strolled down the pitch tapping the ground with the bat and said, 'I have played before, you know, now bowl up, young man!' This I did and the great Lord played some equally great shots in an immaculate style.

I spent a lot of time with Laurence Olivier. He told me that as a boy his father would take him to watch Sussex play County Cricket. He told me that when he was married to Vivien Leigh, if she was away working he couldn't bear to stay in the house on his own. He would wear false noses and other props and go out and be a milkman or a postman for the day.

He also explained the different techniques between acting on film, and on the stage: in film acting you are perceptively aware that the camera can convey the slightest detail of a human face, details which are lost on the stage where your actions must be played on a grander scale. He also spoke of his loathing for award ceremonies, and confided that when he was invited to present the Oscars, all his ad-libs were carefully rehearsed days beforehand. He was primarily an actor who immersed himself in the role, preparing carefully for every part he played, be it Henry V or the dentist in *Marathon Man*. As Dr Spaander he had listened for hours to Dutch recordings, mastering the language – like Anthony Hopkins, he was a master mimic. With his ear for a foreign tongue and his trained capacity to remember lines he 'became' Dr Spaander. He had worn his costume suit for weeks in Civvy Street. 'It's best to wear it, dear boy. There is no other way.' Other modern-day actors such as Robert DeNiro and Al Pacino follow this method. Like Olivier, it works for them, resulting in an even more believable characterisation of the part.

When Sir Richard went to visit him on his first night in the hotel (he had rejected the luxury of a suite in Amsterdam or Arnhem, which many of the other actors had insisted on, for a spare corner bedroom of the old Keizerskroon Hotel in Apeldoorn with no armchair, radio or TV in the room), Olivier had proudly shown him the worn-in-suit. 'It works well doesn't it? One believes I fit into it', and then Lord Olivier showed Sir Richard his shoes. 'I wore those in the garden. It's English mud but I don't suppose it will matter, will it?'

Sir Richard witnessed my friendship with Olivier and decided to give us a scene together. I was to play a badly wounded British para, who had lost a leg in battle. I would be dragged in to Kate Ter Horst's house and the kindly Dr Spaander would attend my wounds.

My line to Olivier was: 'My boots are full of blood', delivered from a sitting position on the staircase. You probably think that speaking one line is a piece of cake, but I can tell you it's much harder to hit the spot with an isolated line than a run in with a substantial speech. As the cameras turned over I looked down at my feet and slowly lifted my head to face Olivier: 'My boots are full of blood,' I exclaimed with as much feeling for the moment as I could muster. I watched his reaction. By a mere dropping of the mouth he indicated the lowliness and humility of Dr Spaander. I looked into his eyes and sensed the weariness of a man who had been under Nazi domination for the past four years.

I struggled with the line. My performance wasn't helped by most of the crew taking the piss and making obscene gestures behind Dickie's back, just to put me off. By take 17 I sounded like a cross between Tommy Cooper and Norman Wisdom. Even more painful was the feeling of having to deliver the line to the Greatest English Actor who ever lived.

Dickie joined Larry to nurse me through my dilemma. 'Think of your situation, now relax, David.' I was becalmed and became oblivious to the war outside and the tension raging through my inside. I felt at ease in the presence of two great actors who directed as well. Larry had triumphed with *Henry V*, his first film as a director, where he had performed all of his own stunts. And Dickie had proved his range by performing opposite Steve McQueen in *The Sand Pebbles*, and in David Lean's *In Which We Serve*. Even as a 19-year-old there was never any doubt that he would direct one day, he clearly had the vision and the leadership necessary. David Lean had given Dickie a piece of advice: 'Of course you must direct, but for God's sake don't direct until you find something you're prepared to give your life for and you know that if you don't direct it you'll die.'

I couldn't have been in better hands. The scene was 'wrapped' and the crew moved on outside to set up the next shot.

Laurence smiled and shook my hand. I left the two Knights sitting on that staircase surrounded by dying privates and wounded paras, lost in their own world. 'My boots are full of blood' never made it to the screen, but my morning spent with the two masters of the art of film acting was unforgettable.

The advent of Robert Redford also swelled the ranks of our cricket team. We became firm friends; a great sportsman and competitor, Bob soon joined in, insisting on being taught the rules. We used his baseball and after he had clubbed a few loose ones over Reg's Honeywagon, I stuck in a bouncer, which shaved his golden head, but left him unmoved. Assistant Steve Lanning did move rather sharply to remind us that Bobby was being paid $2,000,000 for 20 days' work and Sir Richard would appreciate his superstar on the set unscathed. Redford was a hell of a nice chap, a good film actor who had obviously worked hard to master the tricks of his craft.

The secret of the winning close up is to get on with the camera operator. After all, he is the one 'pulling the shots'. We immediately struck up a close relationship with Peter McDonald, one of the world's greatest camera operators who tipped us off as to our best side. In film you're told never to look into the camera. The director will give you an eye line. Not Robert Redford. He used his reflection in its lens to check his hair and make-up, watched closely by his own make-up artist Gary, who had flown in specially.

The APA got on well with the superstars. We played cricket with Laurence 'Call me Larry' Olivier, Robert 'Bob' Redford taught us to throw an American Football. We marvelled at Dirk Bogarde's impeccable delivery of dialogue. We played golf with Sean Connery, hitting balls across the battlefield from a bucket, we witnessed Gene Hackman draw on his massive reserves of strength to lift and carry a man over each shoulder to safety from the Rhine. We listened to Michael Caine moaning incessantly about the amount of tax he paid; there was James Caan who, seeing himself as Steve McQueen, nicked a jeep and roared off to enjoy Amsterdam's night life dressed in full kit as Sgt. Eddie Dohun. Elliott Gould hid his half skinhead, half Afro haircut under his helmet, only to be revealed when it was dislodged on hitting the dirt in crossfire. We saw Edward Fox's always-immaculate appearance among the tanks and explosions, and the people of Deventer's reaction to the reappearance of German uniforms in their town. The young people showed little hostility, but we sensed the emerging bitterness among the older generations, giving Hardy Kruger and Maximilian Schell a hard time.

We loved having our photos taken with Liv Ullman, a beautiful lady with a gentle Nordic spirit.

Anthony Hopkins was our favourite. He was quite simply one of us; he provided beer for our football games and when nothing came from our complaints at getting up absurdly early to go to wardrobe, he fixed for us to change our uniforms in the old folks' home. He talked to us for hours between takes about his career and advised us on ours. His impersonation of Tommy Cooper remains a classic.

And then there was Ryan O'Neal! Wherever we were at war, at 4 p.m. rifles were downed to enjoy a mammoth tea courtesy of Giovanni. It didn't matter if we had been shot to pieces in the heat of battle, at 4 p.m. the cream cakes and Danish pastries loomed large.

At 4.30 p.m. on one particular day, our afternoon delight consumed, Redford and O'Neal were playing an important scene surrounded by extras. It was in an orchard in the searing heat and, just as Bob had delivered his lines, there was a cry of 'I'm f***ing dying' – Chuck 'the spark' from Chigwell had fallen off his ladder. One by one Dickie's crew started to behave in a strange fashion. There were crazy walks and contorted faces, shrill cries and grimaces. Suddenly 'The Bridge' had become Monty Python.

Unconfirmed sources disclosed that someone had put LSD in the crew's cake. Ambulances arrived from all parts to take away crewmen who had probably only tasted junior Disprin or Pro-plus up to that fatal day.

Then there was my one line to General Gavin. I had to tell Ryan that 'General Frost and his men were over there.' To deliver this immortal message, integral to the plot, Ryan O'Neal was winched ten feet off the ground, to be dropped 'on action' as though completing a parachute jump. Obviously because of insurance purposes the Hollywood star was forbidden to jump so he just hung there out of the frame of the camera, grinning and awaiting my line.

The screen was to be filled with action: 500 extras would run about in the background, there would be explosions and parachutists from the 1st Airborne Regiment would fill the sky.

Some of the extras were old hands at war films. They would go from one film to another, A Bridge Too Far, A Bridge A Bit Further and so on. They couldn't care less about the Second World War. They were on the wacky baccy and Peruvian marching dust, wearing tin helmets, Mickey Mouse T-shirts, boots on the wrong feet with a copy of *Mein Kampf* in the pocket. Well what did you expect for 20 guilders a day?

Dickie was ready to roll. He had given the action to the Airborne Division and now it was our turn.

'Sound running, turn over, background action, action Ryan!'

Ryan released himself from his parachute, hitting the ground and immediately twisting his ankle. The sight of General Gavin rolling around the ground clutching his ankle roaring with laughter sent shock waves among the stoned extras who started to run amok. Bombs went off in the background dropped by Stukas and then the whole sky was filled with the mighty First Airborne proudly wearing their Red Berets. Worse was to follow. A sudden wind blew some of the parachutists out of shot, finally dropping our intrepid fighters straight through the greenhouses of a local market garden. The somewhat surprised Dutch gardeners, puffing on their pipes and leisurely watering their tomatoes, confronted by these warriors kitted out in war paint and clutching Sten guns, reacted by putting down their watering cans and lifting their arms high above their heads in surrender.

This, plus Ryan by now apoplectic with laughter, ruined a massively expensive shot.

We had awaited the arrival of the legendary stunt man Alf Joint with a reverence which reverberated around the ranks of the APA.

Was this not the man who had completed the daring leap as Richard Burton's double from one cable car to another in *Where Eagles Dare*? Then there was the Cadbury's Black Magic man, diving from the cliffs, and many other highly touted tumbles.

Alf had carefully planned a dive off Frost's house on to an assembly of cushions 30 feet below. Or, at least it was assumed he was going to dive. For a full hour prior to the jump Alf had informed us how stuntmen always took the minimum of risks. It was always carefully worked out; safety first was imperative. This particular jump was 'very ordinary and routine'. All stunts were paid individually according to the danger and heights etc. involved.

You could hear a pin drop as Dickie cried 'Action!' The whole town had joined us to watch this breathtaking leap by the master. A German soldier shot at Alf on the roof, off the ledge fell 'the Ledge', aaaaaaaaaagh!

He didn't dive – in fact he just fell, missing the cushion and breaking his shoulder. We didn't know whether to laugh or cry.

Cut to hospital and Alf all bandaged up being hand-fed grape by grape, washed down by Lucozade.

The harder they come the harder they fall – for Alf Joint the embarrassment had been the hardest act to swallow.

*   *   *

Big Frank and I were selected to be two of Robert Redford's 'Dirty Dozen' that took the bridge at Nijmegen.

I had just been through the terrifying experience of crossing Waal (Rhine) in a dinghy full of US Airborne with a fair amount of trepidation, looking like a Michelin man because under my uniform I had two life-jackets, fully inflated, in case I went overboard. This safety precaution was taken for two reasons. First, the river is particularly deep with fast-moving conflicting currents and, secondly, my swimming abilities are limited to a width and a half at the Finchley outdoor pool. Undaunted by the perils of the deep we rowed back and forwards across that river with explosions sounding in our ears and six inches of water seeping into our trousers.

The storming of the bridge had to be carefully planned. As a production each sequence had to be carefully choreographed. As the official thrower I was to lead the charge down the road, hurl my grenade and peel off down the bank. Redford would then issue some orders and we would make our way up the embankment, snuffing out a few 'Jerries' in the process. Six of us would finally get on the bridge. Stunt man Paul Weston would die dramatically in true stunt fashion, Big Frank and Jack Mackenzie would attack a machine-gun position and Shaun (Sarge) Curry and I would vault a fence and zigzag across the road before finally getting cut down by a German Spandau. 'Battling Bobby' would single-handedly inch his way along the bicycle track popping off six or seven krauts and then wave on six Sherman tanks. All good action-packed stuff!

So, this was it. Twenty-three weeks in Holland and now the final death on that bridge in Nijmegen. I felt very sad. I had accepted the routine of being a soldier and couldn't imagine it coming to an end. What was there to go back to in England? Anything would be a terrible anti-climax. I had a beer commercial in Birmingham lined up. That final morning in the old folks' home Jacko's thunderous 'come on, my beauties' was replaced by a personal knock and polite 'time for breakfast', there being only six of us, along with Ollie. The summer had gone. As we left Deventer spread out in our coach, the sun was rising behind the twin spires, but it had lost its heat leaving a strange empty chill.

It was bloody cold on that bridge. After Giovanni served up his breakfast with typical flair (bacon sandwich on arrival, and one in my pocket for when I was shot and lying on the bridge), we started to film. I led the charge with every available bit of strength in my body. The grenade hit the target and we stormed the bridge. Vaulting the fence behind Shaun I caught my bollocks on the pole causing a mighty scream of pain which, in the context of the film, may have sounded like a war cry, but in fact had probably put paid to my future marriage plans indefinitely. To regain my breath I lay on the ground for a moment and pretended to be wounded. Then up on my feet I zigzagged towards the Jerry emplacement, firing my Garrard from the hip. 'This is it.' I timed my death barely ten yards from the gun . . . a cry, arms in the air, and down on the tarmac, finished.

As I lay there motionless, eyes closed, half listening to the gunfire, half reminiscing over the past six months, the flood of thoughts began to subside at the sounds of a rumble, metal on tarmac. At first it didn't register; then the realisation that the Shermans were on their way suddenly struck home.

I had seen these great tanks in rehearsal, they were like huge grey elephants, pointing their iron trunks proudly ahead. The noise was deafening.

Oh Christ, they're getting closer, being squashed to death on the last day, what a way to go! Have they forgotten me, I can't get up. A dead man coming alive and legging it off the bridge at Nijmegen might not go down too well with those spending a fortune for this shot. It's alright for those buggers on the other side of the camera, smoking their cigars and safe as houses.

All manner of thoughts flashed through my mind.

'You can get up now, David, we finished that shot three minutes ago.' Slowly I opened my eyes and looked up. Surrounding me were about 15 of the crew having a bloody good laugh. Fifty yards away the Shermans had stopped, but their engines were still running. Such was the penalty for getting into character!

The bridge finally captured I bid my respects to Sir Richard and climbed into the car bound for the airport. The film for me had ended.

A year later I went back to Deventer. Arriving at the station I hired a bike and rode back to where the old folks' home stood. It was boarded up. The doors, windows, everything closed. I was determined to get back in so I tried the back of the houses near to it. Finally I rang the bell of a house four doors away. After a long time a man appeared and after explaining that I had come to take photographs of the home for a magazine in England, he let me in.

Across a couple of rooftops I finally shinned down a drainpipe and a wall and leapt into the garden of the old folks' home. It was completely overgrown. On the forecourt where the sunbathers stretched out the area was now covered with cardboard boxes full of rubbish. Forcing open Ollie's window I climbed inside, my heart pumping as the memories rushed back through my mind. The place had a damp cold smell about it. Feverishly I explored each of the rooms. My linen cupboard still had a few pictures up – a couple of boots and socks were strewn in that corridor. Slowly I climbed the stairs. I was gripped by a strange empty, spooky feeling. The attic had lost its summer warmth. On the floor of the Scarlet Woman's room were a couple of used contraceptives. I left that place of shoes 'n' potties and old folks' belongings and quickly descended the stairs.

MAD DOGS AND THE ENGLISHMAN

In James Wardroper's room I saw some writing scrawled on the wall. It read:

> James Wardroper ate, drank, f***ed, rested, wanked, hid and lived in this room for 4–5 months whilst making the film A Bridge Too Far. The date is 27th August 1976 and my time here is now at an end, I love this room, it is my life at the moment,
> Love Jim
> People must learn to trust one another. Long Live Holland.

As I turned to leave for the last time I'm sure I heard voices, Big Frank Mughan, David Auker, James, Dan, Norman, Tim . . .

'Come on, my beauties, the coach is 'ere.'

'Oh f*** off, Jack!'

'What time is it. . .?'

Attenborough's Private Army may have disintegrated, but its character would linger on in that old folks' home forever.

How did I feel at the end of the film? Well in 2001 Maurice Gibb wrote a song called 'Man In The Middle'. I felt then as though I was the man on the outside looking in. I still do.

YOU SHOULD BE DANCING

'Staying Alive' went to Number 1 in the US charts and the film was a smash success worldwide. The combination of John Travolta's dancing and the Bee Gees music created huge disco fever around the globe. To celebrate the success of *Saturday Night Fever*, Robert staged a massive garden party in the middle of New York. One thousand guests partied all night – all the beautiful people were there. I remember sitting at a table with Andy Warhol, Carly Simon, Paul Simon and James Taylor. Robert, and the Bee Gees came over.

'Look, David,' said Robert, and there above Times Square was our Red Cow flashing in big red neon above the USA Top Ten:

CONGRATULATIONS TO THE BEE GEES, FIVE SONGS IN THE USA TOP TEN

To this day it still stands as a world record. RSO Records was now far and away the world's number one independent record label. Robert made a toast: 'To you, David, you made us smile, knocked down the doors and moved us on down the right road. I told you, you are the one!'

9 YOU SHOULD BE DANCING

I returned to my empty flat and felt lost. I missed the camaraderie of living with a company. Gone were the voices, the laughter and the bravado; I was back in Civvy Street.

Some people cannot handle the switch. My Uncle Tom, a Lt. Colonel in the Royal Artillery and a hero at Tobruk, a leader of men who won the Military Cross for storming Monte Casino, left the army and, two weeks after putting away his medals, was selling insurance, pounding the streets of Twickenham. Nine months later he was admitted into hospital where he passed away. I knew it was through a broken heart. He had been a lion in warfare, and a lamb to the slaughter in peacetime.

So it was back to earth with a bump. There I sat on the floor of my flat, Crestfallen Heights, British West Hampstead, a somewhat forlorn figure (we Pisceans love to plummet to the depths of sadness so we can rise to the exquisite peaks of fun and laughter), surrounded by a couple of para-jackets, my red beret and helmet and a sinister black steel bayonet presented to me by Robert Redford as a memory of 'our lovely war'. Sad September slipped by . . . the phone rang. It was Barry Gibb.

'Dave, what are you doing? You should be dancing!'

'But my legs have been shot away and my boots are full of blood,' I responded.

'Come over to Miami now.'

The voice of high command had spoken, no wonder I call him 'skipper'. Barry has always clearly seen what he wants and goes for it. Like Ian Botham, he has tremendous self-belief and gets frustrated if something or someone gets in the way and obstructs his objective. Suffice to say his clarity of vision and ear for sound is extremely appealing and, almost always, spot on.

It was time to ride the red cow high on the warm tropical breezes to Miami . . .

Hard to think that in the late 1890s Florida was as much a frontier town as the American West had been twenty years earlier. As for Miami Beach, it could be reached only by boat and was still mostly uninhabited swamp, half underwater, infested by alligators and covered by deep tropical jungle . . . Now it belonged to the Bee Gees bonanza. 'You are now entering the Ponderosa of the Brothers Gibb.' The *Children of the World* album cover adorned the walls of the city. Barry's fantastic falsetto had insisted that 'You

Should Be Dancing', and people everywhere had been seduced by the anthem taking to the dance floors, pulsating to the insistent beat.

'You Should Be Dancing' was Number 1 in America. I went to dinner with Barry and Linda. On entering the Art Deco eaterie of sensuous delight, the power of his song made an immediate impact. Achingly thin Brazilian models danced decadently with pony-tailed drug dealers. The floor was heaving with All-American Football stars, movie studio heads, drag queens, Arab zillionaires, Cuban gunrunners and tattooed bikers. Outside, Colombian cocaine barons valet-parked their Ferraris and Lamborghinis before pointing their young model friends towards the floor for an orgy of sizzling dance.

'Baz, you've really done it this time,' I laughed. 'Not bad for a man who never danced a step!'

In April 1977 we flew to Paris and on to the Chateau D'Herouville in northern France to begin work on a new album. The studio was famous for Elton John's recording of *Honky Chateau* in 1972. The Chateau was hardly the fabled palace of Fontainebleau or Versailles as we had expected, more like a set from *The Pink Panther.* Herouville lay in the middle of nowhere; it was seriously haunted and in one of the studio's main rooms an axe had been found embedded deep into the console. The mysterious axe man had not 'forth-cometh' and the room had never been used again. Except, that is, as a keenly sought-after location for badly made porno films like *Gay Boys of the Seine, The Gendarme's Shiny Helmet* and *Kinky Women of Bourbon Street.*

Our cook, Robert, who rarely washed, was permanently pissed and crazily in love with Keith Richards. He joined us at meal times to serenade us with mad versions of 'Honky Tonk Woman', singing wildly through brown teeth and gyrating with a saucepan as a guitar, while we huddled around the long oak table sipping our French onion soup.

This French affair was a ploy from Robert Stigwood. He simply plonked the current No. 1 world songwriting team in the middle of nowhere, with no distractions, nothing to do but just work. And work they did. In the space of just 36 hours, the boys had written 'How Deep Is Your Love', 'Staying Alive', 'Night Fever', 'More Than A Woman', and 'If I Can't Have You'.

A few days later Robert phoned us and said, 'I'm doing this film called "Tribal Rights of a New Saturday Night" based on an article written by Nik Cohn in the *New York Times.* I want some songs. Get them ready, I'll be over in a few days.'

The truth is that these songs were written for the Bee Gees album, not for *Saturday Night Fever.* On his arrival Robert just happened to hear the five songs and insisted they should be used for his film; it was purely coincidence that the lyrics and melodies perfectly fitted the rhythm of the picture. The film was about an Italian kid called Tony Manero who worked in a Brooklyn paint shop, but wanted to make more of his life, by cracking New York's nightlife as a dancer in the clubs. On the back of 'You Should Be Dancing', we knew we were on to a winner. There were 'Tony Maneros' everywhere around the globe, kids who simply wanted to better themselves.

Robert was staying with RSO US President Freddie Gershon at the Beverley Hills Hotel. One evening Gershon was sitting in the living room when he heard Robert screaming from the bedroom. 'Quick! Come quick!'

Freddie dashed into the bedroom and found Robert watching a US sitcom called *Welcome Back Kotter*; he had found his Tony Manero. John Travolta had auditioned for Robert when he was casting *Jesus Christ Superstar* for its Broadway run; Robert had liked Travolta but felt he was too young to fit into the show. But he remembered his name, and, when he saw him playing Vinnie Barbarino in *Welcome Back Kotter*, he called him up and immediately offered him a firm three-picture deal for one million dollars. Once again Robert emphasised his quest to give the young their best chance.

It was Barry who suggested the title of *Saturday Night Fever*; 'Tribal Rights etc.' was far too long. 'You need something shorter, something that young people can remember.'

The rest is history; from our French Connection of intense work in a wilderness of the bleakest surroundings, the biggest selling soundtrack album of all time was created. To date, 50 million albums have been sold. From the moment John Travolta was seen strutting down the street to the strains of 'Staying Alive', the phenomenon of *Saturday Night Fever* was born.

'Staying Alive' went to Number 1 in the US charts and the film was a smash success worldwide. The combination of John Travolta's dancing and the Bee Gees music created huge disco fever around the globe. To celebrate the success of *Saturday Night Fever*, Robert staged a massive garden party in the middle of New York. One thousand guests partied all night – all the beautiful people were there. I remember sitting at a table with Andy Warhol, Carly Simon, Paul Simon and James Taylor. Robert, and the Bee Gees came over.

'Look, David,' said Robert, and there above Times Square was our Red Cow flashing in big red neon above the USA Top Ten:

CONGRATULATIONS TO THE BEE GEES, FIVE SONGS IN THE USA TOP TEN

To this day it still stands as a world record. RSO Records was now far and away the world's number one independent record label. Robert made a toast: 'To you, David, you made us smile, knocked down the doors and moved us on down the right road. I told you, you are the one!'

Saturday Night Fever, Worldwide Promotional Tour. Once again Paris beckoned. We stayed at the Inter Continental Hotel, in the penthouse suite. That afternoon the boys sat through another 100 interviews answering the same questions and posing for the photographer's relentless demands. 'Just one more shot, I promeeese, *monsieur*.'

When the last crew had left I walked to the open window. Outside was a balcony. Far below there were a blur of red tail lights and a cacophony of klaxons as the Parisians careered along the boulevards homeward bound to *les environs* and beyond. The four of us were laughing and fooling around, light-headed after all the interviews.

'Come out here, lads. There's a spectacular view.'

I'll never know what prompted my next action but I climbed over the balcony and started to edge along the ledge, which encircled the hotel. For a man who suffers terribly from vertigo this act seemed even more irrational.

'Come on boys – it's great out here!'

One by one, Barry, Robin and Maurice followed me along the ledge, keeping our backs and hands tightly against the wall, never once daring to look down (my palms are now sweating as I recall this incident). When we came to the next suite we looked in and saw a couple making love. I quite clearly remember the man's white buttocks hammering away and then the girl's face looking over his shoulder. Slowly a look of total disbelief registered as she saw a madman followed by the three Bee Gees inch past her window 500 feet above Paris.

The next day on the plane to London we spotted the couple sitting in First Class. Barry leaned over and whispered to the blushing girl, 'Good morning, sweetheart, nice to see you with your clothes on!'

On reflection Paris had featured prominently in my RSO adventures. Previously I had booked West Bruce and Laing into L'Opera House, the first pop group ever to play at this bastion of Paris culture. The trouble was that 'WB & L' were hardly pop in the Lulu and Her Lovers, New Seekers mould – more like the Demented Disciples from Hell.

Don't get me wrong, Jack Bruce is a big friend and Leslie West is, well, very big ... 20 stone of driving rock power, the lead guitar player from Mountain along with his Cowboy Sidekick the legendary drummer Corky Laing. This was the turbo-charged trio who on playing at the Rainbow Theatre decided to lob a full bottle of champagne into the frenzied audience. As Jack hurled the Veuve Clicquot out into the audience, a million to one chance happened and the bottle landed on Bud Praegar, President of Windfall Records, who had come to the gig to sign them! Bud was stretchered off to hospital and backstage was the only time I've seen Robert Stigwood violent, as he lifted Jack off his feet and pinned him against the wall.

So to the night at the Opera. The French musos sat in their velvet seats, looking through binoculars at the stage awaiting the mighty trio. Backstage all was not running smoothly. Enhanced by a strong chemical intake, the boys were arguing and gesticulating vehemently. It was a volatile mix and quite frankly they didn't look that well.

On went Jack to mighty applause and started up 'Sunshine Of Your Love'. Whether it was the Frog in the front row that had said something to inflame our Jack's troubled state of mind, I'm not sure, but the next thing I saw was the fiery Celt leaping off the stage and scissor-kicking the provocateur in the chest. Meanwhile Leslie and Corky were cooking up a storm. As a full-blown riot ensued the iron safety curtain was lowered dissecting Corky's drum kit. The Texan was cut in two. You could see his cowboy boots poking out from one side as the other half carried on drumming horizontally from behind the curtain. Leslie continued to play full blast. He was on the moon and hadn't a clue as to the whereabouts of his two trusty sidekicks.

The riot police surged through the auditorium brandishing fire hoses and spraying the crowd. Roger Forrester, the group's manager, confronted by the agitated promoter, punched him full in the face – and Leslie? – well, he just kept on playing.

West Bruce and Laing were arrested and thrown into jail.

The next day *France Soir* ran banner headlines 'West Bruce and Laing the first and last L'orchestre to play at L'Opera House!'

That evening, as usual, Robert called me.

'How was the gig? Everything run smoothly?'

'Well Chairman,' I replied, 'put it this way, the guillotine is about to fall and I'll be bringing back three heads to Brook Street!'

I returned to England to appear in two films, *The Lady Vanishes* and *The Silver Bears*.

The Silver Bears was a crime caper involving Mafia financial whiz kids careering around Europe, a rip-roaring yarn starring Michael Caine and Louis Jourdan. The film's director was Ivan Passer, a Czech and a colleague of both Milos Forman and my pal Jan Brychta.

Jan had recommended me to Ivan and I was told to go and see him at his big house in Kensington. On arrival, I was ushered into the garden by the housekeeper, where Ivan Passer, a man in his early thirties, was sitting down drinking tea. He had a strong friendly face and a warm disposition. He also wore a black cape and highly polished riding boots giving him the aura of a Transylvanian Count.

'David, good to meet you. Sit down. Jan has told me all about you. Now watch the birds in that tree. They will eat the berries which will make them drunk and they will fall to the ground intoxicated.'

I sat there fascinated as the blue tits and sparrows fell kamikaze-like to the ground.

'Tell me Ivan . . .'

There was no reply. The Count had vanished. A good twenty minutes lapsed before Ivan returned. He passed me a script.

'Here, read the part of Nigel de Selvigny, a silver broker.'

As I read, I thought hard about Ivan. Before Milos Forman had been seduced by Hollywood and gone on to make *One Flew Over the Cuckoo's Nest*, *Amadeus* and *Hair*, Ivan and Milos had made a classic Czech comedy entitled *The Fireman's Ball*. The Czechs have a wonderful ability to observe in an entirely Eastern European way. Very tongue in cheek with a great eye for detail.

I finished reading and we sat there in the warm sun, just talking. A Kensington garden, the lawn mowers were out and the smell of grass was in the air. The hounds of spring were indeed on winter's traces and the coming summer was rich in promise.

'Tell me of America, David, the record business, the atmosphere,' asked Ivan, stretching out, staring down at his long shiny boots.

'Well, Ivan, I think America represents ambition. If you have talent and want to make it fast. You think like an American. That is what America is about. They appreciate talent.'

We talked and laughed. Lots of stories. I told him of my love of contrast, the fast lane to the Hotel California with its decadent fascination, and Los Angeles with its Hollywood dreams and tragedies. The last stop before you hit the Pacific Ocean. 'But Ivan, a day like today, I'd prefer to sit in Monet's field or lie among the lilies and dream.'

He asked me about songwriting. I told him that I thought stories and emotional experiences made the best songs. Maybe I still lived off faded glories but I felt that the words of Neil Young, Van Morrison, Joni Mitchell and Bob Dylan touched that special nerve.

'For me, whatever idea comes into my head will hit the paper. Sometimes I feel there is gold flowing from my pen.' Then there were the great singers like Barry Gibb and Nat King Cole. To feel the guitar of Clapton . . . I told him the importance of music to film, how it heightened and brightened the story.

During the three or four hours I spent with Ivan Passer, he had made me do all the talking. I had read the words of the script for just twenty minutes and rattled on about life for 3½ hours. My rambling exhausted even the birds, paralytic by now. All this time Ivan the caped crusader and his feathered friends had observed me.

The part was mine. I plucked a couple of berries off the trees. 'Cheers, Ivan! The drinks are on me!'

On the first day of filming, I was reunited with Michael Caine, where, like a couple of old war veterans, we reminisced about *A Bridge Too Far*. Also appearing in the film was Arthur Lowe who suffered from a sleeping sickness. On several occasions he actually 'dropped off' in the middle of a scene. Captain Mainwaring in *Dad's Army* would never be the same again!

Appearances in *It Ain't Half Hot Mum*, *The Professionals*, *Secret Army*, *Squadron*, *Bergerac*, *That's My Boy* and *Emmerdale Farm* all followed. I was on fire and thoroughly enjoying the experience of filming except for the frustration of hanging around between scenes. Believe me, acting is a waiting game. You can wait in your trailer for three hours but when you are called and the cameras roll you have to be instantly 'in character'. I have spent hundreds of hours telling jokes to security men, chauffeurs, cooks, riggers, chippies, extras and anyone who will listen to allay the boredom of the waiting game.

Once again I took the road to Miami, down the West Dixie Highway to Criteria Studios. The Bee Gees were holding a playback party for *Spirits Having Flown*. For years they had told me about Cindy Lee Johnson; 'Just your type, Dave. You'll love her.' Years ago I had only seen her fleetingly back at 461 Ocean Boulevard with Eric. And then this beautiful blonde entered Criteria, laughing and joking with the musicians

Love indeed is a many-splendoured thing. Like inspiration it comes from the very depths of your soul. It is raw and emotional. It tears at your heart and renders you helpless. Its strength leaves you weak. You are out of control but happy to be so. Come to me with your talk of sunsets and I'll take you on magic carpet rides. The wind is high. We'll be dancing on air, locked in each other's arms, racing with the moon, secure and happy to see the world through the eyes of one. A shared dream makes a couple strong.

Cindy Lee went to the ladies' toilet, and, the fire of love flickering in my belly, I followed her in and stood behind her. My heart skipped a beat. She washed her hands and without looking up she said, 'I know who you are. You're David English. The boys have warned me about you!' Outside, 'Too Much Heaven' was playing. She looked at me in the mirror and turned. I held her and looked her straight in the eyes, and said, 'You're the one for me.' I knew it instantly.

She laughed, 'You're crazy.'

I had gone to Miami for two weeks. Two years later I was still holding her. I never went back.

It was not easy winning Cindy's heart. She resisted all my moves, just laughing. 'But I mean it,' I pleaded. 'Please come out with me,' but to no avail. She just donned her straw hat edged with flowers and was gone in her blue Volkswagen convertible with white-walled tyres.

One night I wrote to her about a friend of mine called Billy Steele, a Londoner who had come to Miami Beach to stay with friends. Only 32 years old, he was deep in grief as his father was very ill in a London hospital.

One day, while the rest of the house was asleep, Billy quickly dressed and slipped down the back stairs into the glorious sunlit day. He moved across the road and on to a golf course. From the top of the hill he stood to scan the terrain. Slowly he surveyed the foreground. He could see silver-backed lizards darting in and out of the shrubbery. White-sanded bunkers cut the dew-soaked greens, beautifully punctuated from time to time. In the distance, through a kaleidoscope of colourful fauna and blue and yellow flowers, Billy's eyes rested on this vision and then as if drawn by a magnetic force felt his body being pulled towards it.

Billy found the little house, wandered through the shrubbery and along a path, which led to some wooden steps. His heart beating, Billy's senses were heightened by the perfumed smell of pine and flowers. A strong scented odour, which filled his head and put him in a trance.

The smell of perfumed pine became even stronger as he reached the top of the steps. There, on the balcony, two parrots chatted and played inside a wooden cage. To the right was a glass door with a blue printed curtain hanging on the inside making it impossible to see within. He could feel his palms moistening, the excitement overwhelming.

'What should I do?' thought Billy. 'This is somebody's home. I just can't walk in . . .'

But walk in he did. Carefully turning the handle, he crept inside; his heart beating faster and his mouth by now dry with a mixture of fear and anticipation. The room was decorated like a doll's house, unbelievably pretty. Cream lace curtains fringed the white painted window frames. On the polished floors were rush mats, in the corner a vase of brightly coloured flowers. Little porcelain figurines mainly of rabbits stood on the window ledge and children's books and fairytale stories lined the shelves. There was a breathless hush save for the parrots outside. By now, his heart almost leaping out of his chest, Billy tiptoed to the far room. On the ceiling were golden stars above a large bed with embroidered covers and a wooden headboard. Lying on the bed was someone asleep.

Billy just stood and stared. Still in a spell he saw the body of what he thought at first to be a child, but looking closer he realised it was a woman. An aura of radiance shone around her.

Just then Billy's spell burst. In a moment of panic, he turned and moved back through the lounge, out of the door, breaking into a run down the stairs, back along the path and into the street.

On the crest of the hill, still panting he turned to look back at the little house in the far distance. His mind was rushing with what he had seen. The helpless attraction towards the place, the magic of the little house and, inside, the unsuspecting body of the beautiful girl asleep in her lace and flowers.

The day slipped by without Billy remembering anything except his early morning adventure. He decided to tell no one about his secret.

The next morning Billy retraced his steps. He reached the door of the house and hands shaking turned the crystal knob to the right and peeked in.

The room was the same. He moved towards the bedroom. The bed was empty. He was consumed by a mixed feeling of sadness at finding no one there and relief at being alone in the strange place.

'What do you want?' The voice was slow and positive.

Billy whirled around to see the girl standing in the doorway. Up till then his mouth had been dry, his eyes wide open and his ears straining for any sound. Now he felt like a little boy who had been caught red-handed while stealing something from a shop.

The girl was now staring at him through brown eyes, which peered right through him and knocked him off his balance.

'I . . . I . . . I . . . came here because I thought the place was empty. I didn't think anyone lived here, honestly,' Billy stuttered, shaking with fear.

'What's your name?' replied the girl, moving towards her chair and sitting down.

'Billy Steele.'

'Well, Billy Steele, you shouldn't just wander around other people's property you know . . . it's against the law.'

Billy's mind was racing. He desperately wanted to tell her how he had been drawn so strongly to her house. How for some reason he belonged there and how she looked so beautiful stretched out in her chair.

'Can I sit down?' asked Billy, 'I want to tell you something.'

For the best part of forty minutes he unfolded his story to the girl who smiled warmly and listened attentively. She made him feel relaxed and soon he unlocked the sadness in his heart of his father's illness.

As Billy explained how he had stumbled across her house, the light in the room seemed to change. Sunbeams flickered through the windows and danced on her hair. Then he heard a rushing wind through the flowers outside. All of a sudden the softness in her face tightened to a controlled awareness of the situation.

'Listen, Billy, you must never come here again because I won't be here. You must forget you ever met me . . . that I ever existed. Because, you see, Billy, I really don't.'

'What do you mean?' said Billy slowly.

He had felt he was getting along just fine . . . there was no indication that he was losing his grasp of the situation.

'Billy, come here with me.' The girl got up and took him into a back room. The room was empty except for an oval mirror hanging on the far wall. Out of her pocket she took a sterling silver pen. 'Now go to the mirror, Billy, and write on the surface anything you want. I will grant you one wish. Go on, I'm going back into the other room and you come to me when you've finished.'

Still in a magical trance Billy Steele obeyed the girl and returned to her after ten minutes. He gave her back the pen and she leaned forward and kissed him lightly on the lips. 'Now be strong, Billy Steele, go forward into the world with courage in your heart and your wish and desires will come true.'

Billy tried to speak but there was finality in the girl's voice, which prevented him from saying another word. He took one last glance at her, turned and went out of the door down the steps and into the road. He never looked back.

A week later he returned to England to visit his father in hospital. 'Well, Billy, we've got some great news for you, come this way.' The matron led Billy to his father's ward.

'Well, son, welcome home.' Billy was shocked to see his father sitting up in his bed, smiling.

'Dad, you look great.' Billy embraced his father with all his might.

'Steady on old son, you'll squeeze the living breath out of me.'

'It's quite miraculous, Billy, your father's condition was critical and all of a sudden last week he recovered and now he's almost 100% fit. The doctors could not believe it. There's no medical explanation to such a recovery.'

'Thank you, matron, I'm overwhelmed.' The matron smiled and left the two men together.

'Well, Billy, I'll be out in a week and we can get back to living properly again.'

'You look great, Dad.'

'Yes, son, even had my first shave this morning. Funny thing actually.'

'What's that, Dad?' enquired Billy.

'Well, I was in the bathroom this morning and as I began to shave, the mirror began to wobble. Slowly at first, then it shook quite violently. I thought I was seeing things, having another "turn", but then it stopped and settled back into its position again. Very weird, can't explain it.'

A cold chill spread through Billy Steele. First of all along his cheeks and then across the shoulders and down his back. The blood drained from his face and a large tear fell from his eye.

'You alright, son, anything wrong?' said his father, reaching for his hand.

Billy shook himself together. 'No! No! I'm fine, Dad, I'm just so happy that you're OK.'

That night Billy Steele sat down and wrote to the beautiful girl.

A month later the letter was returned. On the envelope was written: 'Occupant unknown. This address does not exist.'

Ten days after I posted my letter to Cindy, she called me.

'Look, David, I'm going shopping, you can come with me if you wish.'

('Oh dream maker, you heart breaker, wherever you're going I'm going your way. . .')

That night at Barry's house we sat outside under a Miami moon, we kissed, 'Too Much Heaven' played. In a world of romance I had found my soul mate. She took me back to her home up there in the Bougainvilleas. We sat on the balcony, drank coffee and held hands. Later we lay on her big bed and stared at the golden stars on the ceiling.

'Tell me, David, whatever did happen to Billy Steele.'

I drew her to me and brushing her golden hair aside whispered in her ear, 'I've never felt better . . .'

My dad had indeed been ill. Johnny Cousins phoned to tell me he had once again disappeared, so together Cindy and I flew to England to find him. The boys at Mill Hill village told me that occasionally he drank in the Manor Cottage Tavern, Finchley. We quickly made our way to the pub, a dingy affair with a tired appearance, worn carpets, a couple of one-armed bandits and a TV, which flickered intermittently from one channel to another. A couple huddled in the snug and a roly-poly ex footballer was pinning back the land-lord's ears, berating him with past glories.

'Welcome to England, Cindy.' I love England with its pubs, pride and glory. For the Florida girl with sunshine in her veins, it was the first taste of our heritage. She clung on to my arm and reassured me it was fascinating.

At the end of the bar sat an imposing man, distinguished like Douglas Fairbanks. He wore a felt trilby hat and a fine silk bow tie. Next to him sat an elegant lady in her early sixties.

'Pater?'

'Son!'

We embraced.

'Dad meet Cindy, how are you?'

'This is Babs, son, I'm well. Tell me the news.'

It's funny how you must always go back to go forwards in life; a trip down memory lane stimulates the road ahead. So I took Cindy on a grand tour; first on the list was my mum and Bennie the Yorkshire terrier, and then the sentimental journey back to all my childhood haunts, espe-cially the eight schools. To this day if ever I meet a special girl I take her along this route. They probably think I'm a sad old bastard but I draw massive strength from the past. For me all roads still lead to Hendon and just knowing that Hendon Park is there makes me smile and gives me an extra warm glow.

I left England to rekindle my love affair with America, with my new love. We lived in a white house with a tropical garden in Biscayne Park, North Miami. It was subtropical suburbia where good old boys clutched Budweisers and talked about their new boats or the Dolphins game against the Steelers. Barbecues burned and planes flew high in bright blue skies trailing banners advertising 'Hawaiian Tropic' or 'Music on the Beach'.

'Hi, this is Love 94 F.M. and the weather is fine in downtown Miami 88°F – those of you sailing, the ocean is calm except for a medium chop off Key Biscayne.'

It rarely got colder. The postman wore shorts and a white pith helmet and every morning as the air-conditioning unit whirred like a motorbike in the side of the wall, the paper-boy flung a copy of the *Miami Herald*, neatly rolled in a waterproof bag, into our garden.

It was a pretty garden with a white picket fence. We had a lovely maid called Mary, who brought out Viennese coffee as I wrote on a rickety wicker table. I bought a Steve McQueen Ford Mustang 1965 convertible which gleamed white, standing proudly and powerfully in the drive.

I flourished in this domestic bliss. Just sitting there with my pad and pencil at peace, surrounded by the boats and lizards, and safe in the knowledge that Cindy loved me. I had never lived with anyone; I had always been isolated, naked and alone with my thoughts. She gave me warmth. Just knowing she was there, to hear the tinkle of teacups in the next room and a hug at half-time stirred me into action. I was with the girl I loved and had my best friend Bazzer just down the road.

I wrote a book on the Bee Gees called *The Legend*, beautifully animated by Alex Brychta. I told the brothers' story through animal characters; Barry was a Lion, Robin a Red Setter and Mo an Eager Beaver. Every day when Cindy had gone to work at her company, Home at Last, I climbed into my Ford Mustang and gunned it down the I95 Freeway to Miami Beach, and Bazzer's home. We have a prolific, all-encompassing friendship, a deep love and understanding based on laughing a lot and living in an abstract world. Every time we meet we come up with an idea and enthusiastically pursue it till its fulfilment.

For a year we followed the same pattern. Arrive, lie in the sun, laugh, come up with an idea, and drift through to the lounge to write or film. The only time we stopped was to watch any war film that might be showing.

Linda used to glide through the lounge and laugh to see the two of us lost in our own world. 'Look, Mum,' said young Stevie Gibb. 'Uncle Dave is still here. It's a year now, I thought he was only coming for two weeks!'

Miami was a pot pourri of race and culture. In the south you had the Hispanics, Portuguese, Spanish, Cuban and Haitians. North of Collins Avenue the elderly Jewish came to retire. At 65 they would close down their Delis in Brooklyn, pack up their belongings and jump into the Hudson River. They luxuriated in the warm currents which flowed southwards until the hook of Florida pulled them into Miami Beach where they could stretch out and warm their bones or enjoy a coffee and bagel in Wolfie's Café. Then there was South Beach where the bronzed and beautiful worked and played ... where sex and money flowed like the ocean surf, and stately palms swayed above the languid curves and artful angles of a sensuous world of deco delight. But there was a dark and dangerous side.

Back in the Thirties, Forties and Fifties the gangsters had made Miami Beach into what was then America's greatest, albeit illegal, gambling resort. There were elegant gambling clubs and nightspots frequented by hoodlums. First there was Scarface Al Capone who lived on Palm Island, then there was Lucky Luciano, Little Augie Carfano, Frank Costello and most important of all, the Mob's own intellectual Meyer Lansky. Behind his dark glasses he had the appearance of a retired accountant, but until the day he died in 1983, Lansky was under constant FBI surveillance, for he was the brilliant mastermind of the Mob's gambling operation not just in Miami, but in Havana. In fact, Meyer organised crime in America: bribery, money laundering, racketeering, obstruction of justice and homicide were rife. Then there was drug dealing.

Like the snappily dressed gangsters of the Forties and Fifties, squiring around showgirls who looked and dressed like Jayne Mansfield, in brand new pink Cadillac Convertibles, this new breed of drug dealer became the hippest men in town. In the late Seventies and early Eighties Miami was renowned as the drug capital of the USA. Because of its proximity to South America it was the drop-off point for cocaine, heroin and marijuana; the mountains of cocaine, hooking the beautiful people who slept it off by day and became vampires by night, fuelled the club scene.

Dakota aeroplanes overloaded with narcotics from Columbia or Ecuador frequently crashed into the sea off Florida, where ships carrying the stuff stayed seven miles outside territorial waters to prevent being raided by the coast guards.

Because of its intricate network of waterways, powerful speedboats called Cigarettes travelling at 70 mph could reach the ships, load up the illicit cargo and return by nightfall escaping the coastguard's scrutiny.

Every time the coastguards made a kill, a marijuana leaf was proudly painted on the boat's funnel like the swastikas emblazoned on the side of a Second World War Spitfire.

The man who invented and designed the Cigarette lived next to Barry. One day he was in his car waiting for the lights to change, when, in broad daylight, another vehicle drew up beside him and the driver shot him in the head. The dope dealers, puzzled by the sudden escalation in busts, had discovered that he had been making even more powerful Cigarettes for the coastguards, enabling them to make their arrests.

I invited my pal Johnny Cousins to come over and stay with Cindy and me. I'd christened him 'Miami Johnny'. Together we monitored the drug headlines in the *Miami Herald* and watched the dealers as they embraced the Fellini-esque nightlife. They'd sweep into the clubs with their coterie of young beautiful models, who'd once been the pride of the catwalks of Paris and Milan but were now hopelessly hooked and leading a vapid and meaningless life. There they sat, backs to the wall in the VIP section, giving them the best chance to survey and retaliate if a rival gang decided to rush the club, machine guns blazing.

Bodyguards followed their bosses' every move, even into the toilet. The Cuban boys carried shotguns hidden underneath their Versace jackets, living a fast life and plying their illicit trade. Death was imminent, one moment they were heedless and feverish, cavorting in La Dolcevita, the next they would be found, whacked, floating face down in the Miami River with a bullet in their brain.

Together Johnny and I chased these mirages of the night, and, as usual, I reported my sightings to the 'Skipper'. Together Barry and I sat down in the magic lounge and wrote a screenplay entitled 'Whirlpool'. For six months we painstakingly wrote 128 pages of dialogue about drug-dealing and skulduggery in Miami.

We sent the final copy to Robert Stigwood in New York, who called to say he loved it. Barry and I were excited. We knew this could be our first motion picture as writers and producers. Robert passed it on, and then lines from New York went strangely silent. It often seems to happen this way. You create an idea, everybody is in raptures, leaping about in excitement and then nothing happens. You're told that 'The right people have it' and 'It's looking good', which very often is a load of bollocks.

All I can tell you is seven months later *Miami Vice* hit the screens. The characters and storylines were uncannily like 'Whirlpool'. Barry and I were convinced that our script had fallen into the wrong hands, and our idea had been well and truly nicked.

Even today when I watch repeats of the 'Vice', I see Crockett and Tubbs running along the mean streets of Miami, which we had created. Ironically, James Ed Olmos, who played the Lieutenant, is still one of our closest friends.

When Robert Stigwood finally retired he built a big rambling house by the sea in Bermuda. From 'The Wreck', he considered the future. He had always had a love for the sea and decided to purchase the luxury ocean-going yacht RHYC SS *Sarina*. From its moorings at the Royal Hamilton Yacht Club, Stiggy sailed away for a new life on the ocean waves.

The high jinx on the seven seas were chronicled in my book *The Sarinatorium*. The maritime madness that took place on Robert's yacht was spectacular. With the same ingenuity with which he had conducted his business, he planned different parties of pals to join him in different ports around the world.

I was piped aboard in Corfu. Barry and Linda had left a few days before with Tim Rice.

Our party consisted of Earl McGrath and the big guns from Atlantic Records in New York, Bill Oakes, my successor as President of RSO Records, Brian O'Donohue, Britain's number one record plugger and his wife, Robert's lawyer Paddy Grafton Green, and a retinue of voluptuous lovelies to help our voyage run smoothly. The *Sarina* sailed serenely out to sea with her full crew of highly skilled sailors, cordon bleu chefs and Robert's corps of PAs and secretaries all impeccably turned out, ready to serve our every whim. We indulged ourselves in wild parties of Caligula proportions and vivid storytelling which mainly took place at the captain's table just before dinner.

One night, I awoke in my cabin to the sounds of screaming in the corridors; the 'White Lady' was being pitched and tossed in a fearsome gale. There was panic on the decks. 'Abandon ship!' cried Robert. The New Yorkers and co. took to the lifeboats in varying degrees of undress, everybody leaving the boat except Robert and me.

'Don't worry, Robert, I'm staying with you. We'll go to a watery grave together. I can't swim anyway!'

So there I was, left with the most powerful man in showbiz, on a boat which was now being hurled around the seas in the mother of all storms.

Once again in the face of impending doom, I was consumed by a state of calmness. We opened a magnum of champagne and reminisced about the good old days at RSO, and pissed ourselves laughing trying to stay on our feet while clutching at flying ornaments, pieces of expensive furniture and the odd gold record.

After a good two hours riding the cruel sea there was a terrible scraping sound as though we had hit some rocks. When morning came, we discovered we were grounded on the beach of an island. When we came up on deck, there were naturalists skipping about with butterfly nets, staring at us in amazement.

We had hit a nudist colony.

'Come aboard!' laughed Robert. 'Have some champagne. It's alright, come as you are. You don't have to dress up!'

Out to sea the salvage ships were hovering. Apparently, the law of the sea decrees that whichever ship rescues the ailing craft will receive a big percentage of the ship's value. Well I can tell you that a share of the *Sarina's* value would have kept one of those Greek lads in kebabs for the rest of his life!

Robert and I returned to the port, where we were met by the evacuees, sheepishly giving us a hero's welcome.

CRICKLEWOOD TO HOLLYWOOD

'I'm Timothy Dalton,' a deep voice announced. 'I've just returned from fishing in Ireland. I love your script – let's meet.'

Barry and I arranged to take him to lunch at Langan's, along with Steve Lanning.

'James Bond' arrived wearing an old pullover and cords.

I will never forget his words. After exchanging pleasantries about the fishing trip in Ireland etc., Timothy told us, 'I've never come across a script that was as well written. Roy Clarke uses language to such a powerful effect. It is a fine piece of writing, which has great pugnacity, verve and humour.'

'So are you in, Tim?' I said, trying to stop my soup-spoon trembling over my brown oxtail.

'What's your budget?' he enquired.

'We've got to bring the picture in for £4,000,000,' I replied. 'We can afford to give you £100,000.'

Timothy Dalton paused, finished his glass of Chardonnay and shook our hands. 'I'm in,' he smiled. 'Jimmy Sharkey, my agent, will go potty, but I'll do it for £100,000 because it's a terrific story, a worthwhile story.'

10 CRICKLEWOOD TO HOLLYWOOD

Life in the fast lane, taking on the world, can be achieved when you know that you can escape to the seclusion of your own home. However, for some ladies, the notion of the confirmed bachelor living alone behind closed doors presents an irresistible challenge. Foot in the door, they will endeavour to disperse this celebration of peaceful thoughts by announcing that I should 'Come and join the tennis club,' or, 'Meet my friends, they'll love you!'

The overnight bag is a worry; 14 dresses to be hung and the cooking pot on 'for a quiet night in'. My idea of a quiet night in would be a love tussle on the Axminster, fuelled by a bottle of Jacob's Creek (special offer from Costcutter, £4.75). Why do they think they're going to stay? Sometimes, I have to put them on to the 10.05 p.m. to Bromley South, even if they don't live in Bromley.

'Darlink, why are your football boots in the oven?' screeched the lady from Lima.

I had taken her to Paradise. The Curry Paradise is a Bengali restaurant sandwiched between the launderette and a hairdressing salon called Split Decisions. Empty but fulfilled, I stared at the Peruvian delight who proceeded to thumb through the menu with great relish and talk exuberantly at me, giving me GBH of the eardrums for two hours; on the merits of shared experience, and 'how sad it is that you only had two cats to come home to, and it is a waste to sit alone pulling your wonker, darlink'.

I smiled through clenched teeth and suggested enthusiastically that she try the Rat Korma or the Gerbil Vindaloo. Occasionally, Conchita pulled her wild hair back off her caramel face and laughed loudly, puckering her red lips and announcing to the restaurant that she had one week's holiday, and would I take her to Turkey? God, I thought, and all this after one penetration.

It was 10.15 and I was spent, consumed by tiredness. Christ, just think I could have been home watching *Dad's Army,* and then a miracle ... my brothers came to my rescue. Through the ancient Bengali hi-fi system came the strains of Barbra Streisand singing 'Guilty'. Misty-eyed, the broken English cackle ceased from the Latin Quarter as Barbra and the boys harmonised through the papadoms and mamadons.

I've always found the birth of ideas fascinating and stimulating. I have a pen handy at all times, jotting down half-finished thoughts, some of which come in the middle of the night. One idea shines through not only because it was a great laugh but also because it became a great success.

I was with the Bee Gees, in their writing room above Middle Ear Studios, and, once again, they were at the peak of their writing powers. One day we were sitting about having a giggle. 'In all the world, which artist do you most admire?' I asked.

'Barbra Streisand!' was the unanimous response.

The story got to the papers. Within a week, Charles Coppelman, Barbra's manager, called and suggested a few songs to the Bee Gees. The brothers listened, felt they could do better, and wrote five songs. Barbra loved them and asked for five more.

It was fascinating to see them go to work. They simply thought of her singing and it was as if they were writing a script for an actor, or a tailor making a made-to-measure suit; they wrote the tunes to fit her voice. For the Bee Gees the idea is paramount. It will come instantly into their heads. The lyrics, arrangements, phrasing etc. follow later.

The album was demo'd in a week; 12 songs, taking half a day to complete each song.

For me, Barry's demos are as good as the final record. They are fresh and straight from the heart but being a Virgo and a perfectionist he always feels he can produce the song better and better. Letting go is sometimes the hardest thing to do. Barry and co-producers Alby Galuten and Karl Richardson hired the best musicians to lay down the backing tracks. Stevie Gadd on drums, Richard Tee on piano etc. – the hottest players in the business rocked into town.

Barbra flew in. What power! Wearing dungarees and chain-smoking Rothmans she stood at the microphone. The backing track was played and she sang like a bird. Barry, Robin, Maurice and some of the world's finest musicians stood behind the glass and marvelled as 'The Funny Girl' nailed the tunes in one take.

From time to time she would come out to have a cup of tea. I called her Babs, she roared with laughter and always insisted on sharing a teabag.

Success is when opportunity meets hard work. The *Guilty* sessions were amazing. As Barbra sang you knew they were smash hits – 'Guilty', 'Woman In Love', 'What Kind Of Fool', 'Promises'.

Great work stimulates more great work, and I was determined that we should make our own motion picture; watching 'Whirlpool' through the guise of *Miami Vice* convinced me our stories could make the big screen.

Barry loved to drive to the studio in my old Ford Mustang. The rattles, holey floors and dodgy mechanics; the power hood with a mind of its own, going up and down when it pleased – all this appealed to him. The road to Criteria took us along the West Dixie Highway. One afternoon I noticed a 'Barry Gibb lookalike' competition emblazoned across the window of a burger bar. 'Win a free kebab every day for a month.'

I screeched to a halt.

LEFT: A hat-trick of heroes. Sir Tim Rice and Mr and Mrs John Major.

RIGHT: *Absolutely Fabulous*. Joanna leads us out at the Oval. The Bunbury XI versus the Imperial War Museum XI, raising funds for The British Legion – live on Sky TV!

BELOW: The Bunburys Down Under. (From left to right) Chris Broad, James Whittaker, Ian Botham, Mike Gatting, Phil Edmonds, Allan Lamb, Elton John (holding Bunbury), John Emburey, David Gower, David English. At the MCG, Melbourne, 1987.

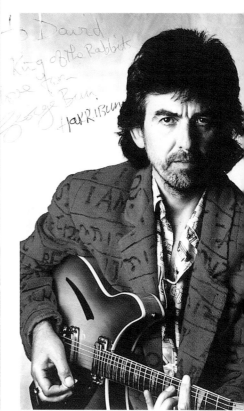

ABOVE LEFT: Three Bunburys in a boat. Botham, English and Clapton. 'Help, get me out of here!'

ABOVE RIGHT: My Swee[t] George. The remarkab[le] George Harrison. A tru[e] Piscean, sadly missed but never forgotten.

LEFT: 'Wiley Will' the leg-break king. Superb batsman, endless laughter and founder member.

ABOVE LEFT: Keeping wicket to Mel.

ABOVE RIGHT: Beef, Boon and the luck of the Irish. Ian Botham's Belfast to Dublin walk for Leukaemia Research, April 1987.

RIGHT: Mel's MC. Melinda Messenger's Big Bus tour.

LEFT: Leading the way into Torino. Strolling with Beefy on the Hannibal walk from Perpignan to Turin, April 1988.

BELOW: Turn again Whittington. The Grand Theatre, Blackpool, Christmas 1988. (From left to right) D. English (Captain), N. Wisdom (Whittington), B. Gibb (visiting icon).

ABOVE: The greatest charity match ever played. PCA Bunburys XI versus Malcolm Marshall XI, July 27 2000, HAC Ground, London. (Back row from left to right) David English, Rory Bremner, Mark Butcher, Justin Langer, John Hurst (umpire), Michael Holding, David Smith, Graeme Hick, Ian Bishop, Phil Simmons, Chris Cairns, Andrew White, Joel Garner, Tim Munton. (Centre row) John Holder (umpire), Phil Tufnell, Deryck Murray, Hugh Morris, Wayne Larkins, Dave Lawrence, David Graveney, Glenn McGrath, Alan Mullally, Shaun Udal, Mark Nicholas, Shane Warne, Alec Stewart, Graham Thorpe, Wasim Akram, Mohammed Azharuddin, Kevin Lyons (umpire). (Front row) Courtney Walsh, Mike Gatting, Brian Lara, Viv Richards, Desmond Haynes, Mali Marshall, Connie Marshall, Robin Smith, Gordon Greenidge, Alvin Kallicharan, Allan Lamb. (Missing from picture: Collis King, Colin Croft, Barry Richards.)

BELOW: A Bunbury Hall of Fame. Viv Richards, Brian Lara and Shane Warne at the Malcolm Marshall memorial match.

ABOVE: A day out at Wimbledon, exchanging gags for twelve hours non-stop

LEFT: All at sea with 'The King and I' off the coast of Brisbane, March 1993.

9 ½ Weeks in the Sunset Marquis, Los Angeles. (From left to right) Mickey Rourke, the legendary John 'Emmy' Altman, yours truly, Johnny Cousins.

RIGHT: My dearest soul mates. Barry and Linda 's' Gibb, Walking ass Productions, ami Beach.

LEFT: 19 June 1993. The day I walked up the aisle. (From left to right) Gary Headley, Naomi Dunckley, Linda Dunckley, Bob Dunckley, Sarah Whitmore, 'Big Bird' Joel Garner, my sweetheart Robyn, Gary Mason, DE, 'Miami' Johnny Cousins, Norman Cowans, Joe 'The Hat' Cuby, Johnny Keeble and Jamie, Ian Botham, Barry Gibb.

BELOW: The Loon, the love of my life, and Beefy.

My princess, Amy Rose.

David English Junior – 'The Zimbo Kic
and heir to the throne.

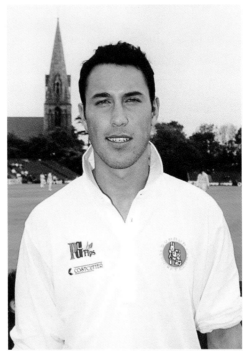

Dedicated to Ben Hollioake, a very
special Bunbury who will remain in our
hearts forever.

'What are you doing!' said Bazzer.

'You've got to go in,' I said.

'You must be joking,' replied the skipper.

I disguised him in an old raincoat and cap, BG walked in and photos were taken. A week later the results were shown in the window. Barry had come fourth. I even took him back into the shop. They still wouldn't believe it was him.

'But I *am* Barry Gibb,' he insisted.

Still carving his kebab off the revolving lamb, Stavros looked up and said, 'Sure, there is a strong likeness, but whoever you are, you've still come fourth.'

It was a Tuesday afternoon, and Miami was on a full hurricane alert. For some reason we decided to drive along the Coastal Road to the studio, turning inland on to the Turnpike.

Out to sea, storm clouds were gathering.

'Blimey, Skip, looks like the end of the world!' Together we peered out from the cockpit of the Mustang at the sight of the impending doom. Momentarily we were silenced by the ferocity of the storm.

'Tell me, Baz, what would happen if we only had a limited time to live, what would you do?'

Barry pondered while I continued, 'Or what would your idea of fulfilment be, if there was not enough time on this earth and you knew it? For some people I think it would be to sit with their families and wait to die. For others, it would be to go out and do everything that they had ever wanted to do.'

The idea was born. Our minds were as one, we knew it was a winner. We arrived at Criteria still talking excitedly about the idea, oblivious to Barbra and the musicians hanging around the foyer.

As Barbra sang in the studio I sat next to Barry in the control room and began to write. My pen flowed, it was easy because the subject matter was close to my heart.

The fact is that people always seem to live and work within the confines of being comfortable. Never stretching themselves, never daring to explore every path to fulfil their promise and dreams. Just think of all those people who go to their grave saying, 'I do wish I had done this or that.' Too late – the chance would have been presented to them but nullified for fear of failure. Content to read about other people's adventures in the pages of a colour supplement. Not me! If everybody felt that way, Everest would never have been conquered, penicillin discovered, Harry Potter written and Ian Botham would not have trudged 5,000 weary miles for Leukaemia Research.

'So, Baz, we've got two guys in hospital. Say it's you and me, we're terminally ill, six months to live; what do we do?'

'Go to Amsterdam,' smiled Barry, twiddling the knobs for Streisand's 'Guilty'.

'How?'

'We'll steal an ambulance.'

'Perfect.'

By the end of the day, 'Guilty' was in the can and we had written our story. We called it 'Going Dutch'.

Now to combine the necessary elements to make the film, here's what you have to do.

To raise the money, first of all you need a red-hot screenplay. The screenplay attracts the actors who love to interpret the work. The better the lines the bigger the star, the bigger the star the more finance can be raised. The other great pulling ingredient was Barry's music soundtrack. He would write the main songs and help to compose the score.

When we concocted the story obviously it was based on ourselves – we were the two lads who were terminally ill and in hospital in England. We had no time left so we decided to escape, steal an ambulance and go to somewhere where life is totally free. There is only one place where you can behave like that and that is Amsterdam. So Amsterdam would become the focal point, our Nirvana at the end of the rainbow.

We would get to Amsterdam and explore its every avenue and canal of pleasure. We would go crazy and out with a bang and a smile on our faces.

However, we were told that we were not bankable as stars. *A Bridge Too Far* and his pal *Saturday Night Fever* would not work. Barry and I were determined to make a truly British film like *Billy Liar*, *This Sporting Life*, *Saturday Night, Sunday Morning*, or the *L Shaped Room*. It must be based up North and have that wonderful Northern humour running through it. A young Albert Finney and John Hurt would be perfect casting. But we were told to get an American – you need one of the men to be an American to sell the film in the States.

I loved putting the film together. In the war I'd have been Mr Fixit in the prison camp. Getting the men out of Colditz or Stalag Luft, organising the tunnels, escape parties, bribing the ferrets with chocolate for ink and cameras, masterminding the forging of the false papers, making the clothes out of blankets and staging meaningless musical extravaganzas as diversions for the boys to get over the wall or tunnel under the wire. I would have charmed the goons as the lads legged it. I would have been the master of chicanery. A cross between Sgt Bilko and gentleman John Mills.

We needed a good hard-working producer to pull together these elements. I had been very impressed with Steve Lanning, assistant director on *A Bridge Too Far*. He had also ensured an extra six-weeks' fully paid stay on the *Bridge* for very little work. Unbeknown to Dickie, each morning we had got kitted out and armed up and slid off the back of the bus on arrival at the location. Steve told us to keep our heads down and 'f*** off to the woods' far away from the action. Each day we returned to the old folks' home under the cloak of darkness.

But first we needed a great script, a screenplay based on our story. I wanted the story to be touching and funny. It's about courage and tenacity and how people deal with life when, through no fault of their own, there is a possibility that it may be taken away from them at any time.

'Going Dutch' was really more about life than death as the lives our two men led had been brought into sharp focus through their illness. The film would be about the course of action they took and how they dealt with it. At first they would both deal with it differently and then because they get to know each other well, they would deal with it together. It would be a film of resilience and courage, humour and kindness bonded by an overwhelming sense of camaraderie. Life is a building process, gathering fragments of information and experience, learning something from everyone you meet and every adventure you explore.

'Going Dutch' was based on the special friendship between Barry and me but in truth probably started on that lonely road to Africa with Mark Strachan back in 1964. It had strong influences from my past; the stay in hospital after the accident, Amsterdam because of my love of Holland with *A Bridge Too Far*, although Copenhagen was strongly in contention after our frolics with Eric Clapton in that dodgy nightclub. And of course the continual quest for adventures with different women.

We needed a writer who could create the dialogue of our black comedy. There was John Sullivan, marvellous writer of *Only Fools and Horses*, Eric Chapell of *Rising Damp* and of course our own Ray Galton and Alan Simpson, writers of *Hancock* and *Steptoe & Son*. But the man we went for was a master of observation and whimsy who, ironically after our Dutch theme, lived in a windmill on the North Yorkshire Moors.

It had to be Roy Clarke. Anybody who could enchant us with the tales of four 'teenage' pensioners cavorting about the Yorkshire Dales in *Last of the Summer Wine* was perfect for our tale.

It was just before Christmas 1981, and Barry and I returned to England. We sent Roy Clarke our story. A few days later the phone rang.

'Hello lads, this is Roy Clarke, I like your story, when can we meet?'

So on Christmas Eve, with the snow lying thick around Beaconsfield, and BG and I sitting in our special room roaring with laughter in front of a roaring fire, there came a knock on the front door.

We opened it, and saw standing on the steps, dressed in a green Barbour coat, khaki trousers and combat boots, a tall, slim, grey-haired and imposing man, with the look of a journeyman, leather satchel slung over his shoulder.

'Hello, I'm Roy Clarke.'

He had fought his way through the snow in an old Land Rover to meet us.

We sat in the kitchen, the engine room of the house, where ideas were hatched. Roy smoked cigars as we animatedly told him how we saw the picture. After three hours he got up to leave and return to his windmill in the frozen wastes of the North. As we bade him farewell at the door, I looked up towards the woods. There, soaring in the sky were two birds of prey swooping in perfect harmony.

'Baz, that could be us up there, our two free spirits. Change the title. "Going Dutch" is now *Hawks*.'

It took Roy six weeks to write the first draft of the screenplay. Our original two characters, two Northern lads, had been changed into Bancroft, a successful English lawyer, and Decker, an American Football player touring Europe. Steve Lanning came through and agreed to be our producer.

Armed with our script I went to Hollywood to meet the movie shakers and makers. My meeting with MGM's head of film acquisition was particularly memorable.

I sat on the couch in his office and I can honestly say that during the hour I was in there he looked at me only once. The rest of the time, he played golf with his back to me, hitting the ball along the carpet into a waste-paper basket. But boy could the tycoon talk! He told me that the chances of a picture getting made by an independent in Hollywood were slim, it was a closed shop. There was a creative circle of six studio heads and big money men who determined if a film actually got to the screen.

'But what of the scripts that outsiders wrote and sent in?' I imagined somebody in bedsitland contriving a masterpiece, penniless but rich in promise.

'OK, we have a script-reading department but very few will reach the top of the pile.'

A rare exception was *One Flew Over the Cuckoo's Nest*, written by a hippy called Ken Kesey from mid-west USA. It had reached the desk of Kirk Douglas. Kirk sent his son Michael to meet Kesey. He bought the rights for a pittance, and the film, starring Jack Nicholson, was made and became one of the biggest grossing pictures of all time. Ken Kesey made nothing from his idea and faded back into hippydom.

However, 'Mr MGM' had read *Hawks* and confessed to liking the story. 'Go and get your two big stars and come back to me,' said the mogul, still with his back to me, concentrating on his next putt.

At that time, Timothy Dalton was playing the part of James Bond in *The Living Daylights*. His work with the Royal Shakespeare Company had confirmed his reputation as one of Britain's best leading actors, but by playing 007 he had become a big star in every country in the world. I knew that if we could get him it would help us raise the finance, big time. Through my network of contacts, I discovered he lived in Chiswick and so one night

I went to his house and pushed a script through his letterbox, together with a covering letter.

Meanwhile Steve Lanning had hired the Californian director Robert Ellis Miller who, like Sir Richard Attenborough, had a reputation as being an actor's director. His film *The Heart Is a Lonely Hunter* starring Alan Arkin had been nominated for an Academy Award. He brought Anthony Hopkins to Hollywood for the first time to star in *The Girl from Petrovka*, and most recently and quite coincidentally had worked with Timothy Dalton on *Brenda Starr*. He had for a long time wanted to work with Anthony Edwards, a superb screen actor, best-known at that time for his role as 'Goose' in *Top Gun* with Tom Cruise (and more recently as the compassionate and troubled Dr Greene in *E.R.*). We told Robert to go after him for the part of the American Footballer, Decker. I told him about my approach to Timothy Dalton.

'If you can get him, he'd be perfect for Bancroft. But he won't come cheap,' said Robert.

I told him about my special delivery to his letterbox, giving his agent the big swerve. Through his agent, Timothy Dalton would cost us £1,000,000 minimum. Several weeks went by when I got a call.

'I'm Timothy Dalton,' a deep voice announced. 'I've just returned from fishing in Ireland. I love your script – let's meet.'

Barry and I arranged to take him to lunch at Langan's, along with Steve Lanning.

'James Bond' arrived wearing an old pullover and cords.

I will never forget his words. After exchanging pleasantries about the fishing trip in Ireland etc., Timothy told us, 'I've never come across a script that was as well written. Roy Clarke uses language to such a powerful effect. It is a fine piece of writing, which has great pugnacity, verve and humour.'

'So are you in, Tim?' I said, trying to stop my soup-spoon trembling over my brown oxtail.

'What's your budget?' he enquired.

'We've got to bring the picture in for £4,000,000,' I replied. 'We can afford to give you £100,000.'

Timothy Dalton paused, finished his glass of Chardonnay and shook our hands. 'I'm in,' he smiled. 'Jimmy Sharkey, my agent, will go potty, but I'll do it for £100,000 because it's a terrific story, a worthwhile story.'

The jigsaw was being assembled piece by piece. We had Timothy, now we'd go for Anthony Edwards. It was like a movie game of tennis with the Atlantic Ocean as the net. We didn't want to Americanise our picture but we knew by adding an American character we had more of an international shot at success. I was determined to get them together. I had watched their acting carefully. Tim didn't like to work technically, you could see that he felt and thought himself through every take, like working in the theatre. He liked to give a performance, working from the depth of his soul and always very honestly. Anthony was more of a film actor, he worked more technically and enjoyed dishing it out in spoonfuls, so he had enough for the next take. He kept it small and interior but it came blazing out of the eyes.

Onwards and upwards, *Hawks* was flying. We had our James Bond and were in pursuit of *Top Gun*. Armed with a first-class screenplay, Steve Lanning and co-producer Keith Cavele would now attack the banks for the necessary finance.

I couldn't afford to rest while this was going on, and as I wasn't needed now, I realised I had to get on with my life. Cindy had returned to Florida to top up her veins with sunshine, so for me it was time to get back and tread the boards. I had always wanted to try a season in Repertory theatre, where you truly learnt the trade. In fact you learned and rehearsed one play in the day, and performed another at night.

I auditioned for the Everyman Theatre in Cheltenham. They were staging five plays during the season, Alan Ayckbourn's *Confusions*, *Outside Edge* and *The Dresser*, an Agatha Christie and *The Rear Column* by Simon Gray.

The auditions took place in Gunnersbury. I went to meet the artistic director, Malcolm Farquhar, a well-built man, flamboyantly dressed entirely in purple. We got on like a house on fire. My varying background fascinated him, we talked at length, I read for him and I was told, 'David, we'll let you know!'

Five days later a letter arrived bearing the purple insignia of the Everyman Theatre. I had been invited to join the company for the summer season.

Driving down the A40, past Oxford and Burford, you enter the enchanted land of vales and hills, where a sense of timelessness prevails. 'Over sun-baked earth and sea by sail, brave men speak of the Dragon's Tail, Fire Red Wing and Sharpened claw raise the fang in the gnashing jaw.' Only the brave will venture over the hills with their ever-changing lights, and there beneath brightly coloured balloons, flying high in a crimson sky, is Cheltenham, tucked away in the Cotswolds. As you descend into 'Harrods in the hollow', with its tea rooms and wine bars and established men's outfitters, all kid gloves and hacking jackets, and hotels with spas and manicured gardens, you are consumed by a sense of blissful peace and warmth, as if you're nestling under the beating speckle-feathered chest of a mother thrush.

I was billeted in Mrs Hancock's theatrical digs at Number 7 Stone Pryors. The circus was in town and I was happy to share my live-in quarters with a dog act, the Great Raymondo, four dwarfs and a red-faced ringmaster with a toupee and a false moustache. Mrs Hancock was a delightful landlady, square of beam with a ruddy countenance and an uproarious laugh. She put me in a big sunny room on the top floor with bright yellow walls and a pear tree outside my window.

There we sat at breakfast time over sizzling sausages, the eyes of the dwarfs barely peeking above the table, flailing vainly for their boiled eggs and soldiers as Mrs H regaled us with tales of her favourite Thespian guests of yesteryear.

'Oooh! My goodness, that Peter O'Toole was a scallywag, Laurence Harvey such a charming man and as for that Richard Harris, well I just can't say!'

Rehearsals were fun. We read on the stage, practised our moves and got into character. Quite honestly, I found it hard to concentrate, Cheltenham was pure heaven on earth. The Ladies College was *Blue Murder at St Trinians* personified. I shared vast amounts of wine and chitchat in the Montpelier Wine Bar with the Fiona Foreskin-Joneses and blue stocking hockey captains. Great girls, great breeding, great sense of adventure. They'd come to the theatre and heckle us in the matinees.

Learning lines was a pain in the arse. Given any chance, I nipped out to play cricket at the back of the theatre with the stage management. Two days before we opened with *Confusions*, during the dress rehearsal, a deep dark brown voice boomed out of the dark auditorium. It was the director, Michael Napier-Bell:

'David, if I were you I'd be a trifle concerned. Keep your mind off the cricket and learn those f***ing lines!'

Interestingly enough, the greatest test in my whole life was just ahead of me.

Malcolm Farquhar, the purple panther, had given me the lead role of Major Barttelot in Simon Gray's *The Rear Column*. This was a harrowing tale of five army men waiting at Yambuya Camp on the banks of the Arruimi River for the return of the legendary H.M. Stanley (of 'Dr Livingstone I presume' fame) from one of his jungle expeditions. It was a powerful drama and an enormous acting role.

The obsessed Major Barttelot ruled over the rear column with savagery. His hatred for Stanley was vented on his fellow officers and the natives. The role consisted of over 3,000 lines and my presence on the stage for 3½ hours. I sat in my sunny room perusing the script and froze with fear. That brown-trousered feeling consumed my body – the enormity of the task, to remember all that dialogue, was insurmountable.

The escape route via the pear tree beckoned. I could shin down its trunk, dodging the dwarfs on the way, and be across the Cotswolds back to the haven of West Hampstead NW6.

A process of self-examination in its most concentrated form took place. I felt pathetic, cowardly. Had I not come up with the idea of *Hawks* precisely about this subject of stretching oneself, and here I was contemplating doing a runner. I called up my agent Susan Angel, a wonderful woman who had the capacity to absorb her actors' insecurities and trepidation, as well as sharing their highs and the exultation of securing the big parts.

'Susan, I've read *The Rear Column*. I can't play Barttelot, there's no way I can remember all those lines.'

I must confess I had expected her to sympathise and help me to escape this onerous task. No such luck!

'Look, David, if you don't play Barttelot, you might as well pack it in. Learn the lines or give up acting. Don't play at it. Do it. You're good enough, so get your head down.'

Fear is a great stimulant, I had no option but to tackle the task. Ostracised in Cheltenham. There was no turning back.

Each night after the final curtain I'd stroll back through the empty streets, stopping for a burger on the way. After midnight at Stone Pryors, I'd sit in my room drinking Mellow Birds coffee and devouring my script. At 4 a.m. I'd get some shuteye, then up at 7 a.m. to see if I'd retained the lines. The secret was not to panic but to relax the mind and give it a chance to absorb the part.

Rehearsals were amazing, native drums and steamy heat provided our setting and hot passion would run wild in the jungle, particularly in the shape of actress Sonya Smyles, the native girl who bared her breasts for the officers. Wow! When Sonya 'Smyled', Major Barttelot was driven to another distraction far away from the cricket field. Talk about the power of a woman. She was sensational. Her smile, the fullness of her body, the raw sex appeal left me gagging for it.

At night I sneaked her back in to Stone Pryors and the privacy of my quarters. There the mad Major and his native girl went crazy, thrashing about on the linoleum floor, scaling new peaks of unbridled lust and passion. Even better, in the afterglow, Sonya would sit cross-legged, wearing just my cricket pullover, hands cupped around a beaker of Mellow Birds, testing me on my lines.

The opening night, I entered stage right and exited stage left three-and-a-half hours later. Having stormed through the tribal atmosphere, lifted by Sonya's presence on stage and the author Simon Gray in the stalls, the combination of adrenaline and fear (plus the other actors' vain attempts to 'corpse me' by placing artificial dog turds in strategic positions and lurid photographs in my view) made my performance in *The Rear Column* the very pinnacle of my career.

The point was I had achieved what I had considered impossible and proved to myself that anything in life could be tackled and won.

Believe me, after eight performances of Major Barttelot a week, for three weeks, everything else is a doddle!

BEEF 'N' LOON IN A STEW

We sat in the back of the taxi, me opposite Beefy, Kath to his side. 'Now, Loon, tell us that submarine joke again.'

'Beefy, I think . . . oooooh! aaaach look out!' I honked all over him, the nuts and carrots brigade covering him from his tie down to his knees.

'Mind the shoes!' cried Beefy, lifting his prize brogues out of the way.

'Stop please, driver!' screamed Kathy.

We disembarked and took Beefy, who now resembled a six-foot pizza, into High and Mighty, Knightsbridge to get fresh clothes.

My mind was in turmoil. I had to get back to Cheltenham for the evening performance of *The Dresser* and here I was miles away, puking over England's finest son.

We arrived at the Motor Show and, suffice to say, to this day I have a framed team photo of Ian, Angela Rippon, Roger Uttley and Glenn Hoddle lined up on the Saab stand, with me in the background, honking up a parabola of puke . . . 'Somewhere over the rainbow'.

11   BEEF 'N' LOON IN A STEW

The summer of '81 saw the homecoming of the Third Musketeer in my trilogy of madness, mayhem and music.

Gibb, Clapton and now Ian Terrence Botham, the hairy one born in Cheshire, hewn from the wild west of Yeovil and Taunton and catapulted to the dizzy level of icon throughout the world.

Not so in 1981. He had just given up the captaincy of England and needed a bit of cheering up. Unbeknown to either of us, our meeting was about to launch 1,000 lost nights. I had met the 'Beefyone' fleetingly on the MCC young professionals' staff. A word exchanged here, a fart there, a beer, a belch and the memorable sight of ITB being staked out naked and white-washed as part of his inauguration to the Lords Staff. It happened to me, too!

I had a couple of days off from the Everyman and decided to go to Lords for the Test Match and on to the Westmoreland Hotel after the game. Ian strolled into the bar with wife Kathy and his entire family, parents Les and Marie, in-laws Gerry and Jan, plus the full Monty.

I walked over to him and put my arm around him. 'Never mind, Beefy boy, you're still the best all-rounder we've got, by miles.'

Ian was meant to be taking his family to see *Evita*. They never got there. I stood on a table and told jokes for the entire evening, boosted by a mixture of every conceivable drink from a pint of Guinness to a Pina Colada that Beefy fed me in mid-performance, sustained by a selection of those hotel nibbles with little sticks in.

It was good to see him laugh. Beefy the Braveheart wore the three lions proudly on his chest and his heart on his sleeve.

'Listen, Loony,' (instantly christened) 'Do you want a new Saab?'

'What?' I said in the middle of my submarine joke.

'Well, the bloke over there is the Managing Director of Saab. Meet me at their Piccadilly showroom tomorrow at 10 a.m. and I'll sort you out. Eh, and thanks for the laughs, Loon!'

I walked out into the night and immediately puked up, pebble dashing the flyover with a selection of nuts, lettuce and carrots – funny, I couldn't remember eating the carrots.

After a night of Technicolor yawns and gyrating ceilings, I got on the tube to Piccadilly. My mouth tasted like a sewer, my head was spinning and my stomach turned like a washing machine emptying its load at every station. Commuters looked aghast as the rhythm of the ride provoked clenched teeth, doors open – 'Mornington Crescent' – empty the load, mind the gap, doors close, clenched teeth, doors open – 'Camden Town' – empty the load, mind the gap, sweating profusely on the Joooooberleee Line to Piccccccadilllyeeeee . . . on the chunderground!

I arrived at Saab's showroom at Piccadilly and enquired politely. 'Has Mr Botham arrived?' Typically, the salesman ignored my plea and went straight into his spiel.

'Just look at the Aero, sir, top of the range, reclining seats . . .'

'I don't feel very well,' I whispered meekly holding my mouth.

'The leather upholstery, the walnut dash . . . Cor, f*** me!'

Another huge volley of nuts and carrots spouted forth all over the shiny Saab revolving in the showroom window. Startled pedestrians passing by pointed their fingers at the window as the salesman went into 'clean up' mode, still telling me the merits of 'the turbo that cuts in at 75 mph'.

At 10.a.m. in walked Beefy, resplendent in England blazer and smoking a large cigar, with Kath on his arm. 'Morning, Loony, sleep well?' enquired the legend, visibly no worse for wear.

'Look, Beef, I think I'm going to pass out.'

'Bollocks to that, Loony!' chirped Mr Cocky Pants. 'Come on, I promised you a car. We're off to the Motor Show. Tell you what, we can stop off for some fresh prawns, go down a treat.' He was showing me his cruel side now.

We sat in the back of the taxi, me opposite Beefy, Kath to his side. 'Now, Loon, tell us that submarine joke again.'

'Beefy, I think . . . oooooh! aaaach look out!' I honked all over him, the nuts and carrots brigade covering him from his tie down to his knees.

'Mind the shoes!' cried Beefy, lifting his prize brogues out of the way.

'Stop please, driver!' screamed Kathy.

We disembarked and took Beefy, who now resembled a six-foot pizza, into High and Mighty, Knightsbridge to get fresh clothes.

My mind was in turmoil. I had to get back to Cheltenham for the evening performance of *The Dresser* and here I was miles away, puking over England's finest son.

We arrived at the Motor Show and, suffice to say, to this day I have a framed team photo of Ian, Angela Rippon, Roger Uttley and Glenn Hoddle lined up on the Saab stand, with me in the background, honking up a parabola of puke . . . 'Somewhere over the rainbow'.

I finally escaped from Beefy and dashed to Paddington to catch the 3.30 p.m. to Cheltenham Spa.

Shovelling back dry toast and black coffee in the BR buffet – there was a party in progress – one of their pork pies was 21! – I arrived at Cheltenham and made for the theatre. After a particularly fragile performance in *The Dresser*, including moves made gingerly to avoid close encounters with my fellow thesps, I returned to Mrs Hancock's, a spent soul, just after midnight.

In the morning, I was awoken by the blurred vision of Mrs H.

'Mr English, wake up! Wake up! There's a man downstairs to see you!'

I stumbled downstairs, bleary-eyed, head still thumping, to meet a smartly dressed man in a blue mohair suit.

'Mr English, good morning, sir, Mr Mike Powell, from Saab City, with our compliments.' He held up the keys. Behind him neatly parked was a brand new Saab Turbo. Mike Powell took me to the car and opened the door. Inside, lying on top of the dashboard was a note:

I promised you a car. Thanks Loon. Love Beefy xxxxx

Two years later I received a letter from Ian Williamson, Managing Director of Saab. It read:

Dear Dave English,

The sky is blue, rivers are deep
We like you, can we have our f. . .king car back?

Ian Williamson, Managing Director.

It had been the longest test drive in history!

Twenty years later I went back to the Westmoreland to meet Beefy. Twenty years down the road, he was slim-lined and controlled, talking about his diet, the best restaurants and sublime wines . . . of golf and the good life.

But, Beef, I'll always remember you taking on the best and smashing the ball to all parts. Locked in that fierce circle of combat that we mere mortals can never enter – good luck to you. LTG – Lost to golf.

Cheltenham over, it was time to let cricket take centre stage. I decided to join 'The Southern Drifters', to play in the West Indies, and so November found me in Barbados, in the wonderfully named Flamboyant Avenue to be exact. More importantly, in the arms of Silvio Osario, a beautiful, tanned Venezuelan girl, who, at this early hour of the morning, stirs gently, nestling her head into the nape of my neck.

Earlier we had tap-danced on the top shelf of the Bel Air Jazz Club and shimmied on the sands to the sound of the steel drums, before clasping each other tight and feeling that magic sneeze between our loins, and knowing the going was right and our time would come again – or not – but at least we had seized the moment. Perfect preparation for the Southern Drifters first game against Banks Brewery, 10 a.m. start the next morning.

You would think our team leader and inspiration Norman Graham, the Jolly Giant from Northumberland, standing 6 ft 7 in, in size 15 boots, would insist on an early night before taking on the world's finest cricketers in their own backyard. Not a bit of it! 'Big Norm' insisted that we consumed vast quantities of Cockspurs in every rum shack on the island, visited all the nightclubs and ramshackle rooms of disrepute, before watching the sun coming up, chewing on Jerk chicken.

'Howay the lads, yer drinkin' like a f***in' budgie. Yer got no f***in' chance against their quicks tomorrow,' encouraged the genial Geordie giant.

10.30 a.m. I opened the batting with Mickey Leishman, a lovely Geordie lad who had never been to London let alone Barbados. There he stood in his brand new kit, helmeted and gleaming, committed to the task, balls steaming.

I took guard and surveyed the backdrop. Typically Caribbean. No sightscreens, a couple of goats copulating in the distance. Vapour trails from 'Shake and Bake' airlines in the sky. Thank you Lord for cricket, always my salvation. The unique mateyness of the dressing room, especially on tour. The moment you walk over that boundary rope you are locked away from the real world, consumed by its all-encompassing nature, which deflects the demons of the day. Just you and your fellow players, a tremendous sense of camaraderie prevailing, we will sink or swim on the day as a team.

As Stamford Clarke Jr marked out his 40-yard run ('I don't go that far on my holidays,' I bawled), my mind drifted. Sadly Cindy and I had called it a day. I was distraught, but she was homesick for Florida. It's crazy but I can never find an English girl to love. I always end up with French waitresses, Polish countesses or Brazilian cleaners. My love life is a long line of holiday romances, I am attracted by their passion and free spirits. Hopeless material for 'settling down' in London; their minds may be with you but their hearts miss their homelands.

It's the same with Indian and West Indian girls. They are joyous, convivial, full of fun, full of love and very sexy. Sunshine makes us all feel happy and sexy. The West Indians are always happy and sexy because for them it's sunny every day. And they live for the moment.

Rum, Bum and Sun, for Stamford Clarke Jr, running in at me like a gazelle, pension plans now a redundant notion.

The first ball zipped past my nose at 90 mph.

'Smell the leather man,' suggested Stamford, pulling up from his run just in front of me, face etched with menace. Seconds later, I heard the ball thud into the wicket keeper's gloves, 30 yards behind me. I looked back and saw eight slips crouched next to the keeper. There was only one fielder in front of me, a token gesture at cover point, and he was only there to relay the ball back to Stamford.

At the end of the first over I had scored 16. Four airy drives which had whistled off the edge of my bat past third man for four. The West Indian lads seemed a little rattled and assailed me with the local patois.

I walked up the middle of the wicket to talk to Mickey. Batting is like a marriage; you are there to support your partner.

'Nice day for it, Mick. Are you alright?'

Mick's face was ashen beneath the grill of his helmet. 'F*** me, Dave! He's fooking lightning!'

Mickey shaped up to face his first ball. He went forward. It reared up off a good length and smashed against his forearm, breaking it instantly.

First time away from home. First ball. Busted arm. Tour over. A sickening finale for Mickey Leishman.

The terrible dichotomy of the West Indies; the most beautiful people off the pitch, killers on it. Mickey was carried off the field and dispatched to the Queen Elizabeth Hospital.

R.M.O. Cooke, small, bespectacled, compact, Lancastrian, Ex-Essex CCC, gift of the gab, great bloke, came out to join me.

'How is it, son?' asked Cookie through gritted teeth.

'F***ing quick,' I replied. 'Can't seem to lay a bat on it in front of the wicket.'

'Never mind, Dave, keep going and keep your eye on the ball from the moment it leaves his hand,' advised Cookie, the helmeted gladiator.

I had reached a very sketchy 36, mostly all off the edge. The opposition was now beside themselves, chattering madly with a combination of rage and mirth. Running around like worker ants, they clicked their fingers and gave me plenty of verbal. 'De Englishman. He crazy!'

It's times like these that you adopt a Noël Coward demeanour; 'Mad Dogs and Englishmen go out in the midday sun' – no wonder he ended up in Jamaica!

The more they ranted and raved the calmer I tried to appear. Sir Dickie would have approved of my performance, especially at the imminent prospect of my boots being filled with blood!

Somehow Cookie and I put on 70 odd. Stamford had been taken off burying his head in his hands and stamping his feet at the injustice of seeing yet another of his missiles disappearing off the edge of my bat for four. It was just before lunch when he returned for his second spell, the ground now at fever pitch. The ladies in the kitchens preparing the goat stew leaned out of the windows and clapped their hands. 'Mercy, man, mercy!'

The elder statesmen in the stands, smashing down their dominoes with long leathery fingers on to Formica tables, swigged their rum and roared with laughter.

Stamford walked up to me. 'Hey Englishman, I'm going to hit you on de head, be ready, man!'

I have never worn a helmet. I smiled, thanked Stamford for his warning and did a bit of gardening in the middle of the wicket.

This time he walked beyond his bowling mark for the extra ten yards. He then turned and started to run, accelerating, his arms pumping like pistons, the gold chains clinking around his neck. The fielders crouched, the ground was hushed. I tapped my bat on the crease and started to concentrate. I never really think about too much while the bowler runs up, I just focus on the point of delivery.

Rearing up like a black stallion, Stamford leapt off the ground and let the ball go with all his might.

It was short, I'd expected that. I shaped to hook, but was too early with my shot. Fatal. Like a cobra the ball rose and smirked at me before spitting its deadly five and a half ounce venom on to the side of my head.

Down came the crimson curtain over my eyes. My legs buckled and I fell to the ground in a pool of my own claret. Good night Irene! The next thing, I was conscious of Big Norm towering over me, holding up his hand.

'How many fingers can you see, Dave?' I couldn't even see his hand!

I was carried off, stunned, to polite applause from the crowd and a sense of relief from the fielders.

So I'm now sitting in the A&E Department of the Queen Elizabeth Hospital.

Mickey Leishman is just coming out with his arm in plaster. 'So, Dave, he pinned you as well!'

The blood was pouring from the side of my head just above the ear. Amazingly they made me fill in a long form and then sat me among my soul brethren.

There was mayhem in Outpatients, a mêlée of domestic spats and drink-related injuries. Admittedly cricketers were treated like royalty on the island, so I should get to be seen reasonably quickly. I sat down next to a man, curled up, fast asleep. I had talked animatedly about the game to my sleeping partner for at least fifteen minutes, when out came the doctor, who looked at me and said: 'Don't talk to Leroy, he's dead!'

Recoiling in shock, my condition became of secondary importance. Just then a fellow lurched in wearing a bright red shirt.

'Here, pal, sit down next to me, don't worry about Leroy. He's dead.'

'I've just been stabbed in the back,' the bloke muttered. 'I've just been stabbed. . .'

I looked and saw a six inch knife wound in his back. The white shirt he had put on that morning was now soaked with blood. Sandwiched between the dead man and the stabbed man. I now felt much better.

'Bring in the cricketer!' shouted the doctor.

The surgery was spartan. Bob Marley blared out of a transistor radio. A single fan whirred in the corner swatting the flies and the operating table was stained with old blood.

'What you do?' enquired the doctor, examining my wound.

'Well, doc, I was on 36 when Stamford crusted me.'

'Hey, man, Stamford, he plenty quick,' smiled the doc, shaving the hair off the side of my head. The doctor continued to talk enthusiastically about his love of cricket as he gave me an injection behind the ear and stitched me up.

Jumping off the table I thanked the doctor and enquired, 'What now? Antibiotics and take it easy?'

'No way, man,' laughed the doc. 'Plenty of rum and pokey pokey!'

As I left the surgery Leroy was still dead and the redman had passed out. Five of my team-mates had staggered in.

'What's the doc like, Dave?'

'Unusual to say the least,' I replied.

That evening, as the bright red sun set over the pavilion of Banks Brewery, Stamford and his pals entertained our walking wounded. Although that day he had put seven of us into hospital, typically all was forgotten as we drank and laughed into the early hours. Banks beer is a great anaesthetic for a sore head and addled brain. Lifetime friendships were forged on the field of play.

'Dave, you can come back here any time. You de happy hooker man!'

And return to splendour I certainly did, many times, to Barbados, Jamaica and Antigua. Sometimes with the Southern Drifters and on other occasions with Eric Clapton.

Life is a tour visiting new origins and experiencing different states of mind every day. The common thread in my life has been the love of cricket. In a sea of possibility, of turmoil, strife, life-or-death decisions, complexity, confusion, love and loss it has calmed me, a stabiliser, acting as my redeemer and salvation.

I have played in Zululand and South Africa, at Newlands beneath the Table Mountain. In Swaziland with the post-match decadence of the 'Why Not Disco' and its mud-hut pleasures, in Zimbabwe, the Middle East, Australia and New Zealand, places I may never have ventured to had cricket not been the key.

A catalyst to the lure of the tour was one Victor Lewis.

Vic is a marvellous man who raised millions for charity through his celebrity cricket side. As an ace wartime bandleader, Vic went on to be the number one showbiz agent for The Beatles, Bee Gees, Cilla Black, Elton John and many other leading stars. During the Bee Gees temporary break up in the early Seventies, Vic had represented Robin Gibb. Elated by his Number 1 hit record *Saved By The Bell*, Vic had sent Robin to New Zealand for a one-night show, a 72 hour round trip for a two-hour performance. To his horror, when he walked on to the stage, Robin discovered the Kiwis had expected the three Bee Gees. After twenty minutes into his act they vented their anger by hurling abuse, bottles and cans that led to Robbo doing a runner and climbing up a tree for safety.

Throughout his life, Vic's undying passion for cricket had led to some other quirky engagements. Elton tapped the ivories in the Bel Air Club, Barbados and Cilla Black performed at the Star of India Club, Delhi.

'Why am I here, Vic?' enquired a mystified Cilla. 'My records don't sell in India.'

Vic's roster of artists quickly discovered that their working itineraries were based around the world's Test Match grounds so that their agent could watch his beloved game.

After my Head & Shoulders commercial and earth-shattering performance in *A Bridge Too Far*, I got a call from Vic to join his showbiz team. On a good day, the Vic Lewis X1 could boast a star line-up including Gary Sobers, Rohan Kanhai, Everton Weekes, Clive Lloyd, Robert Powell, John Alderton, Peter Davison, Rudolf Walker, John Hurt and Godfrey Evans. When we struggled to get a side, we fielded three post-office engineers from Leytonstone who posed as the 'Original Drifters', a Hoover salesman who bore a passing resemblance to John Hurt, the cast of *Please Sir* and the Underwater Badminton Champion of Zambia.

The debacle of Sadiq Mohammed's 'Big Bumper Benefit Day' at Gloucester comes to mind. The 'Original Drifters' decided to drift close to the boundary edge and were well and truly twigged. An impromptu version of 'Under the Boardwalk' did not allay the suspicions of the crowd who turned ugly. This led to a hasty exit off the field by the Showbiz X1 and a lightning departure up the A40 in the team bus.

We idolised Vic. He was thoroughly loved by all the professional crick-eters and led us through many glorious years of showbiz cricket. I watched, learnt and marvelled at the man and in a way I suppose in later years I took over his reins with the formation of 'The Bunburys'.

On one occasion, playing at Worcester, Vic had taken us to Duncan Fearnley's factory prior to the game, which would raise funds for Vanburn Holders Benefit. Duncan, the master bat-maker, hand-made a new blade for each member of the team.

At the ground the crowd were buzzing with anticipation. Norman Gifford, Glenn Turner, Basil D'Oliveira, Roy Booth and the Worcester lads had made us very welcome. Vic won the toss and elected to bat. I opened the innings with John Cleese's agent David Wilkinson. I felt extremely proud taking guard on that magnificent ground and prepared to face the first ball from the West Indian speed merchant, Hartley Alleyne.

In ran Hartley who bowled a fearsome Yorker, which dispatched my middle stump over the vale of Evesham and beyond. Out first ball. You must be joking.

'Hartley, old chap, could you please move the screens a little to the right? I wasn't ready,' I enquired politely.

There was a hush among the fielders as 'the not ready plea' began to sink in. Hartley, after a pause, hands on hips and a look to the heavens, uttered some well-chosen expletives before collapsing in mirth like an unwound rubber doll. He continued to laugh all afternoon as I managed to manufacture 97 for 8 thanks to the generosity of the Worcester fielders. Later Hartley was nowhere to be found.

'Oh, he'll be in his favourite spot, Dave, the airing cupboard. He always goes in there to keep warm from our English summers!' When I opened the door, sure enough, there sat Hartley, still muttering 'Move de Screens, move de screens.'

Vic was a Captain Marvel. The former bandleader orchestrated his players with skill and cunning. However, as a player he struggled. After a shower he resembled a proprietor of a Turkish baths, standing just 5 ft 2 in with jet black hair, a tiny clipped moustache, fair-sized tummy and Savlon around his orchestras (orchestra and stalls, balls), tucked under a Holiday Inn towel. He had all the gear; Gary Sobers' bat, Clive Lloyd's pads, Ted Dexter's gloves, and all fifteen sizes too big for him, which meant that his journey to the wicket resembled more of a waddle than a walk.

And his fielding? Pretty stationary, a perfectly honed and tanned monument. In the case of an emergency, when the ball was skied in Vic's direction, the rule of the team was for the nearest fielder to rush to his aid. This master plan was executed to a fine art for years and years. Until we came a real cropper on a searingly hot day at Edgbaston.

It was Rohan Kanhai's benefit match. The ground was packed and the Sunday afternoon crowd, full of bonhomie and Ansell's ales, swayed in appreciation of the batting skills of Warwickshire's finest. Openers John Jameson and Alvin Kallicharan had put on 40 in double-quick time. Kalli pulled a short one out in the direction of midwicket.

Inexplicably, Vic was the only fielder out there in the distant wilderness, half-asleep, basking in the blazing sun. Kalli and Jamo had run three. Vic was woken from his blissful reverie by the sounds of 25,000 Brummies pissed out of their heads shouting, 'Hey short arse watch that f***in' ball!'

And watch it he did. Panicking, with his arms whirling around like windmills, he shrieked, 'Quick Quick!'

Like lifeboats to a drowning man, Malcolm Macdonald, Reg Scarlett and six other team members were converging at top speed to save Vic.

Kalli and Jamo had run five. The rescue failed to get there in time as the ball, now with icicles on it, fell from the sky straight on to Vic's head.

The Brummies' laughter subsided at the sight of Little Vic spark out. It wasn't a pretty sight, his eyes rotating like Maltesers. As the St John's ambulanceman administered the kiss of life, a massive bump straight out of the *Beano* started to swell on Vic's head. After an eternity he was helped to his feet. Legs visibly shaking, he put back his cap which was now perched precariously on top of the three inch bump.

Alvin Kallicharan was lying on his back hysterical; he physically could not continue to bat.

With his cap now perched on an Eiffel tower of a bump Vic came out with the immortal line, 'I don't know what they're all laughing about, I was nowhere near it!'

It was Jimmy Alldis who introduced me to Finchley CC. 'Jimbo' had been Beefy's Head Boy on the MCC staff. He's always reminded me of Michael Caine, same looks, same keen sense of humour and passion for a practical joke. A fine cricketer, our Jimbo, excellent groundsman, doesn't eat, loves a lager and remembers my gags better than I do.

One day, we were playing for the MCC at Tring. Rain had stopped play and I was in the bar telling my jokes to our great team manager Harry Sharp and the lads. At 4.30 p.m. the pitch was declared unfit to play on.

'Come back to Finchley,' said Jimbo, 'you'll love it!'

I went back to Jim's club; Finchley CC, East End Road N3, one of the finest cricket clubs in the land. It has always been a breeding ground for Middlesex CCC's elite players. The Finchley style of cricket had a reputation as cavalier; the emphasis was on the attacking player, never arrogant but purely naturally gifted. Bob Gale, Ian Bedford, Tim Sellwood, David Hays, Mike Milton and of course Jimbo had gone on to play for Middlesex CCC at the highest level. The pavilion may have lacked the sophistication of its players and staff, but it had a cosy ramshackle charm.

Fired up with Jimbo's lager, I merely repeated the act for Finchley's faithful plus Johnsey's loyal dog, Tammy, who had probably heard them all before.

So 18 wonderful years at Mill Hill Village came to an end, as my transfer to Finchley CC was rubber stamped by more lager. When I finally stumbled outside, the moon was out, the dogs were barking and the pavilion floor was awash in a sea of Stella Artois.

Why am I telling you this? Ah, first you need to know about Viv Richards. To meet the man for the first time is an unbelievable experience. I had met Viv when we took Vic Lewis X1 to play against Somerset CCC for Viv's benefit year. Try and imagine what it's like, to have watched the world's greatest batsman for many years and suddenly you're shaking his hand and playing on the same field. Viv will always be one of my all-time heroes.

It was a Sunday in June 1982, and Beefy and Viv had been staying at my home. I was down to play for Finchley against the might of the Acton and District Sorting Office Third X1, two o'clock start.

'Come on lads, come up to Finchley and have a quiet day, a couple of pints, stretch out and relax, no pressure.' This notion seemed to appeal to the immortal twin terrors from Somerset.

On arrival, the clubhouse was jumping. Murty, the scorer, was slumped over his pint, still mumbling unintelligibly about the night before, and the paraffin fire was still on its last legs. So was Tammy, stretched out sound asleep on the darts mat beneath a flickering TV.

Acton were arriving in dribs and drabs, relating horror stories of snarl ups on the North Circular Road. Their captain, Augustine, and a marvellous Barbadian, wide of girth with a broad smile, welcomed me.

'Hello, man, you gotta good side?' he enquired, clasping a large rum.

'Actually, we're two short, Gus,' I confessed.

'Shame, man, dat means dat me and de boys will give you a good tonking!' laughed Gus.

'Well, actually, I've just met those two blokes in the pub, one comes from your neck of the woods and the other is some long-haired Herbert from the West Country. They tell me they can play a bit. Do you mind if they join us?'

'No problem, man,' boomed Gus, already savouring the prospect of an easy victory.

'Alright, lads, you can come in now, Gus says you can play.' The next moment will stay in my memory forever.

As two of the greatest cricketers of all time stood silhouetted in the doorway, Gus looked up and seemed to enter into a trance. It was too much to comprehend. His jaw dropped. So did his glass, which instantly woke up Tammy, and kick started the TV into working properly for the first time in twenty years.

That day, Viv and Ian scored 326 in 40 overs. The last 10 overs they actually batted left-handed, peppering the rooftops of N3 with an endless barrage of sixes. Viv then kept wicket, while Beefy bowled first-class deliveries to the postmen, right arm, underarm . . . .

The boys from Acton batted with supreme West Indian verve and dexterity but just failed to nick a win. But who cared? Still with stars in their eyes, Augustine and his chums together with Viv, Ian and the Finchley lads retired to the bar to drink Captain Morgan rum and tell timeless tales till two in the morning.

That isolated Sunday in June, Ian and Viv had displayed great technique, with flurries of casual violence. It was thrilling to behold. Although only Johnsey and his dog had witnessed the carnival of carnage, I immediately knew that Finchley was a perfect venue for Celebrity Cricket.

BUNBURY TAILS

To me, Bunbury is the very epitome of what life is all about. It has passion, emotion, excitement and tension, skill, determination, friendship, successes and disappointments, toughness, kindness and a commitment to a challenge. Under 15 captures the moment between childhood and manhood; the players are faintly worldly-wise but with the refreshing outlook of children. They are adolescent, perhaps having experienced their first shave but still peeking over the Coca-Cola cans and dreaming of playing for England. They play with a free spirit, without the fear of failure and oblivious to the demons they'll have to tackle in later years.

I tell the lads, 'Work hard, and you'll get success. The only time success comes *before* work is in the dictionary.'

12   BUNBURY TAILS

In 1982, my cricket committee – Gary Zimmerman, Sid Livesey, Mike Milton, Paul Fowler, Tim Selwood, Tony Mastell, Graham Leggett, Richard and Lyn Johns and I – staged a big celebrity game and have done so every year since, raising valuable funds for cricketers' benefits, Childline and other worthwhile causes. Our benefit matches are less a 'Bridge Too Far' and more the 'Longest Day', and, as such, a test of great stamina – the quantity of alcohol consumed is colossal. The running order is:

- 9 a.m. gates open, coffee and bacon butties on arrival
- three-course lunch, silver service with wine (whole vineyards of Chateauneuf du Finchley are quaffed)
- a slap up strawberries-and-cream tea.

And the cricket? Each company has their own marquee of 20 people, six of whom will represent them on the field. The six-a-side tournament continues non-stop throughout the day. Considered to be one of the best days in this country combining business with pleasure, cricket will end at 9 p.m. followed by a charity auction and a mass exodus to the bar.

It gives the businessmen a chance to pit their skills against the world's finest.

Many classic encounters have taken place. A pal of mine, Bill, a hard-working printer batting in a Mickey Mouse T-shirt and brown boots, was facing England bowler Dave 'Syd' Lawrence off his full run up. Of course 'Syd' was playing to the crowd and was going to bowl it well wide to avoid the pickled printer.

As Dave let go a 90 mph bouncer, Bill the Print, full of wine, swayed into the path of the ball, which clipped his sunglasses, sending them into orbit.

'I don't f***in' need this,' gasped a shaken and stirred Bill. 'Alright, so I can't bat but I bet he couldn't f***in' print a brochure!'

I have seen Wasim Akram bowl boomerangs to the Marketing Manager of McVities Biscuits, full of bonhomie and Burgundy, at 8.25 in the evening.

One year I opened the batting with Mohammed Azharrudin. 'Now, Dave, I'm going to have a little look at the bowling, then we can play our shots, OK?'

'Anything you say,' I replied to the maestro from Madras.

Azha's 'little look' led to the first ball being deposited into the top bedroom window of 171 Briarfield Avenue, a carry of 100 yards. The second soared high over the pavilion, the third was rapiered off the back foot through the covers for four, the fourth landed in the shopping centre in Finchley Central quickly followed by the fifth, and the sixth ball clipped the top of a 143 bus poodling along East End Road some 120 yards away.

All this before Azha played some shots!

I understand how cricketers tick, and enjoy that. Like actors and musicians, they rely on a sense of timing and a sense of fun. They embody a gentle spirit with resolute determination; they cannot be hurried, and will tackle the opposition in their own way. Viv, with all his majesty and finesse, was a master blaster. Gordon Greenidge's awesome hitting was based on a rock solid defence; bowlers throughout the world called Gordon a thug with a cricket bat, but I had known him as a shy 15-year-old playing for England and Berkshire Schools. He was famous for his mighty power but if you examined his technique he played very straight with a full flow of the bat.

Cricket was played with a sense of theatre and Finchley would become our stage. In 1983 we presented the Phil Edmonds Benefit, 1984 Ian Botham, 1985 Graham Gooch and Wayne Daniel and 1986 John Emburey v Joel Garner X1.

First in the car park every year was Courtney Walsh. The West Indies and Gloucester legend would leave Bristol at the crack of dawn and I'd find him having a kip, stretched out in his sponsored car.

The West Indies players, especially under the leadership of Clive Lloyd, were the best in the world. 'Hubert' instilled pride and passion into their game, teaching them how to win, and win with a mental toughness which made them invincible. Cricket kept their islands together; the moment you wore that burgundy badge, you were batting and bowling for five million people. Take Courtney Walsh – that badge was stained on to his heart, he wore it with pride and valour.

The professionals love playing at Finchley because it is a distraction from the intense timetable of games during an English summer. We've had wet and windy days when the sponsor's tent took off and flew away, landing in a neighbour's garden. The sponsor and his twenty guests carried on eating and drinking, oblivious to the misplaced marquee.

It hosed down on Goochie and Wayne Daniel's day, not a ball was bowled. The beneficiaries copped the insurance money, drank themselves into a stupor and spent the day hurling cream cakes at each other. In Goochie's words it was 'the best benefit day they had never played in!'

The following morning, we found the Chairman of a PLC Company hanging off the railings by his braces. 'Big In The City', plastered, had tried to clamber over the fence but had slipped and spent the entire night upside down in a state of suspended animation. The animation appeared in the shape of a large black Dobermann from an adjourning garden who sat two inches from the city gent's ruddy face, all night long, gnashing his teeth.

Where did this impulse to play benefits and charity matches come from? Yes, I'd played in them under Vic Lewis, but this was something I'd been doing all my life. I have always had a deep love for mankind, and in truth the way some human beings are treated moves me to tears, but from this sadness springs great strength and a determination to help those less fortunate and disadvantaged, particularly in the very young.

I started charity fund-raising seriously in 1969, working closely with Princess Anne to support the Save the Children Fund, as my job on the London *Evening News* enabled me to use the power of the paper to stage events and secure revenue by the sale of advertising.

Fund-raising for different worthwhile causes continued by playing for the Vic Lewis X1 throughout the Seventies and early Eighties before the birth of the Bunburys. And once that started, well, then it was like unplugging a Dutch dyke, if you'll pardon the expression.

Valerie Howarth, Chief Executive of Childline, approached me to put on a big Bunbury game for her charity. It was a great success, once again Ian Wright playing a starring role. Childline is the free confidential 24-hour telephone help line for children and young people in danger and distress. It provides a confidential phone counselling service for any child with any problem, 24 hours a day, every day. Just imagine – Childline receives 10,000 calls from children each day, but because of lack of funds they can only answer 3,000 of those calls. They need money to train counsellors and put in more phone lines. I visited Childline's premises to understand the running of the charity, where I heard some of the harrowing calls.

'I used to believe I had a normal family. I thought it was normal not to be spoken to, just shouted at. I thought it was normal to be scared to go home, to be bashed around and worst of all, to be hated. I was afraid to tell you, but now I have, I'm glad I did. I needed to share it. Tell others to speak out as soon as they can.'

This, from a 14-year-old girl. 'He said he would kill mummy if I told. I don't want him to go to prison. I don't want to be put in a children's home. I just want him to stop hurting me.'

These are some of the things that children told Childline's counsellors – 'I had no one else to turn to.' The counsellors help children to talk through their shame, grief and pain. Help to rebuild their shattered self-esteem and encourage them to believe that they have the right to be safe.

The Bunburys continued to put on cricket matches for Childline, but I felt that as an individual I could do more; when Valerie asked me to be Chairman of the Childline Entertainment Committee, I was delighted to accept.

My first two calls were to Robert Stigwood and the Bee Gees, to ask them to donate the takings from the world premiere of the *Saturday Night Fever* stage show; typically, brilliantly, they agreed. Barry even threw in his red Aston Martin for a special auction.

The enthusiasm and commitment of my committee has ensured many starry occasions, Gala Balls and sporting events. I am indebted to each one of them for their overriding passion for the cause.

The Make-A-Wish Foundation is another cause close to my heart. Their objective is very simple – to turn the wishes of children aged between 3 and 18 suffering from life-threatening illnesses into reality. A wish granted is true magic for the child and provides happy memories for the family when, perhaps, time finally runs out.

Having come up with the basis for *Hawks*, I knew that this was a charity I wanted to be involved with. As a patron of Make-A-Wish, I visit hospitals to meet the children. To see the little ones with cancer of the blood or terminal tumours is heartbreaking, there seems to be no justice in life, and yet they welcome each day with a smile of undiluted joy.

Their wishes can be as diverse as flying over New York in a helicopter, swimming with dolphins, seeing where bananas grow and being able to pick them, meeting Postman Pat, taking a penalty against David Seaman or playing a bright red guitar. For these children having a wish come true can bring sunshine into lives that have been dominated by pain and trauma, and can give them the will to keep fighting to get better when everything else seems so bleak.

But of course it wouldn't happen if it weren't for the amazing cricketers, sportspeople and celebrities who happily give up their time to make these things happen. And the more we all did, the more possibilities we began to see in what we were all doing. Come 1986, and our Theatre of Dreams was now well established in cricketers' diaries.

What we needed was some after-match entertainment. I invited the incredible Stan Webb and his band Chicken Shack to come and do a turn. We'd set up his staging and equipment in a marquee and Stan and his boys could come and blast our ears off with his own highly charged brand of blues. Stanley Webb is a legend. He'd played the big blues halls throughout the world. One of his gimmicks was a fifty-yard lead to his guitar, which meant he could leap off the stage and go AWOL, still playing his instrument. I have actually been in the gents at the Royal Albert Hall when Stan has strolled in for a pee, playing his guitar, his music still coming out of the amps on the stage, forty yards away.

12 July 1986: John Emburey's X1 v Joel Garner's X1. Once again Ian and Viv had stayed at my house. We went to the ground at 10 a.m. for the 11.30 a.m. start. By 11 a.m. the ground was packed with a crowd of 5,000. But there was still no sign of Joel and the rest of his side.

'Beefy, where are they?' I asked, starting to panic.

'Loon, you've made a mistake, Joel thinks it's a 2.30 p.m. start,' grinned Beefy.

I was in deep trouble. I'd advertised the game to start at 11.30 a.m. How could I keep the crowd occupied till 2.30 p.m.? I tried all the delaying tactics. Roadworks on the A303; the coach has broken down. I even got Rory Bremner to do an hour's routine on the PA. The crowd was getting restless, there was slow handclapping and sporadic booing.

'Please, oh Lord, help me,' I pleaded.

Just then there was a buzz around the ground.

The door opened and Joel Garner walked in, followed by the entire West Indian side, all wearing their team blazers. Greenidge, Haynes, Holding, Marshall, Dujon, Lloyd & Co., the full world champion team.

Viv and Beefy had stitched me up. They had told Joel and the boys to stay behind the pavilion until I was at the end of my tether with worry. It was a mind-boggling game: 600 runs were scored on that day, the ball dislodging tiles a good 100 yards away from the wicket, and Holding, Marshall and Garner bowled like the wind.

Eric Clapton came along to the game at my invitation; I'd introduced EC to Beefy a year before. We had gone to the Pavilion at Lords but they wouldn't let him in because he wasn't wearing a tie. I phoned the dressing room, Beefy came down and gave Eric his England tie to get in.

The game finished and Stan Webb went into action.

'Tell you what, El, it would be great if you could get up and do a few numbers.'

'No way, Arfur, I haven't brought my guitar.'

Unbeknown to Eric I had asked Lee, his roadie, to bring along his favourite Fender, 'Blackie'.

'Come on, Eric, it would be a tremendous end to a great day,' I pleaded.

Back in the bar, the banter was thick and furious. Suddenly the unmistakable opening chords of 'Layla' could be heard clearly above the noisy din. There in the tent, Eric, Slowhand, the Maestro, was strutting his stuff with the Blues Band. I've never seen a bar empty so quickly.

For three hours, 500 enthralled people rocked to the music as Eric 'exchanged blows' with Stan Webb. There were punch-ups and the occasional flying bottle. 'Marvellous,' said Eric, as a horizontal reveller sped past his nose. 'Reminds me of the good old days in the Yardbirds!'

For the next three years, Eric's appearance after our Benefit Day became a high point on the musical calendar. Blues aficionados from Chicago to Chingford wondered why their bootleg tapes, *Eric Clapton Live at Finchley*, seemed to have been recorded in a beer tent. A bloody noisy one at that, too.

Then in the fourth year I got a phone call from Eric: 'Arfur, I've got to call it a day. I won't be coming to Finchley this year, so don't put my name on any posters. I'm off to Antigua just to get away from you and Finchley CC!'

But it was too late. While lying on the beach with his Italian girlfriend, tanning himself without a care in the world, he overheard the familiar voice of Brian Johnston on the BBC World Service:

'Don't forget to go to Finchley for their big benefit day followed by the usual performance by Eric Clapton . . . dear old Clappers!'

To the astonishment of the assembled bathers on the beach, the usually cool Eric was seen hurling a stranger's radio far out into the Caribbean, followed by a bloodcurdling cry: 'English, I'll kill him!'

February 1986, and down at the Hard Rock Café, I was sitting across the table from Eric Clapton, drinking wine and looking at the girls.

'You know, El, you should get more involved in cricket.'

Still clocking the birds, Eric was only half listening. I reiterated the idea.

'Tell you what, better than that, Arfur, you get it together and I'll turn up.'

So, after midnight in the Hard Rock Café, the EC X1 was born. The formula was simple; I would assemble our own celebrity cricket team and raise as much for charity as possible, rounding up as many famous people as I could to play cricket. They'd enjoy the Sunday afternoon delight, a welcome distraction from their normal lives, the punters would love to watch these famous fish out of water, and the proceeds would go to a good cause. Quite simply, everybody would win.

For the first game I took the team back to Ripley, scene of Eric's childhood. There we stood in a rain-sodden field behind the Ripley Court School, and Eric led us on to the pitch to do battle with the Ripley Nomads X1, in aid of the Royal Marsden and St Luke's Guildford Hospital for Cancer Research.

After that day the game for me took on a totally different complexion. Phil Collins kept wicket, Billy Wyman and Eric stood in the slips puffing on fags, both wearing plastic macs and sou'westers, looking the wrong way through the entire match. Dennis Waterman entertained all and sundry, David Essex charmed the ladies at long off, Gary Mason roared with laughter continuously at square leg, Spandau Ballet's Johnny Keeble chased every ball like a terrier, Norman Cowans opened the bowling with a new ball and 4,500 people stood soaked to the skin, mesmerised by the antics of EC's motley crew.

Chris Cowdrey, the Kent skipper, shook his head in disbelief.

'Down the road we're playing Yorkshire at Tunbridge Wells in front of 17 people and a dog, and yet here there are 4,500 punters standing in the rain watching a bunch of cowboys.'

Ah yes, but they were famous cowboys. The EC X1 would thread its magic anywhere, any time for a good cause and a good slap-up tea. Strangely the rain continued to lash down on our next ten games, but we continued to win. When the sun finally did appear we were totally lost in performance. Ringo Starr and Barbara Bach attended all our games, signing autographs and spreading bonhomie among the Tombolas, bouncy castles and hot dog stands. Our EC X1 matches were indeed fun-filled days for all the family.

'Walter, can you play at Tunbridge Wells?'

'Dave, I'd love to . . . if I can, I will.'

Walter Swinburn won the French Derby before helicoptering back to play in Chris Cowdrey's benefit game on the same day. The champion jockey with the face of an angel jumped out of his helicopter and joined Peter Scudamore out in the deep. Michael Holding and Dennis Lillee opened the bowling for us that day. I felt very honoured. What other captain could tell Whispering Death to 'have a blow' and DK 'to bowl up hill into the wind'?

When the EC X1 tour bus swung into the gates of Northamptonshire CCC to take on Allan Lamb's X1 for his benefit, Australia had just beaten the county side after a hard three days.

'Whato, AB,' I called, as the Aussie charabanc was just leaving.

'Blimey it's English,' shouted Allan Border. All the Aussies, Merv Hughes, Dean Jones, Steve Waugh, the whole side, piled out to meet Eric, David Essex and the boys.

'Fancy staying to watch, AB, and have a few beers?' I enquired.

'Tell you what, better than that we'll join in!' laughed the Aussie captain.

What a game. Dan Essex, aged 11, bowled with Dennis Lillee and Steve Waugh smashed it to all parts. Then there was Derby; after the showers inci-dent (buy me a drink some time and I'll tell you), suddenly having to face Botham and Holding. Quickly grabbing my gloves and bat, I made my way to the middle past the clowning Derek Randall . . . then . . . splosh. Beefy had filled my gloves with cream cakes.

He then proceeded to try and decapitate me with a barrage of bouncers after I'd survived the 'Sand Shoe Crusher' first ball (a 90 mph Yorker at my toes). 'I know what you've been up to Loon with those dancing girls in the showers.'

I pointed out to Beefy that the bumper barrage wasn't a good idea as I had to present 'An Evening with Ian Botham' in 78 towns some two weeks later. A task which would have been made particularly difficult without my teeth.

Two other great brigands in our line up were Gentleman Jack Russell and his trusty agent, Field Marshall Jimmy Ruston. Both being artists, Eric and Jack shared the same spiritual groove. I'd love to see Jack painting to Eric's music and one day I'm convinced they'll produce a canvas of greatest hits under the auspices of Lord Jimmy.

I suppose it was at Beaconsfield that Eric's love of the game took a sudden dive. 'Whatever you do,' said Roger Forrester, our wicket keeper and Eric's manager, 'look after his fingers, he's got a tour of Japan in September, and if he breaks his hands he won't be able to play.' The manager's mind ticked over nervously as EC stood in the gully. It was an idyllic summer's day, the sun beat down and the cows in the neighbouring field chewed lazily on the cud. Gary Mason ran up to bowl, their opener smashed it, Eric took off on a valiant dive and – crunch – his middle finger was shattered.

Well, there are now lawyers and underwriters leaping out of the bushes screaming 'Litigation!' There was deep concern from his team-mates as EC trooped off the field, smoking his fag and clutching the dodgy digit. Then, just as he was halfway between the pitch and the pavilion, a huge bumblebee suddenly stung him on his other hand. Roger and the legal eagles were now apoplectic as lines from Beaconsfield to Tokyo were jammed with the news of the Guitar God's demise.

'Good luck, lads!' cried EC as he was whisked off to Amersham Hospital.

The game resumed. The very next ball was a bouncer, which missed the batsman and struck Roger on his head, sending the ball spiralling towards the boundary.

'Catch it!' cried Rory Bremner, the eternal optimist.

Roger was carried off and spent the rest of the game heavily concussed, flat out in the darkness of the dressing room. EC returned, having met a couple of tasty radiographers, signed a few autographs with his dodgy hand, enjoyed a couple of beers before being discharged, both hands heavily bandaged.

El, our spiritual leader, hung up his boots. Miraculously, he toured Japan, saving the promoter's blushes and millions of dollars in lost revenue. From that day on the team needed a new name – one I was about to provide them with, thanks to the pleasures of a warm evening in a field at Mill Hill Village.

During the summer of 1986, I was sitting on a bench down at Mill Hill Village Cricket Club with my pal Jan Brychta.

I had met Jan while presenting *You And Me* for BBC Children's Television. I fronted the programme, telling stories about 'Duncan the Dragon' and 'Sammy the Seal', while, as I spoke, Jan drew the characters. An extremely famous Czech artist, Jan was the BBC's star animator, creating magical images for *Jackanory* and *Play School*. He had grown up in Prague with the Arts and Film set along with directors Milos Forman and Ivan Passer, and in 1968, when the Russian tanks had rumbled into Prague, he had escaped with his family, wife Lida and children Alex and Edita, to the safety of England's shores. A strong man with a gentle spirit, Jan had left all his possessions back in Prague, but talent prevails and soon he was weaving his wizardry in England. He had an enchanting style full of whimsy and cosy charm. To be in his presence was fascinating and without question I rate him as one of the most talented artists in the world.

As we surveyed the empty cricket field a couple of rabbits scurried across the pitch.

'Ah! That would be Ian Buntham about to bowl to his pal Viv Radish from Bunny Bados.'

As my mind went into dreamland, Jan was busy sketching.

The Bunnies would live in Bunbury where they learned to play cricket. Buntham would captain the team, Vice Captain Golden Hare Gower, Rodney Munch and Dennis Lettuce from Brisbun and Melbun. They would play at Hares' Rock against the Dogs from the Great Terrier Reef, wicket keeper Bob Tailer and little Rajbun from Bungalore, an enthusiastic All Bounder.

I kept 'Bunnying', Jan kept drawing. I could see the first story quite clearly. It would be night-time in Bunbury. The Bunnies had no 'Hop-position', so they called Geoff Boycatt who lived in Whiskertown and told him to bring along a team of cats. They arrived, Pussycat Willis, Imran Kitten, Mike Catting, all under the managership of Chairman Miaow.

The only problem was the darkness. The black clouds scudded across the moon. What could they do? High above in a tree, a wise old owl put his head to one side and laughed 'Owlzat, Cats' eyes to the rescue! Dozens of cats' eyes beamed down from the trees, illuminating the ground.'

By the end of the afternoon we had created 'Bunbury Tails'. Now armed with Jan's dummy, I did the rounds of publishers. Quite a few said 'No'; very complimentary but still the answer was 'No', until we met David Roberts at Weidenfeld and Nicolson who loved the stories.

He signed us up for five books. Of course Ian Botham, Viv Richards and all my cricketing pals helped us promote the stories. In all I wrote 12 books, thus establishing the name of Bunbury to launch my celebrity and school teams. Bunbury, not from *The Importance of Being Earnest*, or Bunbury, a town south of Perth; but Bunbury, the home of the world's most famous cricketing Bunnies.

I am Lord Bunbury, responsible for team selection: on the phone around the clock, catching the lads as they were getting into or out of bed; the art is to know where and when each Bunbury is at any given time of day. Sending the maps to each player with a personal message, wheeling and dealing, securing sponsorships, supplying the kit, planning the fixtures, getting the scorers, Peter Danks and Toby Davidson, two photographers, David Betteridge and Keith Curtis, umpire 'to the stars' Johnny Hurst and commentator Huw Williams, to each game.

All this is achieved by one phone out, one phone in; a knackered fax machine; my rickety old chair, and a desk the size of a postage stamp; in the corner, my trusty Russell & Hobbs kettle, along with an endless supply of PG Tips; and, most important of all, my leather-bound book, containing the addresses of 1,000 superstars throughout the world. From the 30 years of contacts between its covers, I would ensure that over one hundred stars would represent the Bunburys throughout the summer, in order to raise the maximum funds for 20 charities each year.

*   *   *

The danger of injury has always loomed over our Bunbury days.

Both Bill Wyman and Ronnie Wood were rapped on the knuckles while batting, two weeks before a Rolling Stones tour. Rugby players seem to hurl themselves around even with injuries; Dallaglio, Catt, Carling, Lynagh and others have all 'Bunburyed' while carrying injuries. Matt Dawson, England's scrum half, took an amazing catch for us against Cadbury's at Bournville. Fielding at cover, he took off, did a backward somersault before jackknifing on to his already dislocated shoulder.

'No problem, Skips,' smiled the heroic Daws, still clutching the ball.

Heavyweight boxing champion, Big Audley Harrison, used to sneak away from the Olympic camp at Crystal Palace to play for the Bunburys. Two weeks before flying to Sydney he bowled, batted and leapt about the field without any concern for his own safety. Big Aud went on to be our first Golden Olympic Champion.

Alec 'Steve McQueen' Stewart scored a century on his Bunbury debut at Abinger. I was batting at the other end; I say batting, I might as well have sat in an armchair at the non-strikers' end to watch Stewie smack it to all parts of Surrey.

Darren Gough turned up at Chobham to enjoy a rare day off relaxing with the family.

'Do you fancy a bit of a bat?' I asked the Dazzler.

'Don't mind if I do, Big'un,' replied the irrepressible Yorkie.

Fifty in fifteen minutes was the result and when we took the field, I lobbed him the new ball. In ran Goughie off four paces, to bowl flat out to the poor Sri Lankan opening batsman.

The next day I woke up to an international outcry; Sky TV were parked outside my house demanding to know why Goughie had played for the Bunburys and not Yorkshire. Yorks CCC, upset by the media coverage, issued a statement to confirm he had been given the time off from playing in a one-dayer at Scarborough. An innocent day off Bunburying in the country had turned into a national drama – needless to say I issued both Stewart and Gough with Bunbury Central contracts to avoid any future aggro!

The soccer players are a protected breed. High profile, massive salaries and huge insurance prevent the boys from playing cricket as much as they'd like. The days of playing cricket professionally in the summer and football in the winter have long gone, so we won't see the likes of Arthur Milton (Gloucs CCC and Arsenal FC), or Denis Compton (Middx CCC and Arsenal FC), Jim Standen (Worcs CCC and West Ham FC), Mike England (Cheshire CCC and Spurs FC), Steve Ogrizovic (Staffs CCC and Coventry City FC), Ted Hemsley (Worcs CCC and Sheffield United FC), Phil Neale (Worcs CCC and Lincoln City FC), or Jimmy Cumbes (Worcs CCC and Aston Villa FC).

Nowadays, Gary Lineker, Chris Sutton, Phil and Gary Neville, Graham Thorpe and Andy Goram could all have played both sports at the highest level. They have all excelled for the Bunburys along with Dean Saunders, Ian Wright, Mark Bright, Ian Baraclough, Richard Langley, Paul Murray, Danny Maddix, Darren Ward, Glenn Hoddle, Alan Ball, Alan Mullery, Phil Neal, Peter Reid, Gary Pallister, Clayton Blackmore, Brian Robson, Graham Kelly, Graham Taylor and many others.

However, the three most exceptional footballing Bunburys are Gary Lineker, Ian Wright and Matt Le Tissier.

'Gary, can you play for the Buns v Gunner Gould's X1 at Finchley?' I asked.

'I will,' said Gary, 'but we'll have to play it very low key 'cos we're playing against West Ham United this evening. If Terry Venables finds out he'll go ballistic!' That day Gary scored 103 not out, packed his bag and went to Upton Park, where he netted a hat trick for Spurs the same evening.

Then there was the magical day by the seaside against Sussex CCC at Hove. Gary Lineker had trained all morning with Spurs in London before catching the two o'clock train from Waterloo with his lovely Michelle, eight months pregnant with George. He arrived at the ground at 4 p.m. padded up, scored 59 batting with Bunbury debutante Brian Lara, picked up the 'Man of the Match' award before returning to London with sore limbs and an arm aching from signing 10,000 autographs.

'Wrighty', the emotionally charged Pied Piper of Arsenal FC and England, was another true soccer hero.

'Wrighty, it's Dave. I'm up here at Oxford and there are 5,000 kids wearing Ian Wright replica shirts waiting for you.'

'Dave, I can't move. I'm here at Highbury lying on the physio's bench being treated for a dodgy leg.'

I had called the King Gunner on his mobile phone.

'F*** me, Ian, you've got to come – take the A40 on to the M40 . . .' I bleated out the directions and the line went dead.

An hour later my mobile rang. 'David English speaking.'

'Ian Wright speaking, I've just come off the Cowley Roundabout, where are you?'

Wrighty had told Arsenal physio Gary Lewin he was nipping (hobbling) up to the canteen for a quick cuppa. He in fact had squeezed himself painfully into his Aston Martin and made all haste from Highbury to Oxford. Wrighty arrived and was mobbed by his adoring fans. He looked like a pint of Guinness with his peroxide hair.

'What number, Dave?' smiled Wrighty with his gold tooth flashing.

'You go in three. Johnny Keeble will run for you.'

That afternoon Wrighty scored 86 one legged, signed all the boys' shirts, kissed all the girls, cuddled the mums and laughed with the dads, before disappearing into the hubbub of the M40 back to the Smoke.

Wrighty has been a true champion over the years. He's helped us raise thousands for charity, arriving in helicopters with his loving family. The thing about Wrighty is he is totally whole-hearted; if he likes you he loves you.

Recently I was conducting a radio interview when Wright and Bright burst into the studio live on air shouting, 'Come on you Bunburys!'

Wrighty leapt on me, gave me a big kiss, and ran out of the studio, much to the amazement of the producer and 1.5 million astonished listeners.

Matt Le Tissier, a little more understated than Wrighty, arrived at Paulton's Park to play for us against Hampshire CCC.

'What do you do, Matty?' I asked.

'Anything you like, Skip,' said Matt quietly. Matthew Le Tissier batted at number three scoring 79, beautifully playing shots all around the wicket.

After tea I said, 'Who wants to keep wicket?'

Nobody was forthcoming.

'I'll give it a go,' said Matt.

The quiet genial genius from Southampton proceeded to leap about like a dervish, keeping wicket impeccably and urging the Bunburys to field out of their skins. We beat the county side handsomely after Robin Smith had threatened with a blistering 85. Matt took three catches and a leg side stumping reminiscent of Jack Russell in his pomp.

After the game, an unassuming 'Le Tiss' signed autographs and shook hands with everybody before returning to The Dell for an evening's training session. Gone but never forgotten. Matt Le Tissier, pure class, totally natural.

And then there was 'Wemberlee!'.... Bunburee! Wemberlee! Yes, the impossible had happened. The Bunburys had reached Wembley, the *only* team to have played cricket in the world's greatest stadium. As the rain slanted down, the name of Bunbury reverberated between the Twin Towers. Joe 'The Hat' Cuby weaved his magic with his towering spinners giving the 'air a bit of ball', Mark Nicholas stood at cover and, sweater pulled over his head, resembled a polar bear. Johnny Morris peppered the stands with well-timed pulls and drives, so did Chris Broad and Roland Butcher before Joel Garner leapt into action, ripping the ball off the matting before retiring to the boundary to sign autographs in the pouring rain. Rory Bremner ran around enthusiastically commentating in a thousand voices, Errol Brown bowled with style, Dickie Bird looked on incredulously and I, as the captain of this extraordinary outfit, watched in complete wonder.

We were raising funds for the Leonard Cheshire Homes and as we climbed the red-carpeted stairs to the Royal Box to receive the award from Group Captain Cheshire, I surveyed the ground where so many famous FA Cup Finals had taken place. And now, to think that I, a cricketer, would lead such a team on to this hallowed turf!

*   *   *

The Bunburys bring together all factions of sport. We have played from schoolyards to the Test arena, in front of group captains and lords. Lord Sam Vestey in Gloucester, Earl 'Georgie' Porchester, Lord de Lyle at Penshurst Place, Earl de la Warr in Wythyham, home of A.A. Milne and Christopher Robin. As William de La Warr played an aristocratic cover drive, Gary Mason was heard to say, 'There's two there, M'Lud!' Castle Ashby, where Dennis Waterman and I told gags all night to the Duke of Northampton, me giving them the cuff links gag, the Duke and his Minder falling about underneath the Castle's Coat of Arms.

We've played in front of queens and kings. Every year we perform against the Royal Household at Windsor Castle. Her Majesty poodles down to watch with her Corgis, and the Queen Mum used to drive up and down the Long Walk beneath the trees to get a glimpse of the flannelled fools. And the kings? Well King Viv Richards has captained the side with our own King, Collis, batting at four. Sovereign of the Mountgay Rum, believe me, when Collis walks into the bar, the top shelf rattles!

Prince Hakeem of Brunei is a keen Bunbury supporter. So too is the Duke of Marlborough. After a meeting with the great duke, he agreed that we could stage a Bunburys v Bill Wyman's X1 at Blenheim Palace. Proceeds would be split between the Oxford Association for Young People and the Royal Marsden Cancer Appeal.

'Let's go big on this, sire,' I said, sitting with the Duke in the Palace's main hall.

'David, I'll leave it to you,' was the noble reply.

I quickly called my pal 'Radio One' Richard Grieves.

'Grievsy, I'm here at Blenheim Palace, get the Road Show down here in a month's time. Two great charities, we'll stick you in the main meadow.'

Whether you are running a record company or a cricket team you have to put on a show, it's all about contacts! 'Radio One Rich' went into action, resulting in the biggest Bunbury crowd ever. 100,000 revellers watched Bill and I do battle in front of the Palace before leaping about to Chris Evans & co. on the Radio One Road Show in the back meadow.

Before the game Bill and I were bursting for a pee. So we relieved ourselves up against a nearby tree.

Later that afternoon, the Duke commented, 'I saw you two watering my oak.' An amazing observation as that tree was a good 500 yards from the Palace bedroom!

Once again, the rain started to lash down, making the meadow musical and very muddy. But nobody cared, they were happy bopping to Bill and the Bunburys at Blenheim! The cricketers fled to the marquee where Bill and Ronnie Wood 'reformed' the Rolling Stones, with Phil Cool doing an incredible Mick.

Group captains, lords, earls, dukes, queens, kings and prime ministers!

For twelve years I've taken the Bunburys to Alconbury to play against Norma Major's X1 for Mencap, hosted by John and Norma Major. It remains a magical day on our Bunbury calendar. Timeless trips up the A1, past the perennial roadworks, seeing the welcome sight of the church spire peeking over the hill, and then the sign to the Alconburys. The drive through the village (never a soul in sight) and the sound of the Tannoy crackling in the distance 'one, two . . . one . . . two . . . Welcome to Mrs Major's cricket match here at Alconbury CC.'

Then to be met by Dave Pilling and his mighty team who usher you into the pavilion overflowing with star names. Gary Lineker, Imran Khan, Ian Wright, Rob Duncan, Mark Ramprakash, Alvin Kallicharan, Fraser Hines, Medha Laud, Ned Larkins, David Smith, Phil Robinson, Rory Bremner, Isabelle Duncan, John Altman, Jamie Hart, Charlie Dagnall, Joe Cuby, Naynesh Desai, John Rice, Jamie Theakston, Rudolf Walker, David Essex, Graham Cole, Dave Beasant, Josh Gifford, Jimmy Greaves, Allan Lamb, Lloyd Honeygan, Trevor Brooking, Leslie Grantham, Dave 'Syd' Lawrence, umpire Dickie Bird and my opposition skipper, the one and only Brian Close, not the Reverend by the same name across the fields, but the 69 years young, former inspirational Captain of England.

Mr and Mrs Major arrive to enhance the day with their special warmth and friendliness. The team photograph is taken and Emma Noble bowls the first ball and the magic of Alconbury unfurls.

I've seen legendary South African batsman Barry Richards fly in especially from Queensland to play. On arrival he had no gear, just a well-worn pair of golf shoes. With hastily borrowed equipment and a bat so old, cobwebs still adorned the handle, 'Bazzer' proceeded to score a peerless 52. I've witnessed the magician Mohammed Azharuddin hit Imran Khan off the back foot over the 'Mr Whippy' ice cream van at the far end, a carry of 95 yards. Azha remains one of my favourite Bunburys, a soul mate and deeply spiritual man.

I've stood next to Bill Wyman in the gully when he caught Brian Close left-handed off the bowling of Ian Wright, while clutching his favourite Benson & Hedges in his right hand.

One lad, an Aussie, Ryan Campbell, scored 90 before retiring hurt. Not himself but our hands. He had hit the ball so hard there was absolutely no chance of the Bunburys getting him out, even if we did have 23 fielders.

In 1999 Wasim Akram opened the bowling for us. Standing at mid off I gave Wasim his orders.

'Go on, give him your inswinger or give him the outswinger.'

'Certainly,' replied the Wizard. 'Watch this, Captain.'

Sure enough, Wasim bowling from the bouncy castle end swung the ball left and right making the poor batsman jump like a firecracker.

'Thanks, Waz, have a blow.'

W. Akram – 9 overs, 5 maidens, 0 for 4.

On I came to bowl to the same batsman who promptly hit my first three balls over the church.

'What can I do, Waz?' I enquired in desperation.

'Just keep your chin up, Captain,' smiled the great man.

Same game, same batsman, different bowler, different class.

I have never taken the field with 11 men. There was the Bunbury 23 at Alconbury and the Bunbury 17 at Finedon where Viv found it unnerving to bowl to 12 slips. 'Brother "D", what's going on? You've got all those slips drinking red wine, you've got Samantha Fox bowling, her bouncers swinging both ways, this isn't cricket, man!'

'It's Bunbury cricket, Viv,' I pointed out.

'Ya, man, but play with pride, play properly, where's the respect?'

We all froze . . . until Viv collapsed into fits of giggles.

Since that day, whenever Viv captains the team, there are only 11 on the field and we play properly as a mark of respect to the King. The magnificent Ashwells game, in aid of the Sargent Cancer Care for Children charity, at Chelmsford, was one such occasion.

Our record, however, was the Bunbury 27. Bunbury CC v Imperial War Museum X1, to commemorate the 50th anniversary of VE Day, played at the Fosters Oval.

A chance visit to the Imperial War Museum, along with my partner-in-dreams Barry Gibb, led to a meeting with Dr Christopher Dowling, the director of the museum. As we chatted, Christopher told us he was keen to stage a cricket match to celebrate the 50th Anniversary of the end of the Second World War.

There were five Victory Matches hastily arranged between England and Australia in 1945 to celebrate VE Day. German prisoners of war actually helped to repair the bomb-damaged grounds. Three games were played at Lords, one at Sheffield and one at Old Trafford. Large crowds turned out to greet the resumption of cricket after the war years, and the matches were played in a carnival atmosphere. Many of those taking part were still in the services and some had recently been engaged in front line duties; two members of the Australian team had been prisoners-of-war in Germany.

One of the Aussies, the dashing young Flying Officer Keith Miller, had been the player of the series. He would return from bombing raids on Germany to strap on his pads and walk out to bat for Australia, all on the same day.

It was a great idea to stage such a match – once again I was driven. I felt a huge feeling of goodwill swell up inside; we could raise funds for the British Legion, helping needy ex-service people, their families and dependants financially, practically and emotionally.

We could fly Keith Miller over to be reunited with his old pal and adversary Denis Compton. They would be our guests of honour. We'd invite the remaining living players from that series, Alf Gover and Dougie Wright from England and Bob Cristofani from Australia.

Dr Chris and I went to see Paul Sheldon, Chief Executive of Surrey CCC, to present the idea. Paul was instantly supportive, especially as such a game would tie in with Surrey CCC's 150th Anniversary. By a miracle, the Oval was available on the day we needed it, 6 May 1995.

In order to maximise coverage, awareness and fund-raising, we needed to televise such a historical match. I went to see Vic Wakeling, Head of Sky Sports, and typically he immediately agreed to cover the whole game.

6 May 1995, 50 years to the day since war ended, the Bunbury 27 took to the field at the Oval in front of an emotional crowd, rows and rows of war veterans, a galaxy of stars and media people, and, high up in the Committee Room, Keith Miller and Denis Compton, reunited over an outstanding bottle of red wine.

The dressing room was buzzing. My two strike bowlers, Joanna Lumley and Samantha Fox, changed with the lads. Super Sam Fox plonked her whites down in between Clive Mantle and Tony Meo.

''Ere, Tone, give us a hand with these pads.'

Sammy is a regular Bunbury, a master of line length and fine leg. She is sexy, fleet of foot, a great sport and extremely popular with the crowds.

'I think I'll change round by the basins,' purred Purdey, pulling on her immaculate flannels, held up by a silken sash.

I don't know who was the more graceful, David Gower, my opposing captain, or Joanna Lumley, who bowled the first ball with great panache.

We were all wired up for sound, live on Sky TV. We had 17 blokes in the slips chatting away as Dave 'Syd' Lawrence ran into bowl to Graeme Fowler. It was a fearsome bouncer, which nearly decapitated 'Foxy'.

'F***in' 'ell, Syd, mind how you go!' cried Foxy as the Sky switchboard was jammed with complaints. Needless to say the 17 slips, who were engaged in the most lurid of conversations now being beamed into millions of households up and down the country, didn't bother changing positions at the end of the over, resulting in 17 mid-ons!

'There's f***ing 27 on the field,' shrieked Sky executive producer John Gayleard into my ear-piece, 'we can't get all their f***ing names on to the screen!'

Bill Wyman, who is the only bowler I know who has a pile of fag ash instead of sawdust to mark his run-up, never waits till the end of the over to come on and bowl. Whenever the mood takes him, he comes up to me, says 'now' and proceeds to bowl.

In walked Gary Lineker, quite miraculously. I had arranged for a fast car to fetch him from the BBC as soon as he had finished his lunchtime *Football Focus*. Instead of going upstairs to watch *Match of the Day* with Trevor Brooking and the boys, Gary had nipped out to the waiting Saab limo and travelled flat out to the Oval, changing into his whites on the way.

If Des Lynam had turned over to Sky he would have seen his star presenter taking guard to wiley Bill Wyman at the Oval.

In ran Bill smoking his beloved Benson & Hedges and delivered one of his looping leg breaks. 'Crack!' Lineker was caught in the deep by Liam Botham. Next in was Trevor McDonald. Whoosh! went *News at Ten* Trev, thick edge, caught behind by Johnny Keeble. Two in two balls, Bill was on the verge of a hat trick. The crowd was on the edge of their seats. Out came Sky's own Charles Colvile, mumbling about 'this Bunbury bunch of cowboys, I'll show 'em' and swishing his bat.

Charlie took guard. Bill pulled on his fag and ran in. Up went the ball into the sun. Charlie blinked and smacked it . . . straight to Rory Bremner fielding at cover, hitting him full on the chest. The crowds were on their feet as Rory, on his knees, caught the ball one inch from the ground.

His 26 team-mates mobbed Billy.

'I think I'll call it a day now, Dave,' smiled Bill.

As we walked off the ground, the pile of fag ash blew away towards the Vauxhall End and with it the memory of an EC/Bunbury founder member. Bill Wyman never played again.

To this day, Bill Wyman remains the only bowler to have performed a tele-vised hat-trick in the history of the Oval.

People always ask me why I over-recruit my teams. Well, I suffer from the endless nightmare that one day the lads will not turn up. This paranoia was firmly installed after the 'Derby 4' and 'Hampshire 7' games. At Derby, only Gary Mason, Peter Scudamore, Fraser Hines and myself turned up to take on their First Team. The Derby lads were magnificent and supplemented the Bunburys with some of their Second X1 squad and Committee members. The nightmare of the Hampshire 7 was played on Fathers' Day and the day of the World Cup final. When we arrived at Paulton's Park, Robin Smith had his entire First X1 on duty. All I had was Audley Harrison, Peter Bowler, Joe Cuby and a couple of others.

'Sorry, Judge,' I apologised to Robin. 'Leslie Grantham's got a sore throat, Steve Tompkinson is filming, Fathers' Day etc.'

'Never mind, Loon,' said the Judge, 'we'll have a good day.'

Robin Smith would always be at the top of my All Time Great Blokes X1, closely followed by Sir Tim Rice. I quickly recruited a couple of youngsters from the crowd, plus David Betteridge, our scorer. I managed to swipe John Rice from the Hampshire ranks, an inspired transfer deal which has seen

Ricey stay with us ever since. It was a great game. Peter Bowler scored 147 not out, Audley and I bowled 25 overs between us, and the Hampshire lads were magnificent.

Every year we play 20 Bunbury games starring over 100 celebrities. An average Bunbury squad comprises 15 players. But I still live with the fear of not being able to turn out a good team, which leaves me sometimes exhausted and totally insecure. That is why I make all the team selection phone calls, maps etc. myself, to make sure I never turn up one day with 'The Bunbury One'!

The Bunbury One? How about the Bunbury 48? It is a desperate shame that tragedies turn out to be the catalysts for the world's biggest charity events. I admired Bob Geldof's inaugural concept of staging the biggest ever musical event in aid of a good cause, Live Aid, linking the world together through music and raising millions for Ethiopia in the process. When our friend Malcolm Marshall, the great West Indian fast bowler, passed away, I decided to stage the biggest ever charity game in his memory to raise funds for his little boy, Mali.

I say 'biggest', not in terms of people watching, but in the coming together of so many of the world's greatest cricketers ever to play in one game: 48 Test cricketers including 32 Test captains took part in the PCA Bunbury X1 v Malcolm Marshall X1 at the Honorary Artillery Club, London on Thursday, 27 June 2000. The first person I called was Robin Smith in South Africa. I spoke to the Judge, who was socialising with Top Bun, Rod Bransgrove, in a bar in downtown Cape Town.

'No problem, Loon, I'll be there. I'd be proud to captain the Bunbury X1.'

My next call was to Viv Richards in Antigua.

'Viv, big game, special match for Macca. Are you in? Will you captain Macca's X1?'

'No problem, Brother D, I'm there,' came the Master Blaster's reply. The third call was to Malcolm's County captain, Mark Nicholas, and the fourth to Richard Bevan, the charismatic MD of the Professional Cricketers' Association.

Out came my Bible of contacts. One by one the legendary names agreed to play. I had to find them in every cricketing corner of the world. Years of experience in chasing the boys at the right times confirmed Lara, Wasim, Greenidge, Haynes, Warne, Garner, Stewart, Gatting, Lamb, Walsh and Azharuddin. The greatest names in the game coming together to cherish and honour the memory of their friend Malcolm.

On the eve of the game Glenn McGrath called me. 'How many players you got for the Macko game tomorrow, mate?'

'Well, Glenn, we've got 47.'

'Make that 48,' said McGrath, 'wouldn't miss it for the entire world. See you around lunchtime, bye for now.'

Blimey, I thought, *I'll never fit them all into the dressing room!*

So there we were, a day later, jammed into that tiny dressing room. For me, one of the greatest moments of my life – to be inside the sacred inner circle of the legends. To see Big Joel Garner complain that his shirt was too big, Mikey Holding still wearing flannels with a 31 in waist. To watch the 'youngsters' Langer, Warne and Thorpe soaking up the atmosphere in that small room, listening to the conversations, the banter, the reunions, turning back the clock and imagining what it must have been like to play with these immortals.

To watch 48 fantastic cricketers from each corner of the world standing side by side along the edge of the square at the HAC.

A trumpeter's haunting interpretation of the Last Post allowed a long emotional silence to say all that was needed about a special man. Malcolm Marshall, the buccaneering cricketer with the eye of an assassin on the field and a heart filled with love for his fellow men off it.

I will always remember the standing ovation that welcomed Viv as he walked to the wicket with that familiar swagger and the resulting cameo that followed, including a one-handed hit for six clearing a sight screen, much to the delight of the huge and happy crowd. Watching Mikey ('Whispering Death') Holding coming into bowl with that unmistakable fluent and graceful run. Seeing one of the greatest opening partnerships of all time in Gordon Greenidge and Desmond Haynes, playing quite superbly against the bowling of Alan Mullally and Dave 'Syd' Lawrence. Rory Bremner bowling Brian Lara with a real beauty. Courtney Walsh and Collis King laughing and embracing the crowd and the Mark Butcher Bunbury band playing late into the night and sending us home happy with the stars still in our eyes. Up to now, £50,000 has been raised for the Mali Marshall Trust and in years to come those that experienced that magical day will proudly smile and simply say, 'We were there, we took part.'

Give the children the roots to grow and the wings to fly. Give them the time of day and the space to cultivate their dreams. Give them encouragement and instil hope in their heart. Give them a guiding hand, protect and love them. Never stifle or rule out but enhance the talents that God gave them. If they believe they can fly and touch the sky, do everything in your power to let them reach out and touch . . . This has been my philosophy, and that's what brought about another amazing step in my cricketing career.

In 1986 I received a call from Ben Brocklehurst, the visionary proprietor of the *Cricketer* magazine.

'David, come down to Beech Hanger, there's someone I want you to meet.'

As I pointed the Saab through the twisting lanes of the Garden of England, I wondered just what was ahead, and, when I arrived, Big Ben met me with a broad grin and warm handshake.

'David, I want you to meet Cyril Cooper, the General Secretary of the English Schools Cricket Association.'

Cyril Cooper sat, sunk deep in Ben's comfy armchair. He had the appearance of a wise old owl, eyes twinkling behind thick-lensed glasses. He wore a grey suit and a blue tie bearing the Red Rose motif of the England Schools, while by his side lay a grey trilby hat.

'David, our Under-15 Festival will cease to be if we don't find a sponsor. It is a crucial competition which has discovered 95 per cent of all our test players, including Gooch, Gower, Gatting, Atherton, Hussain and Ian Botham. Now the Festival will sink without trace. Can you help?'

I looked at Cyril and felt the passion of the man who ran the Association of School Masters, unpaid talent scouts who were always first to spot a 'new Ramprakash' at the age of seven because they were in the playground and could start 'him' on the road to the Test arena. From his home in Winchester, Cyril had travelled the network of schools throughout the nation, keeping ESCA together, covering thousands of miles on the train. He must have been through Crewe more times than Dario Gradi!

Never have I said 'yes' so quickly.

'Put it there, Cyril, you're on!' I extended my hand and lifted the 'pocket battleship' out of his chair.

Ben boomed with laughter and cracked open a bottle of champagne. 'Let's raise our glasses to the Bunbury ESCA Festival!'

The Festival represented a 'cricket-for-all' opportunity, with no time for elitism. Whether a boy or girl attended a public or state school, they would have the same chance 'to Bunbury'. They would play for their school team, then the county and finally, after a further trial, represent their region.

The four regions, North, South, West and Midlands, would then converge on a different county each year, where the 44 best players at the age of 15 would contest their skills against each other in a 'Round Robin' Tournament. The selectors would then pick the best 11 who would represent England.

We are fortunate indeed to have David Graveney, Chairman of the England Selectors, to present the lads with their regional caps and to give a stirring speech on 'What it takes to play for England'. Each year 'Gray', accompanied by England heroes like Graham Gooch, Robin Smith and Ian Botham, kick starts the Festival, having driven hundreds of miles clutching maps to far-flung locations to stir the passion in the young Bunbury hearts.

We played our first Bunbury ESCA U15 Festival at Harrow, Middlesex, July 1987. I saw John Crawley (Lancs. Schools) score an unbeaten 154, batting with the grace of a right-handed Gower! I witnessed Ronnie Irani from the North running in and bowling flat out to Aftab Habib from the South.

Over the past 16 years I've seen the young Buns blossom into full England cricketers. Sixteen golden summers of patrolling the boundary's edge of the country's finest schools with Ken Lake and my ESCA pals, watching our future Test stars develop their ability, aptitude and athleticism. I've seen Marcus Trescothick score six centuries in one season at the age of 11. I've watched Phil and Gary Neville excel in the 1991 Festival before going on to play football for Manchester United and England, having to make the difficult decision as to which sport to follow. Some years have reared a rich vein of talent. In 1992 the wheel of fortune brought us Liam Botham, Andy Flintoff, David Sales, Alex Tudor, Ben Hollioake and David Nash.

In 1992 we brought over the first cricket team from South Africa after the lifting of apartheid, to play the Inaugural School Boy Test Matches between our countries. To see Gift Pedi from Soweto make Liam Botham an honorary Zulu, winding up the son of Beefy into wearing war-paint and beads, dancing before both teams and so breaking the ice, resulting in explosive laughter and a wonderfully friendly series.

In 1996 we staged the first-ever Junior World Cup, the 'Lombard World Challenge', the final at Lords live on Sky TV.

We witnessed the riot between the Indian and Pakistani spectators. Passions running wild between the Under 15s? They had no birth certificates and I definitely saw the Pakistani captain drive the bus in, sporting a full beard and smoking a pipe!

The light will always burn brightly in my window. In 1996 the glimmer of hope shone in the hearts of children around the world. No lifetime is long enough for a person to discover the full extent of their capabilities, so the younger anyone pushes out the frontiers of experience, the better. When you are close to something so special, you know that if you reach out for it, life is certain to be changed.

Ask Hasan Raza, Lombard World Under-15 Challenge finalist, 20 August 1996; a full Pakistan International Cap (24 October 1996) aged only 14 years and 227 days.

We repeated the Junior World Cup in 2000 – the 'Costcutter U-15 World Challenge' final at Lords between Pakistan and the West Indies. One of the Pakistani lads actually bowled left arm and right arm in the same over.

With all these events the securing of sponsorship is vital. The secret is to find the Top Man in the company who loves cricket with a passion; at least then you have a foot in the door and a responsive ear. On a personal level enormous thanks must go to: John Morgan of Lombard, Colin Graves, chairman of Costcutter, Ray Merridew and Steve Adams of Unilever Best Foods, to Paul Thwaites, boss of the Ashwell Group, Andrew Varley, Director of Next Plc, Joe Cuby, chairman of EMP, Kevin Twomey of Canada Life, and the whiz-kid sporting lawyer Naynesh Desai, his partner Neil Patel and the wonderful John Goldsmith, Lord of Liverpool.

I'm proud to emphasise these blatant plugs because without their generosity of spirit and kindness a great deal of youth cricket in this country would never have seen the light of day.

To me, Bunbury is the very epitome of what life is all about. It has passion, emotion, excitement and tension, skill, determination, friendship, successes and disappointments, toughness, kindness and a commitment to a challenge. Under 15 captures the moment between childhood and mánhood; the players are faintly worldly-wise but with the refreshing outlook of children. They are adolescent, perhaps having experienced their first shave but still peeking over the Coca-Cola cans and dreaming of playing for England. They play with a free spirit, without the fear of failure and oblivious to the demons they'll have to tackle in later years.

I tell the lads, 'Work hard, and you'll get success. The only time success comes *before* work is in the dictionary.'

There is a great comfort in the knowledge that today's young Bunburys will continue to play in our Bunbury Charity X1. Vaughan, Trescothick, Sales, Flintoff, Peng and Bell will take over the mantle from Botham, Gooch, Gatting and Gower, helping to raise vital funds for charity.

In January 2001 I was called by Nasser Hussein, on tour in Sri Lanka. 'Dave, we've been sitting here and just worked something out. Nine out of the eleven of us here in the England dressing room are Bunbury Old Boys.'

That's what makes it all worthwhile.

A THOUSAND LOST NIGHTS

'Ian, would you mind signing this for my little boy, Bruce?'

'My pleasure,' said Beefy. 'Tell you what, in return, could I take over the controls?'

'It would be an honour,' said the unsuspecting Biggles.

Fatal, now we're in for it, I thought. Far down below was a beach.

'Come on, Loon, let's take a look!' Beefy went into a dive. The pilot started to sweat visibly, Mickey Budden vomited and I just held on. If you gotta go, you gotta go!

On the beach, girls were leisurely stretched out, basking topless in the sun, Ambre Solaired, transistors blaring. The next moment they were desperately reaching for their tops as Top Gun Beefy kamikazed towards them. At the last moment, he pulled out of his dive and soared upwards.

Needless to say an interesting aroma filled the cockpit. 'I think we're lost,' squeaked the pilot, picking himself up from the floor.

'Never mind,' chirped the ever-helpful Beefy, 'we'll drop down again and read the road signs.'

13   A THOUSAND LOST NIGHTS

Interestingly enough, 'Beefy' Botham had not made the England U-15 side; Liam did but not the Braveheart. When I address the lads on the first day of the Bunbury Festival, I always tell them to keep playing with passion and fervour. Even if you don't get into the England team now you will develop later – after all, Ian Botham didn't do badly, did he? The same applies to academia; it's nonsense to suggest that if you fail your 11-Plus exams you are a duffer, some of us just blossom later.

The thing about Beefy is that he's a winner. He has the most enormous sense of self-belief, which propels him through life on a tide of victory. He always thinks he's right and ensures that those close to him will feel the same. He is a super-salesman of 'The Beefy Way' to tackle life and I can confirm that from the day I met him I became a convert and disciple of the nutcase. And to think the King of Psychopathy calls me the Loon!

Above all, he makes the mundane fun. Undoubtedly he will go down as the supreme cricketing hero of any age. He is a person of the people who tackles life like the game he played, with enormous gusto and the sole desire to entertain and have fun. I know how he ticks, I have been by his side through colossal adventures by day, merging into a thousand lost nights. I have accompanied him on all of his walks for Leukaemia Research – granted, sometimes in the back of a taxi – and MC'd 189 of his shows around the world. The trouble with 'Beef' is, if you are his pal, it is for 24 hours a day. You are a prisoner of his pleasure.

The 2 a.m. phone call is a favourite.

'Loon, it's Uncle Beefy. What are you doing?'

'Sleeping, Beef, strangely enough.'

'Don't be a wimp, Loon, come and see me.'

2.15 a.m. – it could be a hotel room in Abu Dhabi, or Alice Springs. Out comes the red wine and in we go for the soul-searching stuff.

The fact that Beefy is an insomniac doesn't matter. I have sat up with him and enjoyed the experience, satisfying our souls and making plans till dawn. We could be howling with laughter and suddenly he'd stand up.

'Do you know what, Loon, if someone came in here with a machine gun, I'd stand in front of you and take the bullet.'

'But, Beefy, it's peacetime.' Gawd knows what he'd have been like in the war. Certainly been the first out of the trenches, probably would have wanted to take on the entire enemy single-handed. Once he has a notion in his head, he will pursue it with a single-minded focus unparalleled in modern times. If Mike Brearley told him to go out and beat the Aussies single-handed he would, and in 1981, he did.

One day, while we were clambering up some Alpine road, walking for Leukaemia Research, he was asked by a journalist, desperately struggling to keep up with him (Beefy walks at 4 mph whatever the terrain), what other walks would he entertain?

'Loon, who was that bloke who stormed the gates of Moscow?'

'That was Napoleon, Beefy, in 1812,' I replied.

'Then it's about time we went back to Moscow again,' boomed 'Metal Mickey', 'or maybe I'll walk along the Great Wall of China or around Australia backwards.' Beefy's prognostications became the headlines of the next day's papers, as the scribes hung on to his every word. The journalists took him seriously because they knew he was capable of such conquests; Beefy could turn the stuff of dreams to mere mortals into real epics.

I suppose it was in 1986 when the 'Beef 'N' Loon' partnership really stepped up a gear.

'Listen, Loony, we're off with Gatt down under to play for the Ashes. Come and find me any time and we'll have some fun.'

The Legend had spoken. The England lads had played the 'up country' games and were now ensconced in the Menzies at Rialto Hotel in Melbourne.

'Room service for Mr Botham,' I chirped in my best Aussie drawl.

Kathy opened the door. 'David!' her mouth dropped a little. 'What are you doing here?'

'Is that the Loon?' came the voice from inside. I gave Kath a big hug and went in. 'Beef', wearing his shorts, was lolling in an armchair, swigging a beer and surfing the TV channels. Without taking his eyes off the TV, he smiled. 'Whato, Loony, I knew you'd come.'

The first night, fuelled by a couple of glasses of Chardonnay and the excitement of seeing my pal, I was put under hotel house arrest for lobbing an entire bowl of peanuts across the bar at Allan Lamb. It had all started with a leisurely aimed nut at 'Daffy' DeFreitas (my adopted son aged 21 on his first England tour) and Lamby. This had prompted a hasty return of the odd cashew, climaxing in a rapid line of fire, and me hurling the whole contents over the two players.

News had filtered back to Beefy in his lair. He rarely came down to the bar because of the attention seekers. I was escorted to his room, which by now resembled something out of *Apocalypse Now*, dark with a low fan whirling above.

'Bring in the convict!' boomed the Legend. Beefy was sitting drinking with Aussie skipper Allan Border and Greg Ritchie. 'Loon, I want you to meet a great friend of mine.' To qualify as 'Beefy's great friend' wasn't difficult. It could have been anybody he had shared a bottle of wine with and arm-wrestled to the ground. A thinnish bloke with a pale complexion stood up to meet me with an outstretched hand.

'G'day, Dave, my name is Mickey Budden. I'm a promoter from Berri, South Australia. Do you fancy doing a two-man show?'

'Listen to him, Loon. You'll love it and it could be a good earner.'

'Yeah . . . right,' continued Mickey. 'I'll take you both to the Berri Sports Club for "An Evening with Ian Botham". Basically, Dave, you tell the jokes and Beefy can answer some questions.'

So there we were, banged up in the lightest of light aircraft, 'Starship Beefy', on a one way ticket to . . . where? Berri, South Australia. Me and promoter Mickey in the back, Beefy and the pilot in the front. As we were in mid flight, the pilot, as if by magic, produced a copy of *Botham's Ashes* from under his seat. (This happens everywhere you go with Beefy.)

'Ian, would you mind signing this for my little boy, Bruce?'

'My pleasure,' said Beefy. 'Tell you what, in return, could I take over the controls?'

'It would be an honour,' said the unsuspecting Biggles.

Fatal, now we're in for it, I thought. Far down below was a beach.

'Come on, Loon, let's take a look!' Beefy went into a dive. The pilot started to sweat visibly, Mickey Budden vomited and I just held on. If you gotta go, you gotta go!

On the beach, girls were leisurely stretched out, basking topless in the sun, Ambre Solaired, transistors blaring. The next moment they were desperately reaching for their tops as Top Gun Beefy kamikazed towards them. At the last moment, he pulled out of his dive and soared upwards.

Needless to say an interesting aroma filled the cockpit. 'I think we're lost,' squeaked the pilot, picking himself up from the floor.

'Never mind,' chirped the ever-helpful Beefy, 'we'll drop down again and read the road signs.' Off we went into another suicidal dive, pulling up sharply just above a family in a beaten-up Ford Falcon full of kids, beach balls, buckets and spades, waltzing down the coastal road to the billabong. Beefy hovered above a big road sign. 'There you go, Loon, Berri – that way!'

When we finally landed on a deserted airstrip, the town's mayor and his committee were there to meet and greet us. 'Welcome, Ian, this is indeed an honour and a great day for Berri. Come on, we've got a reception for you.'

Beefy and his three shaken pals were whisked away to a boat on the River Murray. Mickey was wobbling vomit down his shirt, and the pilot was still in a state of shock, as we were piped aboard the river cruiser. The beers started to flow as the Legend did the rounds, shaking the hands of the blacksmith, postmistress and all the town's dignitaries.

The problem with the old boy is he gets bored easily. 'Wouldn't mind a go at the wheel,' he said, putting his arm around his new 'best mate', the captain. 'No worries, Beefy, it's a pleasure,' came the reply.

The trouble is nobody says 'no' to him. It wasn't as though the ship was being handed over to the venerable Lord Nelson, instead to a seriously demented psycho, who instantly became the captain from *Apocalypse Now*, wrapping a roll of toilet paper around his head and lighting up a big cigar.

We had just cruised around the bend when we came upon one of those brightly decorated Martini boats coming towards us. On board a jazz band was playing and a company, all in suits, were enjoying a corporate knees-up away from the rigours of the office.

Now the rules of the river state quite clearly that you keep to the left. Not Captain Pugwash!

'Beef, mate, keep to the left,' said the captain a little nervously. Beefy sailed straight on full throttle regardless. 'To the left, Beef!' The captain's voice had reached a crescendo. It's the right one, it's the left one, it's Martini!

As our boat collided with SS *Martini*, the entire jazz band, including the stand-up bass player, tipped over the side, followed by the corporates.

The Berri and District Urban Council's finest hit the floor, as King Beefy wrestled with the controls and continued to sail on, full speed, up the river, singing 'The Sun Has Got His Hat On'.

Blimey, I thought, *all this and we've still got a show to do!*

The Berri Sports Club was a typical Aussie affair, the great outdoors crammed into a compact indoors. Wonderful facilities for all the family to play all sports. On the door there was a poster.

MICKEY BUDDEN PRESENTS

AN EVENING WITH IAN BOTHAM

M.C. – THE LOON

ONE NIGHT ONLY

We were seated on the top table. I was next to the mayor's wife to whom I immediately took a shine. Being with Beefy, you are subjected to essentially a man's world, so any female who remotely shapes up is for me like a Red Cross parcel. As we got stuck into the meal, the mayor slipped his hand under the table into his loved one's, only to find my hand already there, warming up her Threepenny Bit.

This act of instant attraction didn't go down too well and Beefy spotted the forthcoming altercation. Quickly he held my leg, and gave me a big kiss. Totally confused, the poor old mayor whispered to his deputy, 'Bloke's trying to root my wife, and that Botham geezer is holding his leg. They're probably a couple of Pommie poofters!'

The show went very well. I launched myself into my full repertoire of gags, giving it full animation and big volume. Fortunately, I was on top form and when Beefy sat on the stool to commence his Q&A, the Berri Sports Club rocked with applause. A little girl who had been watching him all evening came and sat on his knee and kept pulling on his nose. She had seen him so many times on television and couldn't believe it was her hero in the flesh.

All was well. Mickey Budden was beaming, thinking about his rosy future as an impresario, when a big voice boomed out from the back, 'Hey, Botham, you fat git. If you nick it do you walk?' All went quiet as Beefy deposited his little friend from his knee.

'I'll tell you what, mate, I'll walk over there and put your lights out.'

As Beefy strolled through the crowd to meet his 'new great mate' I sensed it was time to start our great escape. The place was humming and I could foresee a Wild West brawl. I bid our farewells, kissed the mayor's wife, and legged it, followed by a shocked Mickey, the pilot and eventually the Swashbuckler himself.

Back at the hotel the drink came out and was hosed down in great proportions. The last time I saw Mickey Budden, he was kneeling over the toilet with his head in the pan.

Apparently he was found in the morning passed out on the floor. His trousers had mysteriously caught fire and now hung sadly at half-mast. Mickey Budden's Promotions, 'One Night Only', closed down and he was never seen again. But the idea for 'An Evening with Ian Botham' had been born.

Back to the cricket and England, under the inspired leadership of Mike Gatting and manager Mickey Stewart, won the Ashes. For years, Mickey, who affectionately calls me 'The Nutter', used to invite me into the England dressing room.

'Come in, Nutter, and gee up the troops, give 'em five minutes of your best gags then hop it!'

It was a happy and triumphant tour. Edmonds and Emburey spun the ball prodigiously, Dilley and Foster bowled with fine control, Gower and Lamb batted with flair and power, 'cousin' Gladstone Small kept the spirits high and Beefy and Chris Broad belted the ball to all parts.

'That's it!' said Beef at the end of the tour. 'No more cricket. Come on, Loon, we're off to Brisbane to have some fun!' Beefy, Chris Lander from the *Daily Mirror*, photographer Graham Morris and I packed ourselves into a vehicle and roared up the Pacific Coast Highway to Brisbane. Halfway stage, we ventured off along the dusty trail to Coff's Harbour. We checked into a lovely hotel situated right on the beach. Beefy immediately retired to his wolf's lair to watch his favourite films, *Conan the Barbarian* and *The Hawk Slayer*.

I decided to play cricket on the beach with Chris and Graham. Beefy can't stand to be on his own for too long, and we could sense his restlessness. After half an hour he appeared on his balcony and lobbed all his day/night gear in the air (quickly snaffled up by me. To this day I still have more of Ian's cricket gear than he does. Sometimes he'd come to my house to 'loan' back his equipment).

'Free, I'm free,' he shouted. 'I can't believe you tossers are playing cricket!'

'Crash' Lander (a dearly loved D'Artagnan character now rampaging in heaven), 'Morrow' and I laughed, and purposely ignored him. Sure enough after another ten minutes we saw his face behind the curtains. As we continued to play he walked out with his beer, sat on the bottom step and watched us; we could physically feel his competitive spirit rising to bursting point.

'That's it!' cried the Beef. 'I'll take you all on. Me against the rest!' Beefy, after his declaration of No More Cricket, scored 276, the last 50 left-handed. We threw everything at him including rocks, but he still hit them for miles.

News must have got out that he was there because hundreds of kids emerged from the sand dunes to witness the Legend getting us all out for 15.

So fierce was his bowling that when he had delivered the ball he followed through and stood nose-to-nose with me and marked a cross on his forehead. 'That's where you'll get it, Loon!'

'Do you do that in Test matches, Beef?' I asked.

He looked back and smiled. 'What do you think?'

The game was finished and Beefy was on a roll. 'Come on, Loon, we'll walk down the beach as far as the eye can see. If we come across any obstacles we'll tackle them.'

Blimey, I thought, and this is his first day resting from Test cricket.

We must have walked for five miles when we came to some rocks and steep cliffs. Beefy sprang across the rocks and began to climb.

'Come on, Loon!'

'But Beef, I'm terrified of two things, you know that. Heights and deep water.'

'Don't be a f***ing wimp, Loony, now come on.'

I started to climb the cliffs. All was going well, I actually overtook Ian. The secret was not to look down. I must have been twenty feet from the top when I was struck with vertigo. I literally couldn't move, stuck to the cliff, completely terrified.

'What's up, Loon?' panted Beefy, coming up behind me.

'I can't move, Beefy. I'm stuck. I told you I'm afraid of heights.'

After a brief volley aimed at me 'not to be such a poofter', he suddenly realised that I was locked to the cliff side in a state of fear. With enormous power and speed Beefy came in front, took my arm and pulled me to the top. As I lay there panting he proceeded to walk to the cliff's edge and pound his chest like Tarzan.

'Come here, Loon, it's the only way you'll overcome your fear.' Seeing him teetering on the edge made it even worse. I broke out into a heavy sweat.

Finally, I stood and said, 'Come on, Beefy, let's get back.' Then, as we strolled along the cliff path, we were confronted by a snake coming straight for us.

The cricket, the walk, the cliffs and now the deadly serpent, I couldn't believe it.

Spontaneously, we clasped hands and leapt as high over the snake as we could. If you had freeze-framed this moment it would have been a scene from *Butch Cassidy and the Sundance Kid*. So great was the feeling of relief, Beef and Loon leapt down the cliffs, ran across the sands and dived into the sea. *From Here to Eternity* with IT Botham, Action Man of the Twentieth Century!

When I returned from marauding across Australia with Beefy, I was greeted with the wonderful news that Steve Lanning had raised the necessary finance to make *Hawks*. Principal photography commenced at Pinewood Studios and locations were in England and Holland. Timothy Dalton and Anthony Edwards were magnificent in the roles of Decker and Bancroft, which were really based on Barry Gibb and me.

The press loved the film. 'Moving ... thought-provoking, howlingly funny,' said the *Sun*. 'Greatest British movie I've ever seen,' added Whoopi Goldberg. The Gala Premiere was held at the Odeon Leicester Square – champagne, pomp, red carpet and all the glitterati were there.

Super-slim starlets, 'wearing' backless, sideless and frontless dresses, all hair and teeth, boobs bursting out of tanned chests arrive. Film bosses, their heads nuzzled in the cleavage of some plastic surgery exhibit, chomp on cigars. It's silicone valley – don't sit next to the radiator, girls, or you'll melt. With the paparazzi spilling on to the red carpet, fighting with each other to capture tomorrow's headlines, BG and I nipped out and went down into the underground just to look at our names on the poster. Standing there in our DJs and bow-ties, we stared and saw 'Barry Gibb and David English present Hawks'. We had made our first motion picture.

On the poster, it said: 'In this life, people are either Hawks or Pigeons. Meet the Hawks'. We took out a blue felt tip pen and added:

Let them go, let them fly, refuse them not a mortal glimpse of all that is.
Allow them still their swoop and wondrous altitude
Redeem them in their chosen path, soaring, soaring, silhouetted forms of life
   against a summer moon
Beautiful in sight and we are left in silent fear that they arrive too soon.

LOVE IS IN THE AIR

'DoDoDoDoDo yooooooo take this ssssss . . . woman to be . . . be . . . be . . . your wife?'

'I do, I will, I want to.'

'Nobody Gets Too Much Heaven No More' was reaching a crescendo when the organ suddenly stopped playing . . . but the song continued with that familiar lead vocal. We looked to our right and there, standing next to Ian and Kath, was Barry Gibb, singing his heart out.

Barry and Linda had flown in from Miami, as a surprise.

'I wouldn't have missed this for the world,' smiled Bazzer, receiving another rapturous round of applause.

The Rev. Parsons was beside himself with excitement. He launched himself into some gags which received a thunderous reception from the congregation, before frantically trying to get all the stars to sign his hymn book.

'Only just made the church on time,' said Bazzer. 'I was bursting to do a pee so I sneaked into the graveyard. Only trouble was a lady passed by walking her dog and said: "'Ere, aren't you that Gibb fellow? Go on, Barry, give us a bit of 'Night Fever'."

14 LOVE IS IN THE AIR

A shared dream makes a couple strong?

Are we searching for a soul mate, to link hearts and minds, and to have children, the natural fruits of our love? Or, why buy a book when you can join a library?

Would you rather spend a lifetime with one partner or ten minutes with a million? Fear of commitment, the lust for liberty. Some people need the emotional security of marriage, but you face the contradiction, the struggle between commitment and freedom, the need for domestic solidity and the simultaneous desire to run away.

The truth is I've never needed to be with any one person. I have a love for everybody. Why get married when you can race with the moon – and there's always the possibility of meeting somebody better? It's best to be honest in this quest for perfection, than be tied in a loveless marriage.

Subconsciously I suppose I learnt this from my grandfather and father. If you are going to see the world through the eyes of one it must be better for both of you, otherwise what's the point? And so it grinds on, like an agony column in *Cosmopolitan* magazine, all the sensible bollocks about relationships and marriage.

However, if you find love all this rhetoric goes out of the window. Feelings will always supersede commonsense. Love takes you on an emotional roller-coaster through the mountains and lakes, stretching like a ribbon in the ever-changing light. But often we are much deeper than the water we skate on.

To see a yellow windmill on a hill and a child clutching a red balloon with clenched resolution. To watch the silver tipped gull soaring northwards, white as a kite, against anthracite skies, unshackled, free-searching for the furthest horizon through rain and sun, taking us on a rainbow ride, lifting us to a higher plain where we can dance and sing, filled with the joys of a stolen kiss and the expectation of eternal bliss. There's no point uttering platitudes in the foothills when there are still peaks to climb, but it was 1992 and I was fed up dancing to my own waltz.

4.15 p.m, 14 February 1991. I climbed the escalator at Baker Street Station. In front of me was a blonde head in a long blue coat and a velvet collar. Immediately drawn to 'my type', I accelerated to rendezvous with the pale rider at the top of the escalator. If she looked as good from the front as she did from the back, I was on to a winner.

From the moment my eyes fell on Robyn Grace Dunckley I fell in love with her. There we stood in our own silence. A chance meeting, so fleeting; seize the moment because we won't pass this way again.

'Where do you come from?'

'Zimbabwe.'

'That's a long way to take you home!' Out tumbled the nonsense as we walked and talked. I asked her for her number. She refused. I gave her mine, but as the train came in I pleaded for hers again and she gave it to me.

That night she came to my flat. Wearing my cricket sweater I opened the door.

'Can you park my car?' she asked.

I did so. Mr Patel passed by and I gave him the thumbs up. She had run upstairs. Later Robyn Grace told me she had wanted to case the joint, to make sure I was kosher. For all she knew I could have been the Hampstead Cavalier, but she felt at home with me wearing my cricket sweater. She had been brought up with cricket – her former boyfriend Charlie Lock had played for Zimbabwe.

She possessed all the elements I'd been searching for, sexiness, vulnerability, fire, and a gentle spirit. Maybe we were two lost souls who had met each other at the right time, I basked in her beauty and tenderness. You know when it's love when you're apart and the sense of missing tears through your body. Above all we laughed. My father loved her and so did my mum.

I called Barry and Linda and we flew to Miami to see them. We stayed in the Michael Jackson suite (MJ always slept in the four-poster when he visited BG, gawd knows where he kept the chimpanzee!).

4 a.m. one morning, as the moonlight danced outside on Biscayne Bay, we lay in that massive bed, lost in our own world. I asked her to marry me, and, in that soft Zimbo lilt, she accepted. At 46, I was twenty years older than her. The boy from Hendon Park had found his barefoot soul mate from the dusty trails out of Africa, just three months after meeting her at Baker Street, on that stairway to heaven.

When you fall in love, you are filled with optimism and the whole world takes on a beautiful look. A new love blows your head off, and your heart leaps out of your chest. Your tummy is tingling, your balls are steaming and your helmet's gleaming!

Saturday morning in Golders Green, Peter Mellor and I used to chat up the au pairs. They were in a different class, blonde, smelling of pine, with eyes as blue as a Finnish Lake and skin as pure as the Nordic snow. Laughing and uninhibited, a million miles from the po-faced English birds, who were all so predictable and humdrum. It was Saturday Morning Fever outside the tube station, the same ritual. Meet an Eva from Budapest or Maria from Stockholm, arrange to see them in the Bull and Bush at nine that evening after we'd played football down at Mill Hill Village and then take them to a dance at the University of London with the promise of a portion early Sunday morning.

I always took the best ones to meet my dad. I was terribly proud of him and I loved to see his face as a long line of au pairs used to troop into his lounge to sit and listen to his adventures. He had found peace of mind, living with Babs in Golders Green. There he was, ensconced between the Isaacs and Sollys, quite content to potter about his garden by day and to play his cello long into the night. I had led the scented trail of blondes along the High Road past Grozinski's the bakers and the kosher butchers, to my dad who sat there in his semi-detached armchair, immaculately dressed, looking like Douglas Fairbanks. He had never fulfilled his wonderful talents as a musician and an artist, but he was a born *bon viveur* with a dazzling sarcastic wit; the girls adored him. Babs would keep popping into the front room with biscuits and tea as my dad held court with tales of his worldwide escapades.

Every time the hot pants and clogs brigade went up the stairs for a pee, he always asked me the same question: 'Stinker, you really should settle down.' It made me laugh, because it came from a real ladies man; he just lacked the confidence.

His marriage to my mum had left scars and crippled his spirit. My mother was a fantastic woman, but they simply had not been right for each other. I always imagined my dad as a younger man with a French woman, in bohemian bliss in Paris. Two lovers caught in a moment of timeless passion in a bustling Parisian café. The evocative image of him playing a bluesy saxophone, telling gags, charming the *mademoiselles*, making them laugh. Love on the Left Bank. The nocturnal life of the artist with his free spirits, drifting from bars to nightclubs to cafés in search of sexual adventures and intoxication.

Like an actor, he did not cope too well with life, with marriages, relatives, offspring, domesticity or involvement with affairs of the world. He was blessed or cursed (you can view it either way) with a need to be another person in public, to pretend, to be part of a show and the staged brightness that's never challenged by the real light of life.

In a way I'm glad he never became famous. Celebrities are particularly vulnerable. They are forced to spend time with people they don't care about and who don't care about them. They also have to live up to expectations – both their own and the public's. No genius is worth too much heartache. So my dad ended up in suburbia just half a mile from Hendon Park where we had all started.

As the weeks slipped by and the leaves of autumn covered summer's traces, his health began to fail rapidly. You could tell it was an effort for him to get through the day.

Of course he had met Cindy and co., but when he met Robyn he sensed it was special. For Dad, she was like a breath of fresh air. Her sense of fun, so young and invigorating, lifted his spirit. The touch of her hand, laughing together, the semblance of a smile. At last he felt he could let go. I had found true happiness and that satisfied his soul.

One morning, Babs phoned me to tell me my dad had passed away. I sped around to the house and leapt up the stairs to his room, and there he lay, in his blue-and-white striped pyjamas, quite still, with a smile on his face.

I just sat there in his room, as quiet as a churchyard, holding his hand. I was consumed by uncontrollable grief as I stared into his face, and felt isolated, naked, alone with my thoughts. He had gone down dark alleys and shining valleys but he had always loved us.

I had never seen a dead person, and now I had lost my dad. Life would never be the same. I kissed him and went to the door. I took one last look at the troubled dreamer who had fallen, smiling, into a beautiful timeless reverie. It was 17 August 1991.

When you lose a parent your whole life changes. You feel as though you've lost a limb.

I arranged the funeral through Grimshaws in Brent Street.

When I arrived at Hendon there were only a few mourners assembled outside the Chapel of Rest. A miserable clutch of crows, dressed in black with faces as solemn as bleached parchment stretched tautly over sculpted cheekbones. There was Pedro, my pal from the library, the lads from Mill Hill Village, Aunt Maud and Uncle Sid, cousin 'this' and nephew 'that', members of my family who I had only known through the odd card at Christmas. It's funny how families and friends only come together at weddings and funerals, the start and finish of a world together.

'Your father was such a character,' sobbed Aunt Maud tearfully into her lace hanky. 'We'll miss him, I can't believe it. Do you remember when he—'

Just then my mobile phone rang.

'Meester English?' came a nasal voice crackling down the line.

'Speaking.'

'Oh, it's Grimshaws here, the undertakers.'

'Where are you?' I enquired.

'I'm afraid we're in a bit of bovver. Cock-up with the 'earse carrying your father.'

'Cock-up?'

'Yers, 'fraid the old 'earse has broken down 'ere in Brent Street.'

'Where are you?' I continued, mortified.

'Well, we're currently parked on a double yeller outside the post office.'

'What about my dad?' I said in a state of shocked horror.

'Oh! 'Ee's alright. Good as gold. All boxed up in the back. Put it this way, he's not goin' anywhere.'

'Aren't you a member of AA Relay?' I suggested in desperation.

By now the clutch of aunties and uncles were showing more than a keen interest in my dad's dilemma.

'Bloody stupid if you ask me,' piped up Uncle Sid.

'Who's heard of a hearse breaking down? Next he'll get clamped!'

I tried to lighten up the situation. 'Never mind, Sid, it could be worse. They buried the bloke who compiled the *Times* Crossword here last week.'

'Where is he?' said a surprised Sid.

'Four down, three across!'

It was then that Pedro went into action in his usual all-encompassing enthusiastic style. 'Tell you what, pogler, I'll go and get your dad in my van. It's the least I could do for dear old Ken.'

An hour later my dad arrived in the Hendon Borough Council mobile library. There he lay boxed in between the Dickens and D.H. Lawrence. Worse was to follow. As we stood around the graveside, the vicar had just got to his 'ashes to ashes' speech when my Auntie Mildred, who had downed a couple of pre-service sherries too many, caught her high heel in the green matting and half fell into the grave, landing on top of my dad.

So my dad had passed away, but I had found Robyn. It was time to leave Kingdon Road. Farewell old house, goodbye Mr Patel, thanks for the memories. I took my fiancée to Finchley where we lived by a viaduct and the tube train, which rattled along the end of the Northern Line to Mill Hill East. We lived just four doors away from my artist partner Jan Brychta. It was a leafy cul de sac where Robyn and I laughed all day and made love all night, or a combination of both.

Jan and I worked hard on the Bunbury books which were doing well. What we needed was music. How about the Bunbury album?

Barry Gibb was staying at his English HQ.

'Baz, can you help, we need some Bunbury tunes.'

Together we sat down with Robin and Maurice and wrote 'We're the Bunburys' (we recorded this track later in Miami at the Bee Gees Studio, Middle Ear. I phoned up George Terry, from Eric's old band, to play guitar, Maurice Gibb on keyboards and Barry and Robin on vocals). The next day I was playing cricket for Finchley against Amersham. By the time the last ball had been bowled, Barry had come up with the melody for 'Bunbury Afternoon'. We wrote the lyrics, which seemed to capture the essence of summer:

Young lovers holding hands
Babies in prams
A little bit of Heaven on the village green
And the Bunbury Eleven you've never seen.

Next we wanted the anthem for the team. The notion of fighting the good fight, and then the long road home after some hazardous missions. It would need a strong driving melody and a rousing lyric driven by a great guitar; fortunately, we knew the best. We trapped the master as he was eating lunch at a polo match in Windsor.

'Let's ask him now, Baz.' As Eric ploughed through his hors d'oeuvres we plonked the walkman on his head and played the demo:

'This is it, El.' As 'Fight' sunk in, the Legend smiled and tapped his knife along in time.

A week later he stood in producer Dave Mackay's little studio among the trees in deepest Surrey. As Eric's guitar soared he was oblivious to kids and dogs that wandered into the studio to watch in wonderment. The session had started at 2 p.m. The Bee Gees and Ian Botham backed him on vocals, and by 9 o'clock EC had packed his case to go and play with Prince in London. Have guitar, will travel!

The following day we recorded 'Seasons', the Bunbury carol, with the group No Hat Moon. Cheryl, Sheila, Pete and Paul from Swansea did a wonderful job. The two girls sang like birds to capture the warm Christmas feel we required. Great credit must go to Dave Mackay who, after working with Barry, had taken just two days to record 'Fight' and 'Seasons'.

We left the magic of Toftrees to return to the real world. Next it was on to India! Little Rajbun had ridden off Jan's drawing board into our lives from Bungalore on top of his faithful elephant Ellie. We needed a song from India to capture the mystical feeling of wizardry and great history. Where else could I possibly go but to George?

'George, I need a song from India for my Bunbury album. Can I come and see you? . . . . and, George, think curry house!'

The drive to Henley gave me time to think of little Rajbun's background and how he would fit on to the album.

On arrival, George Harrison introduced me to his son Dhani. We played cricket on the lawn and talked briefly about Rajbun's character. That evening when I returned home the phone rang.

'Listen to this,' said George excitedly. Down the line came this haunting melody featuring the sitar. It was the first time he had played the instrument since the Beatle days. It was great. The next day I returned and we put the words to the tune.

It was quite daunting, writing with a Beatle. In his studio George played me the track and told me exactly where the lyrics should fall.

'I need a bridge here, chorus there and then the harmonies.' We stood side by side as if in a tailor's; he had supplied the cloth and now I had to make the cloth into a suit.

It was great fun. George had a fantastic dry wit. Nine-year-old Dhani sang the lead vocals, George sang the chorus and I warbled away as the Evil Katman of Katmandu. Two nights later, George went to see Ravi Shankar at his hotel and recorded his sitar on to the track. It was the stroke of a master, and Rajbun could now ride into the sunset, his song firmly in place. George was so enthused by the song, he actually flew tabla players, drummers and flautists in from India to complete the track.

Eric Clapton had first introduced me to George. He was a man full of love and compassion. A great soul, very spiritual but with the common sense of a man in touch with people. He reached us with his music. Away from all the business heads, just an acoustic guitar and a sunshine spirit, he found solace and great relief in writing his songs. 'Something', 'Here Comes The Sun', 'My Sweet Lord'. That's how I'll remember him, but above all, for his wisdom, wit and humour smiling through. At one point we considered merging our groups of special friends – yes, The Travelling Bunburys; now that would have been something very special!

When I met The Beatles I soon realised that although there were four of them they were the same person; just four parts of one. John, the angry one, Paul, the charmer, Ringo, the joker, and George, the thinker. Like the Bee Gees they had magical telepathy and when their hearts were beating as one the genius of their melodies flowed and they could encapsulate a story in four minutes. And like Barry, Robin and Maurice they never ceased to be thrilled at being part of the Great Adventure. In a world at war they wanted to Give Peace A Chance. And now, although two of their hearts have ceased to beat, their music will live on forever.

Viv Radish, and his golden island of Bunny Bados, deserved a happy calypso/reggae song. For a long time I had liked the idea of that Coca-Cola commercial with the aerial shot of all the children singing 'I'd Like To Teach The World To Sing'. We wrote 'Up the Revolution' in a day. The Bee Gees asked Aswad to add that Caribbean quality, and a really happy recording session took place. Now for the lead vocal. I had made friends with Elton John on the 1987 England cricket tour to Australia, and not only was he one of the funniest and most sensitive fellows I had ever met, he also played a good game of cricket, belting the bowling of Beefy Buntham and the England players in the nets at Melbourne. I got a message to Elton. Two weeks went by and I received a card from China. It read

OK. Wing Commander Bunny, I'll sing your tune, Love Elton.

He arrived at Mayfair Studios at 2 p.m. one Tuesday, dapper as ever, wearing a trilby hat and a silk bow-tie. It was clear to see that Elton and the Bee Gees were delighted to see each other; obviously there was a deep mutual respect for each other's music, built over 25 years. After making everybody fall about laughing, Elton sat at the piano, a bottle of Mouton Cadet was opened, and the backing track was played. It was breathtaking to see the keyboard wizard at work; within thirty-five minutes the vocal was completed perfectly.

Over the years I have watched Barry produce the best in the world. A true perfectionist – he has that special ear for a great performer. A great job done, his face will break into a smile of approval. I have seen that really special grin only twice; once with Barbra Streisand, the other with Elton John.

The Bunbury sessions completed, Barry and I got a deal with Island Records and later on Polydor. *We're the Bunburys* was released at the end of 1991 and went to Number 20 in the charts. For me, the real thrill was the success of the second single, 'Fight', which reached the Number 1 spot in the American AOR Charts (Adult Orientated Rock).

The prestigious *Rolling Stone* magazine gave the record a glowing review; 'The Bunbury Band, from England. Songs from some cricket playing rabbits . . .' True enough, recorded deep in the Surrey Hills with a little help from some extra special friends!

Success is seeing the opportunity based on your instincts and then working hard to bring all the elements together. But as in all the projects I've conceived, it was the fun in the making which gave me the real buzz. Armed with my six books and hit record, I went to see Andrea Wonfor, Head of Arts and Entertainment at Channel 4 TV, who commissioned Jan and me to make a series of cartoons. It took a year to produce 12 five-minute films with Bob Godfrey and when they were finally shown at 5.55p.m each day ('adults/children of all ages' spot), the ratings approached three million viewers.

But, after the euphoria of the Bunbury album . . . my mother's time was running out.

As a fighter in the war and in peacetime she had been a champion. She was my friend and the one who answered my needs. She was my field, which I sowed with love and reaped with thanks, giving me my board and fireside. I went to her with my hunger and I looked to her for peace. Night and day, you were the one. Yes, Mum, all those times when I came to you with my troubles and left you feeling strong again. Your silhouette at the window waving to me, always reaching out to reassure and to love.

In December 1991, she complained of a pain in her back. By March 1992 she had gone.

I took her to the Royal Free Hospital in Hampstead, where they discovered a small cancer in her lung.

'We've found it in time, Mrs English, we can remove it.' They operated but the growth had spread. They removed half of her lung and then the other half.

She lay in intensive care and only the machines kept her alive. I know she smoked twenty cigarettes a day in the same flat that Al Green had sung to her, but the specialist told me it must have been more like 60 cigarettes:

'Your mother's lungs are like the inside of a chimney.'

Robyn and I visited her every day. Then one Wednesday the doctors told me she was going back on the wards, which usually meant that she had improved and would be sent home.

'Good news eh, doc?'

The doctor looked uneasy, avoiding my stare. 'We've done our best for your mother.'

The following day we went to see her in her single room. The doctors stood in a line, with their backs against the wall. She was slipping away. She reached out to me to hold my hand, her name tag around her wrist, and then with her fingers stretched and shaking she felt Robyn's tummy, smiled and was gone, lost to the world.

She knew Robyn was pregnant. One mother's psyche to another. It was 9 March 1992. In two years, I had lost my mum and dad, gained a fiancée and a Bunbury in the oven.

It was time to take the three of us down the 'Aisle of Man'.

'Beefy, it's the Loon, I'm going to get married.'

I waited for the five minutes of uncontrollable laughter at the other end of the line to subside. 'Would you like to be my best man?'

'When is it?'

'June 19, 1992.'

'It's the day before the Test Match at the Oval. We'll have nets.'

'Speak to Mickey (Mickey Stewart was England team manager). He'll give you a couple of hours off.'

'Alright, Loony, I'll be there.'

I wanted to get married in Hendon, specifically Hendon St Mary's, which sat proudly on Greyhound Hill. The parson was the Rev. Richard Parsons who incredibly lived in Parson Street where I had gone to school at Hendon Prep. Under the light of a summer moon Robyn and I found the parsonage and rang the bell.

'What do you want?' came an angry voice through the intercom.

'We want to get married.'

'Do you know what time it is? Give me your number and the Reverend will call you tomorrow.'

Mrs. Parsons sounded like a nightmare, but when the phone rang the next day the Reverend was very friendly, although he struggled to talk with a stammer.

'Your . . . your . . . your . . . name . . . name name?'

'David English.'

'Your . . . your . . . your . . . best . . . best . . . man . . . man?'

'Mr Ian Botham.' That's one Ian Botham, Reverend, not seven!

When the big day arrived Beefy drove me to the church.

'Loony, do you know what you're doing?'

'What do you mean?'

'Well, you're not the marrying kind, you love everybody.'

'Well, you're alright, Beef, you've got Kath, now it's my turn.'

I've never been more certain in my life. I couldn't wait to get up that aisle with my young Zimbo bride. When Rev. Parsons met us at the vestry it was like a scene from *The Godfather*. The Rev. lifted up his gown and took out a copy of *Botham's Ashes*. (I told you this happens everywhere!) 'Coo . . . Coooo . . . Could you pl . . . pl . . . pl . . . please sign this, I . . . I . . . I . . . I . . . Ian?'

'Certainly, Vic, it will be a pleasure,' smiled Beefy Corleone. 'Now, while we're here what's your wine supply like?'

The Rev revealed some bottles of dodgy Bulgarian red probably costing £1 per gallon. If you'd belched you'd have taken paint off a door from twenty feet.

'I can do better than that, Vic,' said Beefy, opening the boot of his car to reveal a winery of considerable pedigree. So there we were, on the biggest day of my life, and Beefy and the Rev were wheeling and dealing.

The Church hung heavy in incense and personalities. It was like a light entertainment show. In fact Sky TV filmed the ceremony. All we needed was Des O'Connor to MC the event. But we didn't need Des when we had the Rev. Parsons and David Essex, Gary Mason, John Keeble from Spandau Ballet, Mr Patel, Johnny Cousins, Joe 'the Hat' Cuby, Gary Headley and Joel Garner who had flown in specially from Barbados.

There was a flurry at the door and there was Robyn, radiant, gliding up the aisle like a young swan on the arm of her Rhodesian dad, Bob, whom I'd never met. In fact all her family were there, pew by pew, all 1950s and refreshingly innocent.

'Go on, Loon . . . It's your turn,' whispered Beefy with a shove. Intoxicated by the heady mixture of scent and the sounds of the organ playing my favourite Bee Gees song 'Too Much Heaven', I stood in front of the Rev. and awaited my bride.

'DoDoDoDoDo yooooooo take this sssss . . . woman to be . . . be . . . be . . . your wife?'

'I do, I will, I want to.'

'Nobody Gets Too Much Heaven No More' was reaching a crescendo when the organ suddenly stopped playing . . . but the song continued with that familiar lead vocal. We looked to our right and there, standing next to Ian and Kath, was Barry Gibb, singing his heart out.

Barry and Linda had flown in from Miami, as a surprise.

'I wouldn't have missed this for the world,' smiled Bazzer, receiving another rapturous round of applause.

The Rev. Parsons was beside himself with excitement. He launched himself into some gags which received a thunderous reception from the congregation, before frantically trying to get all the stars to sign his hymn book.

'Only just made the church on time,' said Bazzer. 'I was bursting to do a pee so I sneaked into the graveyard. Only trouble was a lady passed by walking her dog and said: "'Ere, aren't you that Gibb fellow? Go on, Barry, give us a bit of 'Night Fever'."

'Not now, love,' said Bazzer in midstream. 'I'm not meant to be here!'

We were swept away in a white Rolls-Royce to Bill Wyman's Sticky Fingers Restaurant for the reception, where Beefy made his speech before returning to the Oval. Rory Bremner dashed in, to give us thirty minutes of his magic. Showered in confetti we bade our farewells and flew to the South of France where we stayed in Bill's villa at St Paul de Vence.

Just Rob, 'The Bun' and Dave on their HoneyLoon!

To find remoteness, wild woods and isolation where you can dream under a starry sky beneath the mantle of the moon and still be only seven miles from Hyde Park would indeed be a right result, but Robyn and I found our hideaway cottage in Mill Hill along a leafy lane to serendipity.

I knocked on the door. A city type answered. It had been thirty years since I had done the same in West Hampstead but if you don't ask you don't get.

'Excuse me, but if you ever consider selling your house I'd be very interested.' We were invited in. I made an offer and 'Lane End' was ours.

Even now I look out and marvel at the ponds and Highland cows. Riders on horseback pass my window, as do the weekend Barbour Brigade, walking their red setters, tramping through damp leaves and mottled light . . . just the sound of the wind through the trees . . .

The only way I'll leave here is in the back of the Hendon Council mobile library, wedged between the Wisdens and D.H. Lawrence.

THE LOON'S OUT, THE DOGS ARE BARKING

Capt. Beefy is at the helm wearing his Oakley sunglasses, which reflect the mighty seas. Viv is cooled out on deck, soaking in the rays. All is well until the boat slows down and begins to trawl. The pirates cast their lines into the surf to catch the Marlin. To their surprise a parabola yawn bearing my breakfast quickly follows suit. I have never felt so ill, my senses are slipping away. Viv is genuinely concerned and gives me the last rights Antiguan style, followed by a hearty rendition of 'The Lord is my Shepherd'. 'Viv, all I want to be is alone,' I plead to my soul brother. 'Brother D, you look dead, man.' Eventually, Beefy persuaded the pirates to turn the ship and plough through the seas back to Brisbane. Half gaining my sea legs I staggered back to the hotel – only to find Beefy had installed a water-bed in my room.

15 THE LOON'S OUT, THE DOGS ARE BARKING

'Loonatic, it's me, Beefy. Get yourself ready, we're off again, you, me and Viv, 36 nights on the trot. De Luxe coach, best hotels, the works.'

'But Beef . . . Beef . . .'

The line was dead. I had received the call from His Highness. Another adventure. Hell on wheels. Mind you, I was now a hardened campaigner of the road show; since we'd returned from Australia, 'Beef and Loon' had completed 75 evenings of chat, film, and questions-and-answers, all born on the premise of 'You get it together, Dave, I'll just turn up.'

First night had been Stourbridge. A packed town hall full of Beefy's BBC TV *Question of Sport* fans. Mums, dads, grannies, kids, candy floss. First question out of the barrel.

'My name is Kate Williams, I live at 96 Cambridge Street, is it true you are hung like a rhino?'

Unfazed, I looked at Beefy from my stool and said, 'Was Michael Holding the quickest bowler you faced?'

Unknowingly, Beefy answered. Next question: 'Do your balls swing more off a green wicket, in a heavy atmosphere or with "Miss . . ."'

'Mike Brearley, the best captain you played under?' I lied, thinking, *Blimey, I've got another 74 nights of this and it's meant to be a family show!*

As 750 punters idolised the Legend, hanging on to his every word, I stuck a trembling hand into the barrel to pull out the third question. By now Beefy knew something was wrong, as I kept putting the dodgy questions into my top pocket.

'Loon!' he boomed. 'I hope you're reading out those questions properly. Come on, give that one to me.'

Right! Well he asked for it!

'Did Mike Gatting bonk the barmaid?'

There was a hush in the auditorium save for a couple of sniggers.

'No, he certainly didn't!' laughed Beefy. 'Cos anything that goes into Gatt's room after ten o'clock he eats!'

Massive laughter all round. A relieved MC and Beefy putting his hand over the mike and whispering, 'Loony, I told you to read 'em out!'

That evening, on the way to the hotel, Beefy and I walked through a graveyard. On one of the headstones it was written 'Here lies a cricket writer and an honest man.'

'Funny, Loon. Strange to see two blokes in the same grave!'

And now, add the most powerful batsman of all time, and you're on to a real winner.

'Good evening ladies and gentlemen, welcome to the King and I.'

Viv ('Cool on a Stool') was the King, Beefy ('Heat on the Seat') was 'I', and me, well I was just happy to be 'and'.

After the show, back into the mobile home to travel to Maidstone or St Austell, or some other remote location. I'm sure to this day that our promoter Mick 'D'Artagnan' Leigh sat in his office and threw darts at the map to decide on the itinerary. The moon is out and the dogs are barking as the lights of the 'Beefy mobile' catch the startled look in the badger's eye. Have you ever prepared a prawn korma at 65 mph in a gale going over Shap Fell on the B1245? Let me tell you, there is an art to preparing this high cuisine. Up front, Ian watched *Peter Alliss's Golf Video* or the *The History of Liverpool FC* for the 36th time. Viv was stretched out, semi-comatose, and Clive (ex-manager of Guns 'N Roses), our intrepid road manager, was at the controls of the nightclub-on-wheels, valiantly trying to keep us on the tarmac. The hazards were many; a sharp turn of the wheel could prompt a flurry of activity in the kitchen area, bottles of Chardonnay flew out of the lockers, along with the occasional saucepan and kettle. It was common to be nodding off, only to be awoken by the *Best of Botham's Ashes* smacking you on the back of the head.

25 November 1992, we had just come off stage at the Hexagon Theatre, Reading. The phone went. It was Robyn's mum, Naomi, who had been staying with us as Rob was about to have our baby.

'Dave, Robyn's gone into labour. We're at the Hillingdon Hospital in Middlesex.'

'Right,' I gulped. 'I'm on my way!'

'Good luck, Loon!' said Ian and Viv. 'Hope it's twins!'

I sped to the hospital in a state of nervous excitement. Robyn was sitting in a big bath; she had always wanted a water birth. She looked beautiful. Morning came, but nothing had broken, so the sister said they'd have to induce the birth. Robyn got out of the bath and the nurses went to work.

'Push! Push!' and out flew our little princess, Amy Rose. I caught her at third slip and held her tightly to my body. It is the greatest feeling I've ever experienced.

The UK tour successfully completed, the next stop for the 'King and I' was Australia – Wagga Wagga to Wollongong to Warrangul – 31 cities in 35 days, more than 5,000 miles, driving along red dirt roads, through tumbleweed towns in the middle of nowhere.

Beefy had gone on first. Viv and I followed and here are extracts from the diary I kept on our tour 'Down Under'.

February 1993: Tuesday

I'm sitting in my dressing room in Whyalla or is it Broken Hill? One town seems to roll into another. 31 cities in 35 days. It seems an eternity since I met Viv at Heathrow and boarded the Jumbo to Perth. Breakfast over Warsaw with the man who had blasted 120 centuries worldwide, lunch above Moscow and high tea roaring across Islamabad, finally brought us down to Penang. It should have been Bangkok, but due to fog we were diverted to Penang with its airstrip hewn out of the jungle.

We were prisoners of Penang for what seemed an eternity. Everybody recognised Viv, they always do, wherever we go, be it a shopping mall in Adelaide or an airport terminal in Thailand. When we finally landed at Perth we were met by the press, TV and dear old Beefy who stood in his shorts, saluting us with a wide grin. 'G'day, boys. Welcome to Oz. No worries, six weeks of bliss!' You must be joking, I thought. More like prisoners back in the old penal colony. And to think he was thrown out of Australia, most people get thrown in! That was back in 1987; after being arrested on the plane with the Queensland team, Ian had been banged up in the East Perth lock-up. Talking about it now, on stage, Beefy laughs. 'Not the best net before a final. I'm sitting in a cell wondering what on earth I'm doing there, when Dennis Lillee walks in to bail me out. He's got with him a six pack and a bottle of Bundaberg. We disappeared down to the beach for a few hours. I've never prepared for a final quite like that.'

The questions come in fast and furious. 'Did Viv shave his head so he could run quicker between the wickets? Do you tamper with your balls?' Sitting on the far stool, Smokey is in fine form. Answering, 'What was his most embarrassing moment?', he replied there had been two. His first game for Antigua playing against St Kitts: 'I was the new kid on the block. Walked out to the wicket for my first knock and was given out caught behind. I knew I had not hit it so I showed a little dissent, enough to get the crowd going. And they did. They set fire to the stands and play was abandoned. I was back in the pavilion. The administrators were panicking. "Viv, would you like to bat again?" "Wouldn't mind," I replied. I went out and scored another duck. The crowd was disappointed. I was devastated as a youngster would be, but looked forward to my proper second innings. I went out and scored another duck. So I had the unhappy distinction of scoring three ducks in one game! My second most embarrassing moment was after scoring the quickest century ever against England. A streaker ran on to the pitch and asked me to sign her boob!'

Monday, 7 pm, Bunbury

We were happy to get the first show under our belt. We drove to Bunbury, south of Perth. Was this the Australian home of my Bunbury Tails?

Upon arrival at the theatre, the management asked us to sign a back stage door which carried the signatures of the stars who had appeared at the Bunbury Entertainment Theatre. It was good to join the list which included Gene Pitney, Barry Crocker, Gerry and the Pacemakers, Warren Mitchell and, inevitably, Rolf Harris. A near-capacity audience was mesmerised by the candour of the couple. Viv was 'cool on the stool', and Beefy 'heat on the seat'. First there was the tale about the Test in Christchurch, New Zealand, when Beefy ran out Boycott, the captain, under orders from Bob Willis. He, like the rest of the team, had become angered by Boycott's excruciatingly slow batting.

'As I walked out to bat, Bob told me to run him out,' said Beefy. 'I said I can't do that. This is only my third bloomin' Test Match, and that is Sir Geoffrey out there. Willis said if I didn't do it, I wouldn't play anyway. Richard Hadlee bowled to me and I pushed it into the covers. I called out "Yes", "No" and left him stranded. He couldn't believe what I had done. I looked up at the pavilion and my team-mates had fallen over laughing like dead ants. He didn't talk to me for the next six weeks, which was pretty hard seeing as he was captain, but I quite enjoyed it.'

Thursday: Alice Springs, the heart of Australia

Staying in another motel with a fridge that roars like something driven by Nigel Mansell; welcome to Cell Block H.

And another great audience. Viv recalls his childhood under the intimidating influence of his father, a deeply religious man who banned his son from playing cricket on Sundays. 'I was so scared of him. He would never come in the ground with me when I was playing local matches. He would sneak in and stand on a hill behind a tree. As soon as I played a rash shot you could hear his booming voice yell out "Concentrate!". I would hear him but never see him.'

Wednesday: Darwin, Northern Territory

Had an hour to fill, so Beefy suggested we walk through a crocodile-infested mango swamp. Gingerly, I moved along the boardwalk, ready for the impending death sentence of a poisonous snake or man-eating spider to slip down my shorts.

Arrived at theatre. Once again Rolf Harris had been there, he seems to have daubed every theatre wall in Australia. Outside my window, electric storms crackled over troubled waters, highlighting the fishing boat speeding for home. Shades of Key Largo with a tropical set on stage. Lush green plants hung over us as the audience was allowed behind the scenes once again, this time into Geoff Boycott's bedroom.

One evening Beefy went to his room in Calcutta after Boycott had said he was too ill to continue the tour. After hearing he had played golf when he should have been at the ground, the team had voted for him to be sent home. 'I felt sorry for him and went to his room to say "goodbye" with a flask of brandy,' Beefy recalled.

'He answered the door dressed in nothing but his England cap and his batting gloves. He was holding his Slazenger bat and practising his strokes in front of a mirror. He wanted to know if his knee was bending correctly!'

Monday: Brisbane, day off

First day off and Beefy had organised a deep sea fishing trip with a man called Brown and a man called Green, whose nickname is, of course, 'Blue'. They met us at the airport. Lively to say the least, and certainly related to Long John Silver and Ben Gun. After exchanging umpteen 'G'days', our two salty sea-dogs drove us to the harbour, past the endless prefab buildings which remind me of Florida, bearing names like the 'Gobble and Go' and 'Morry's Motors'. Out to sea we roar, 25 miles out we were flanked by some dolphins, playfully dipping and diving in the wake of the SS Capt. Barnacle.

Capt. Beefy is at the helm wearing his Oakley sunglasses, which reflect the mighty seas. Viv is cooled out on deck, soaking in the rays. All is well until the boat slows down and begins to trawl. The pirates cast their lines into the surf to catch the Marlin. To their surprise a parabola yawn bearing my breakfast quickly follows suit. I have never felt so ill, my senses are slipping away. Viv is genuinely concerned and gives me the last rights Antiguan style, followed by a hearty rendition of 'The Lord is my Shepherd'. 'Viv, all I want to be is alone,' I plead to my soul brother. 'Brother D, you look dead, man.' Eventually, Beefy persuaded the pirates to turn the ship and plough through the seas back to Brisbane. Half gaining my sea legs I staggered back to the hotel – only to find Beefy had installed a water-bed in my room.

We are now into day 20, or is it 21? I have lost count. Outside, the moon is out and the dogs are barking. I lie on my bed listening to the fridge rattling and the air-conditioning revving up. It's the start of the mosquito Grand Prix; suddenly the air fan roars into life, propelling 350,000 mosquitoes across the room like surfers on a wave. My brain is addled with jumbled memories of skyscraper hotels, outback motels, tumbleweed towns and aboriginal settlements where little children stare at Viv and Ian as though they were from another planet. We were touched by their kindness, as they offered us didgeridoos, boomerangs and hand-carved emu eggs.

There was the night in Port Pirie where a doctor's beeper went off in the audience. Laurel and Hardy were in fine form describing Derek Randall's antics. By the time we had wrapped up the show, the doctor had come back stage. 'Sorry lads, I had to slip off to deliver a baby, but I was back in time for the end.' Then there was the little girl who had been brought up watching Ian on TV, believing that every time he smiled while playing, he was smiling directly at her. Now she stood in front of her hero, who signed her T-shirt and left her in wonderment.

In Adelaide the porter's TV flickered a live show from America. There was Eric Clapton, winning his six Grammys. It took my mind back 20 years to RSO. Well done, El!

Life was so hard in Iron Knob that we had to put out the chairs. The windows had no curtains and we had to wait till darkness fell to show the video.

The ache of homesickness is tinged with the feeling of being lost to the rest of the world. Yesterday we travelled through three states in 15 hours, experiencing the different time changes. We travelled down a road and saw eagles, dingos and the Murray river, but still not a kangaroo in sight.

Life is hotting up on stage as the brothers-in-arms exchange memories of the early days together. One night Viv decided to recall Beefy's arrival in Jamaica, when he was offered a rum punch and declared it easy to handle. The fruit obscured the 150 per cent proof rum and, after several, Beefy was slumped comatose in his room. Viv found he could not wake him. 'I took some ladies' make-up and applied a little blusher, three layers of lipstick and some mascara.' He told his Aussie audience: 'I took some photographs. Maybe one day if he makes me real mad I'll let you all see them.'

'Right,' roared Beefy. 'The gloves are off! We all know Viv's reputation, old angel-guts, never-touch-a-drink Richards. Well, let me tell you about the time we won two finals at Somerset and 160,000 fans lined the streets of Taunton as we paraded the trophies atop our double-decker team bus. We were thrown up bottles and it seemed a shame not to drink them. We got stuck in and by the time we arrived at the town hall, Viv could hardly walk. I had to hold him up as the team was introduced to the mayor, but as soon as I let him sit down he snored his way through the rest of the presentations.'

Another 15 nights to go. No doubt there will be a wag in Wagga Wagga and a wit in Wollongong to keep Beefy, Smokey and the Loon down by the billabong.

Looking back, I had enormous love and respect for Ian and Viv. Beefy for his self-belief and fighting spirit, and Viv for his deep-rooted pride and passion. As 'and' in 'The King and I', I was happy to be the bridge between the two mighty personalities. On some occasions I had to diffuse some hairy moments as their temperaments clashed.

'Brother D. Stop sitting on the fence,' said Viv.

'Dave, *you* talk to him,' huffed Beefy.

No wonder Somerset won all those cups in the mid-Eighties. When Viv and Ian batted, their competitive spirit burnt through the innings. I'm sure they tried to outscore each other. If Viv hit a sublime cover drive, Ian would try to top it. Very often it was the same on the road and the stage.

One day after driving for miles down a dirt road we got a puncture. Freewheeling into Pooncairie (pop. 50) we pulled up outside a garage.

'Can you help us?' I enquired.

The mechanic continued to tinker under a car. 'Sorry, mate, but I'm a bit busy at the moment,' came the reply.

'That's a shame, because my two pals and I have to do a show in Iron Knob tonight and we've still got a way to go.'

The mechanic, still on his back, begrudgingly pulled himself from under his car.

Whether it was the silhouettes of the world's two greatest cricketers that brought him to life, or the prospect of free tickets to the show, I'm not sure, but boy did he spark into action.

'Jeepers, fellers, it'll be a pleasure.'

By now the other 49 inhabitants of Pooncairie had heard we were in town, and Ian and Viv were mobbed. Cakes and beers were brought to the garage, and for the next two hours we had a street party.

When we hit the one-horse town of Iron Knob our welcome was less than enthusiastic.

'Don't know why you're doing a show here, lads. Nobody comes to Iron Knob. The Abos are queuing up to jump off the cliffs,' said the promoter who doubled up as the town mayor. 'Do you mind helping me put the chairs out? And as for your video, we'll have to wait till it's dark as we haven't got any curtains.'

'Charming,' said Beefy.

The three of us went to the dressing room to prepare for the show. Beefy was watching golf on television and as usual Viv was looking at our video of his and Ian's *Greatest Cricketing Highlights* that introduced the performance. There were about one hundred punters in the audience and half of those were from Pooncairie! Plus a kangaroo and the odd Emu.

'That was a bit unprofessional,' said Beefy to Viv at half time.

'What?' replied The Master Blaster.

'You, walking behind the screen when the video was on.'

Tempers were already frayed from days on the road. Viv confronted Ian face to face.

'Are you talking to f***ing Liam?' he said menacingly.

As the two men squared up, the promoter put his head around the door. 'Everything alright, lads, you're on in two minutes.'

As I went out to resume the show you could quite clearly hear some pretty fruity verbals from backstage. It didn't seem to faze our audience who were probably used to a bit of rough house on a Saturday night. The kangaroo ate nuts from his pouch and the Emu was well 'emused'.

'Did you hear that Imran Khan's wife has just given birth to a little boy?' I continued. 'Yeah, he came out rough on one side and smooth on the other. And Jemima's dress fell off as she walked up the aisle. Imran had been picking the seams.' All good topical material. By now sounds of hooting and hollering from backstage were at fever pitch. Even the screen on the stage began to sway. 'Anyway, ladies and gentlemen, how about a big hand for Ian and Viv?'

The monumental racket had subsided as Smokey and the Bandit walked out arm in arm as though nothing had happened.

'Great to be in Iron Knob, ladies and gentlemen. Are you enjoying the show?'

That night after we drove out of Dodge City nothing was said about the flare up. It was always the same, friendship conquers all. Blood is thicker than water.

'Beefy, pass me the red wine'.

The last Bunbury game has come to an end, the tannoy has ceased to crackle and the sounds of summer and children laughing are locked away inside the bouncy castle until next season – and I am left to ponder the road ahead. Yes, it's another marathon stroll with my pal, Beefy Botham. This time the endless tarmac takes us from Land's End to Margate, a mere bagatelle compared with other hikes, 535 miles in 22 days, raising money for Leukaemia Research.

It all started years ago on the march from John O'Groats to Land's End. I had just staggered through Bristol, my knees were creaking, the old thighs chapped 'neath my thermals. My eyes were misting over with pain. Blurred ahead, I could just make out our Leader, Captain Sensible, waving to all and sundry. Or was it Monday? You lose track of time.

There was Beefy blazing the trail, lifting up kids, blowing kisses to secretaries and old ladies alike as we passed through yet another town as though it were D-Day.

''Ere guvnor, you're struggling, do you wanna lift?'

The words percolated through the pain barrier like drops of salvation. It was a London cabbie. 'Go on, get in, nobody's looking.'

Briefly my mind was in turmoil. A dilemma: to cheat, or die. Being a man of enormous fortitude and moral fibre I was in the back of the cab within three seconds.

'Good on yer, pal,' I blurted, 'just drive slowly behind the walkers and keep your eye on the Messiah with the blond mane up ahead.'

For five days our ploy worked. As we entered each town I would slide out of my cab, hobble up to the front rubbing some dirt in on the way and report to Beefy.

'Where have you been, Loon?'

'I'm struggling a bit, Beef. But I'm at the back keeping the lads' morale going. You know, nothing like a few gags to keep the old legs pumping.'

'Good lad,' beamed Beefy, his face ravaged by the snows of Scotland, the winds of Cumbria, a thousand lost nights, and the odd tot of 'Fanta sunrise rocket tonic', which fuelled his desire to trudge southwards.

Guiltily, I returned to the warmth of my cab and the cockney banter of Raymond, my chauffeur.

'Anuvver tea and sandwich, Dave, or perhaps it's time for a beer?'

On day six, disaster struck a fearsome blow. Whether it was the burnt-out clutch or the prospect of a juicy fare in the next town which prompted Ray's burst of acceleration, I'll never know, but suddenly the tortoise from Hackney turned into Nigel Mansell and decided to overtake the legions ahead, led by Beefy.

Ian glanced into the cab and saw me sitting on the floor reading the Sunday papers and pulling on a large Havana cigar. Within a split second Conan the Barbarian had lifted me out of my sanctuary and hurled me into the River Tome. My ruse had been rumbled, my reputation as a walker was in tatters. From that day on the blisters on my backside slid down to the soles of my feet as my leader kept me under armed guard for the rest of the walk.

After liberating Land's End, we moved on to Guinnessland, and the march from Belfast to Dublin. I was familiar with Dublin as Beefy had insisted on a 'recce' a few weeks before; coincidentally, this took place just as England were to play rugby against the Irish at Lansdowne Road. Another misadventure by the Demon King had been constructed and we found ourselves crammed into an aeroplane the size of a motorbike heading westwards. We somehow landed broadside in a field outside Dublin, more by luck than judgement. Beverages had been served and not stirred by the man with shaky hands who doubled as the pilot.

As ever, the team had been handpicked by Beefy. It spelt danger. G. Cook (Northants CC and England), D. Pringle (Essex CC and England), Miami Johnny, Ian's father-in-law Gerry Waller, the master and yours truly. At 7.30 p.m., Friday night, we checked into the Burlington Hotel. The lobby was littered with aficionados of the pear-shaped ball, some wreathed in flags, others singing 'Danny Boy' in varying keys. We engaged the Dark Stranger at 7.35 p.m. It tasted like nectar, and four pints of it slipped down and propelled us into the street. We turned right. The first bar was called 'O'Brien's'. We entered its dimly lit portals at 8.15 p.m. The fact that we reappeared into the blinding sunlight the following Wednesday lunchtime says a lot for Irish hospitality.

Well satisfied, Beefy led us away from O'Brien's Bar with the sounds of prose and limerick, its marbled counters and madness caught in the gilt-edged mirrors reflecting a large lump under the carpet. To this day I'm certain Miami Johnny still rests there as a shrine to the 'Beefy Six'.

The trek over the Alps took us from Perpignan to Turin. Hannibal had covered the distance in his sandals with the elephants thousands of years before us. Day one, the rains slanted down covering the traces of time. There were no arrowheads, bits of tusk or Roman feathers to be seen, just the constant pitter patter on our anoraks as we stood in the town square listening to the mayor wishing us Godspeed.

There was 'Hannibal Beefy' standing next to the town's dignitary in front of his greengrocer's shop, the little man in his shabby suit, proclaiming through a brown-toothed smile what an honour it was *'pour Monsieur Bootham et ses camarades de commences La Marche des Alpes . . . avec les éléphants'*.

'Les éléphants', however, had more immediate priorities to mind. As the mayor rambled on, their trunks entered his shop and started to suck up the contents. *'Monsieur Boootham, très courageux . . .'* On went the mayor as the last turnip was devoured. Beefy's eye wandered just in time to see 40 Pyrenean potatoes being hoovered up.

Weeks later, and with the odd ride in the back of farm lorries, snatches of sleep in timber yards and frantic attempts to hitch-hike under my belt, Beefy announced that I could lead his army into Turin. Where was the catch? Had Attila the Hun finally weakened? Impossible.

'No, Loon. I mean it. You can ride the lead elephant as we enter Turin.'

This was it! There would be all the paparazzi, media attention, my big moment. Up I leapt like Sabu and straddled the elephant's head in the proper riding manner. All was well, until Nellie moved off; it was like riding a gyrating coconut. In a jiffy my shorts were ablaze and my manhood was sorely tested.

I don't know who laughed the loudest, Beefy and the boys or the elephants linked tail to trunk.

But for now it's Land's End to Margate and the call of the wild. As for the future, who knows? The Great Wall of China? Australia backwards?

Help!

THE PRINCE, THE FOX HAT AND 'ALL THAT FOR A SHAG'

'Now listen, gentlemen, when His Royal Highness comes in, you stand up, and when he sits down, you sit down.' In walked the nephew of His Majesty Sultan Haji Hassan Al Bolkiah, 29th Sultan and Yang Di Pertuan of Brunei, aged just 21.

'Your Highness,' I piped up. 'If you lie down, do we all lie down?'

There was an uneasy hush among the sporting greats. The Prince looked at me, startled at first. 'And who are you?'

'David English, your Highness, they call me the Loon.'

Prince Hakeem of Brunei burst into laughter, much to the relief of the assembled legends. Even the Gurkhas guffawed. So I went into my repertoire of gags: I must have done three hours of dog jokes, blind rabbis, one-legged Indians, cufflinks, football stories for Arsene and Kenny. The one about Geoff Boycott's car being stolen in Paris, which tickled Schumacher. But it was 'Prince Charles and the Fox Hat' gag that really hit the mark for the Prince.

'Prince Charles goes to Newcastle to open a plastics factory. He's wearing a fox hat. The mayor asks, "Howay, Your Royal Highness, why are you wearing a fox hat all day long?"'

(In my best Prince Charles) 'When I awoke this morning my mummy asked me where I was going. And I said "Newcastle", and mummy replied, "Where the fock's that?"'

16 THE PRINCE, THE FOX HAT AND 'ALL THAT FOR A SHAG'

'He's going to love you!'

'Who, Jimmy?'

'His Royal Highness. You'll crack him up!'

Jimmy Pearson, lifelong pal, Scottish footballer and former top dog with Nike, was now working for Prince Hakeem, nephew of the Sultan of Brunei. Ian and Viv had already formed a close relationship with the Brunei Royal family, spending time each year coaching the Princes.

'Look, son, I'll send a limo round for you tonight. Come and meet the Prince and tell him a few gags.'

That evening, a long black limousine purred down the leafy lane to my dwelling. A very smart chauffeur came to my door and I was whisked away. First stop was to pick up my neighbour, Arsenal manager, Arsene Wenger.

'Davide, do you know what these eese all about?' asked the immaculate Frenchman.

'I haven't got a clue, *mon ami*,' I answered quite honestly.

The limo pulled up outside one of the Sultan's hotels, the Dorchester in Park Lane. We were met by six Gurkha soldiers in full battle dress who swept us through the foyer to a special lift marked 'Penthouse Only'. Arsene and I zoomed to the room at the top where we were met by 'Jimmy P'.

'Hello lads, great to see you, come this way.'

We were shown into a splendid room. Seated around a long mahogany table were some of the most famous faces in sport. Bernard Gallagher, Michael Schumacher, Javed Miandad, Jahanger Khan, Kenny Dalglish and Boris Becker. 'Jimmy P' was super-animated:

'Now listen, gentlemen, when His Royal Highness comes in, you stand up, and when he sits down, you sit down.' In walked the nephew of His Majesty Sultan Haji Hassan Al Bolkiah, 29th Sultan and Yang Di Pertuan of Brunei, aged just 21.

'Your Highness,' I piped up. 'If you lie down, do we all lie down?'

There was an uneasy hush among the sporting greats. The Prince looked at me, startled at first. 'And who are you?'

'David English, your Highness, they call me the Loon.'

Prince Hakeem of Brunei burst into laughter, much to the relief of the assembled legends. Even the Gurkhas guffawed. So I went into my repertoire of gags: I must have done three hours of dog jokes, blind rabbis, one-legged Indians, cufflinks, football stories for Arsene and Kenny. The one about Geoff Boycott's car being stolen in Paris, which tickled Schumacher. But it was 'Prince Charles and the Fox Hat' gag that really hit the mark for the Prince.

'Prince Charles goes to Newcastle to open a plastics factory. He's wearing a fox hat. The mayor asks, "Howay, Your Royal Highness, why are you wearing a fox hat all day long?"'

(In my best Prince Charles) 'When I awoke this morning my mummy asked me where I was going. And I said "Newcastle", and mummy replied, "Where the fock's that?"'

Just before midnight, the Prince, still in hysterics, stood (so did we), bade us farewell, and left the room flanked by his giggling Gurkhas.

Arsene and I went downstairs to the restaurant for a beer. The whole evening had been alcohol free. Just Coca-Cola and a few Royal sandwiches. 'Jimmy P' joined us.

'I told you he'd love you!'

Seven days later I was at Finchley CC watching the cricket in my shorts and T-shirt. The players' attention wandered when a big black limo snaked into the drive and parked next to Johnsey's tractor. We were living in a scene from James Bond as two large, expensively dressed men approached me, took my arm and led me to the limo. I was driven home, told to get my passport and an hour later I was sitting on the Sultan of Brunei's Royal Jet. For 18 hours I was waited on hand and foot by some beautiful girls who fed me every delicacy imaginable . . . just me, still in my T-shirt and shorts . . . there was even a golden toilet.

When we landed at Brunei's Darussalam Airport, I was escorted through to another limo and driven to the Royal Palace. Breathtakingly opulent, with golden domes, the Palace stood shimmering by the East China Sea. I was led into a magnificent dining room, where dignitaries sat at a table with golden plates and cutlery, under glittering chandeliers that would have put Versailles to shame. In walked Prince Hakeem, everybody stood.

'Ah! David, welcome to Brunei. Now please tell my friends the joke about the Fox Hat.'

For the next ten days I was treated like a king. The Prince had his own football team, managed by Jimmy P. He would fly in Chelsea or Liverpool FC to play them. He had the world's best polo team, made up mainly of Argentinians. In the Golf Centre, legends of sport sat chatting, awaiting the Prince's whim, whether to play golf or tennis. If he wanted to moonwalk he'd fly in Michael Jackson. In fact MJ, Elton John, Whitney Houston and many others performed free concerts for the people of Brunei, who loved the Sultan and his family. His magnanimity was unrivalled: every boy at birth was given a free house, all the islanders had jobs and medical care. They were happy and friendly folk who worked hard, paid no income tax and availed themselves of the generosity of their leader, who would take care of them from the cradle to the grave.

I was Prince Hakeem's official court jester and he took me everywhere. If he fancied playing golf at 2 a.m., the sporting stars were summoned and we would tackle the floodlit golf course. I always accompanied him on his buggy, telling him gags and having a whale of a time.

On one occasion, he drove me to two massive doors. Using a remote control they opened, revealing an enormous underground car park, where stood rows and rows of magnificent brand new cars. Rolls-Royces, Bentleys, Ferraris; hundreds and hundreds of the world's most expensive cars, some still unopened in waterproof wrapping. It was amazing. Then, the Prince flicked another button, which opened a secret entrance in the wall, and, as we drove by, laser lighting shone down on different racing cars. The winning car from every Formula One Grand Prix is flown direct to Brunei, and there they stood, shining under the spotlight, Ferraris, Maclarens, Williams and, right on the end, a London taxi and a Mr Whippy ice-cream van. That Prince Hakeem . . . he's a lad! I half expected to see Johnsey's tractor.

Over the years the Prince and I have enjoyed many adventures. He calls me from time to time for the latest gag. My mobile can go at any time.

'Fox Hat, where are you?'

'Just parking my car outside Costcutters in Mill Hill Broadway, your Highness.' Hoots of laughter from the other end of the earth. 'And where are you, sir?'

'I'm just about to attend the State Opening of Parliament. Loon, what's that one about the three-legged pig?'

'I'm dreaming of a white Christmas, just like the ones I used to know.'

It's 25 December 2001, 6 a.m. I awake to that wonderful muffled hush that descends in the night, an unearthly glow from behind the curtain; moonlight spreading through the pines, and the wonderment of snow on the meadow. Soon bobble-hatted juniors, having wrestled with parcels from Santa, will crunch along, pulling their sleighs, from Legoland to Lapland. To see the sheer unadulterated joy a white Christmas brings to children, many of whom have never seen snow . . .

Certainly not in the Marondera Maternity home in deepest darkest Africa, where Robyn delivered Harry Thomas David English, 'the Zimbo kid', weighing out at just 5 lb 2 oz on 24 December 1993.

And now as I look through the frosty patterns on my window, the iridescent whirls like Nordic Knitwear crystallise before my eyes, taking me back over the past few years. Sadly our marriage dissolved, not through a lack of love but Robyn's homesickness for the dusty trails. From time to time she'd give me the 'Air Zimbabwe look'. I couldn't conjure up giraffes or the lions that ran alongside the wooden train from Bulawayo to Victoria Falls. I would always encourage her to go home and see her family but missed her the moment she'd gone. We tried to make it work, commuting between England and Zimbabwe; she would return with our two babies and the old purple bag full of hope. But it was not to be.

When I think of my children, I'm overcome by a sense of grief, of loss and missing. It comes over in waves. To be honest I feel emotionally crippled, as though half my soul has been ripped from my chest. Tears are never far from the surface. 'How many sleeps before I see you, Daddy?' You cannot lock in a restless spirit. Better to leave the door open, and let the person return of their own free will.

As she left, Robyn said, 'Promise me, if you ever write your book, when it comes to the chapter marked "marriage", you'll call it "All That For A Shag".'

So the English family now live and flourish in Cape Town, safe in the knowledge that their old dad loves them. And I am left, the Loon beneath the moon and the three African stars that twinkle in the silent night. 'Silent Night, all is calm, all is bright.'

It's 3.15 p.m and I'm just on my way to the Seaman's Rest for my Christmas lunch. A pork pie with a sprig of holly. A bowl of broth, paper hat and crackers with Riff McKoy and Panama Jack and the boys from the *Big Issue*. An evening of *Morecambe and Wise*, *Hancock* repeats and *The Great Escape* beckons when the phone rings. It was my soul-mate, the skipper 'Bazzer' Gibb in Miami.

'What are you doing?'

'Just having a think, Skip.'

'Well, think about this. The limo's on the way. You're coming home. See you in a few hours.'

My heart beat quickly; once again Barry and Linda had pulled me back to my second home. The Bee Gees mum, Barbara, always says that I am the son she never had, and I am deeply proud to be an 'Hon. Gibb'. Every time I think of their family, I feel a real glow and sense of belonging. And my 'sister' Linda. . .? My love and respect for her are unbounded. Her sense of caring for others and generosity of spirit are timeless. Soon I'm winging my way first class to Florida.

Near my destination, I see Santa, in his Bermudas, flying high over the Interstate on 195 down to the palms of Miami Beach, gently swaying under a deep blue cloudless sky. Swooping in on a smooth groove, hip to trip in sneakers and a beard flecked with white, dropping his gifts to all those 'Hairy Potters' stretched out on the golden sands, waiting all night with dreams of a PlayStation or a Barbie doll or the 'Dolphins' latest shirt.

The Bee Gees' strength is built on a deep family tradition full of love and generosity. A big jigsaw but, when several of the pieces are missing, the picture can never be the same. This year we lost George Gray, Linda's dad. A marvellous ex-naval man who, along with his wife May, had made the engine room – the kitchen – tick. We always met there for a laugh and a little spurt of bonhomie to get us through the trials and tribulations of the day. For all Barry's children, Stevie, Ashley, Travis, my godson Michael and daughter Ali, May and George had kept the engine room watertight with affection.

Back in March 1988 we had lost Andy Gibb, aged just 30. He was incredibly talented. A Piscean Peter Pan. But although his first three singles on RSO had rocketed to Number 1 in the USA, he felt he was always living in the shadow of his brothers. A terrible misconception, for Andy was super-versatile, a brilliant sailor and a first rate pilot. He once flew us single-handed from Los Angeles to Miami at the age of 22. He was just like a Barry Junior; very keen, very funny and extremely enthusiastic. He just lacked that self-confidence that makes you survive in the Great Adventure. We will never get over the loss of the Young Spirit Having Flown.

When I walked into the engine room this Christmas I was greeted with the news that Barry, Robin and Maurice had been awarded the CBE. It's the first time that three brothers have gained such an accolade, a wonderful commendation for forty years making great music.

Looking back, I've always been most comfortable in the company of musicians.

Songs touch us in a way that no other art form can, and they become the soundtrack of our lives.

One night, I went to see the Temptations at the Odeon Hammersmith. I visited their dressing room and sat down as they towelled off after another wonderful performance. Years before I had seen them at the Apollo Theatre in Harlem, where old ladies knitted and chewed the fat and kids danced in the aisles to the doo-wops and breathtaking harmonies. They were compelling showmen, sharp outfits, and with a smooth demeanour. 'My Girl', 'Since I Lost My Baby'. They enunciated the songs wistfully, they saw beauty surrounding the gloom.

I sat down with Melvin Franklin. Boy could he dance, he felt fire in the soles of his feet. With the strength in his heart and power in his singing, no-one got down so lovingly as Melvin.

As I talked to him we got deep down and soulful. He asked me if I felt fulfilled. I told him, 'There were only two other things I would have loved to have been in my life; one was to be a great lead guitar player and the other was to be the deep voice in the Temptations. Yes, Melvin, I'd love to have been you.'

Suddenly and still perfectly in sync, the other Temptations broke out into an exhibition of laughter, clicking of fingers and wild high fives.

'What's so funny?'

'What's so funny, brother David? I'll tell you what. There's you wanting to be me and all this time my real name is David English!'

How could this be true? How could the Emperor of Soul from Detroit's Motor City be called David English?

But true it was. A ten million to one chance?

Or Just My Imagination?

THE HALL OF FAME: ROLL CALL OF BUNBURYS PAST AND PRESENT

Chris Adams
Jimmy Adams
Steve Adams
Usman Afzaal
Wasim Akram
Roly Alexander
Tim Alldis
Clive Allen
Martin Allen
Hartley Alleyne
Mark Alleyne
Paul Allott
John Altman
Curtly Ambrose
Ian Anderson
Jerome Anderson
Dick Ashby
Mike Atherton
Mohammed
  Azharuddin

Rob Bailey
Ian Baraclough
Gareth Batty
David Beasant
Ian Bell
Joey Benjamin
Don Bennett
David Betteridge
Janis Betteridge
Richard Bevan
Dickie Bird
Ian Bishop
Alan Border
Ian Botham
Liam Botham
Peter Bowler
Stan Bowles
Rod Bransgrove
Richard Branson
Rory Bremner
Tim Bresnan
Graeme Bridge
Mark Bright
Chris Broad
David Brook
Ali Brown
Keith Brown
Jan Brychta
Neil Burns
Gary Butcher
Mark Butcher
Roland Butcher

Chris Cairns
Tim Cansfield

David Capel
Michael Carberry
Will Carling
Paul Carrack
Mike Catt
Chris Chittell
Eric Clapton
Sylvester Clarke
Graham Clinton
Richard Clinton
Brian Close
Graham Cole
Paul Collingwood
Phil Collins
Nick Cook
Arthur Cooke
Ray Cooper
Wendell Coppin
John Cousins
Ashley Cowan
Norman Cowans
Chris Cowdrey
Lord Colin Cowdrey
Graham Cowdrey
John Crawley
Buddy Holly & the
  Cricketers
Joe Cuby
Joshua Cuby
Samuel Cuby
Kevin Curran
Keith Curtis
Les Curtis

Charlie Dagnall
Lawrence Dallaglio
Roger Daltrey
Suzanne Dando
Peter Danks
Toby Davidson
Paul Davis
Winston Davis
Matt Dawson
Richard Dawson
Ralph Dellor
Grahame Dene
Naynesh Desai
Lee Dixon
Martin Dobson
Jason Dodd
Damian D'Oliveira
Matt Dowman
Isobelle Duncan
Robert Duncan
Keith Dutch
Simon Dyson

Steve Smith-Eccles
Phil Edmunds
Ross Edwards
Richard Ellison
John Emburey
David Emery
David English
Robyn English
David Essex
John Etheridge

Georgie Fame
Paul Farbrace
Rod Farrant
Gary Fellows
Robert Ferley
Andy Flintoff
David Folb
Darren Foster
James Foster
Neil Foster
Steve Foster
Neal Foulds
Graeme Fowler
Samantha Fox
John Francis
Paul Franks
Angus Fraser
David Frith
Barry Fry

Chris Garland
Joel Garner
Mike Gatting
Rohan Gavaskar
Devang Ghandi
Barry Gibb
Linda Gibb
Maurice Gibb
Robin Gibb
Ed Giddins
Ashley Giles
Graham Gooch
Andy Goram
Darren Gough
David Gower
Norman Graham
Danny Grantham
Jake Grantham
Leslie Grantham
Spike Grantham
David Graveney
Colin Graves
Peter Graves
Jimmy Greaves
Gordon Greenidge

Frankie Griffiths

Aftab Habib
Richard Harden
Dusty Hare
Roger Harpur
Mel Harris
Audley Harrison
George Harrison
Jamie Hart
Paul Hart
Basher Hassan
Jean de Havilland
Paul Hawksbee
Desmond Haynes
Peter Hayter
Dean Headley
Gary Headley
Mike Hendrick
Graeme Hick
Fraser Hines
Michael Holding
Adam Hollioake
Ben Hollioake
Lloyd Honeygan
Lloyd Honeygan
  Junior
Geoff Howarth
Merv Hughes
Geoff Humpage
John Hurst
Nasser Hussain

Richard Illingworth
Mark Ilott
Kevin Innes
Ronnie Irani

Andy Jacobs
Mick Jagger
Samantha Janus
Paul Jarvis
Terry Jenner
Elton John
Jilly Johnson
Joe Johnson
Paul Johnson
Peter Johnson
Mike Mahoney-
  Johnson
Richard Johnson
Kenny Jones

Alvin Kallicharan
John Keeble
Graham Kelly

Nigel Kennedy
John Kettley
Robert Key
Amer Khan
Imran Khan
Wasim Khan
Collis King
Nick Knight
Karl Krikken

Chris Laine
Ken Lake
Allan Lamb
Dave Lambert
Glenn Lamont
Stuart Lampitt
Justin Langer
Richard Langley
Brian Lara
Wayne Larkins
Buster Lawrence
Dave Lawrence
Geoff Lawson
George Layton
Neil Lenham
Matt Le Tissier
John Lever
Dave Levy
Chris Lewis
Dennis Lillee
Gary Lineker
Clive Lloyd
David Lloyd
Mal Loye
Joanna Lumley
Michael Lynagh
Monty Lynch
Steve Lynott

Gary Macdonald
Will Macdonald
Danny Maddix
Darren Maddy
Devon Malcolm
Tony Mant
Rod Marsh
Steve Marsh
Malcolm Marshall
Ross Martin
Robin Martin-
   Jenkins
Gary Mason
Tim Mason
C. Matapuna
Matthew Maynard
Martin McCague
Anthony McGrath
Glenn McGrath
Keith Medleycott
Tony Meo
Ray Merridew
Geoff Miller

Lance Milligan
Andy Moles
Richard
   Montgomerie
Tom Moody
Ben Morgan
Piers Morgan
Tom Morley
Alex Morris
Hugh Morris
John Morris
Zac Morris
Alan Mullally
Tim Munton
Tony Murphy
Dereyk Murray

Graham Napier
David Nash
Gary Neville
Phil Neville
Phil Newport
Mark Nicholas
Emma Noble
Wayne Noon
Richard Nowell

Donny Osmond
Nick Owen

Min Patel
Neil Patel
Tony Penberthy
Nicky Peng
Stephen Peters
Robert Philip
Ben Phillips
Tim Phillips
Roy Pienaar
Adrian Pierson
Elliott Pigott
Tony Pigott
Keith Piper
Paul Pollard
Mark Powell
Michael Powell
Prince
Lawrence Prittipaul

Trevor Quo

Neal Radford
Clive Radley
Mark Ramprakash
Derek Randall
Chris Read
Carlos Remy
Steven Rhodes
John Rice
Sir Tim Rice
Barry Richards
Dean Richards

Mali Richards
Sir Vivian Richards
Richie Richardson
David Ripley
Bruce Roberts
Phil Robinson
Graham Rose
Mike Roseberry
Jack Russell

Nick St. John
Charlie Sale
David Sales
Ian Salisbury
Dean Saunders
Reg Scarlett
Chris Schofield
Mike Scudamore
Peter Scudamore
Tom Scudamore
Graham Seed
David Sels
Richard Sels
Owais Shah
Nadeem Shahid
Chetan Sharma
Gary Shaw
Mo Sheikh
Arnie Sidebottom
Ryan Sidebottom
Phil Simmons
Judy Simpson
Anurag Singh
Andy Sinton
Gladstone Small
Ben Smith
Chris Smith
David Smith
Neil Smith
Paul Smith
Robin Smith
Jeremy Snape
John Snow
Sir Garry Sobers
Vikram Solanki
Ben Spendlove
Henry Spinetti
Ringo Starr
David Steele
Billy Stelling
Darren Stevens
Alec Stewart
Ed Stewart
Ian Sutcliffe
Luke Sutton
Alec Swann
Graeme Swann
Simone Sweeney
Walter Swinburn

Jonathan Taylor
Paul Taylor

Geoff Theakston
Jamie Theakston
Dave Thomas
Ian Thomas
Steve Thompson
Jeff Thomson
Graham Thorpe
Steve Tompkinson
Chris Tremlett
Marcus Trescothick
Alex Tudor
Phil Tufnell
Rob Turner
Steve Turnock
Kevin Twomey

Victor Ubogu
Shaun Udal
Derek Underwood

Andrew Varley
Michael Vaughan

Vic Wakeling
Matthew Walker
Rudolf Walker
Courtney Walsh
David Ward
Ian Ward
Trevor Ward
Shane Warne
Russell Warren
Atul Wassan
Dennis Waterman
Phil Waters
Steve Waugh
Paul Weekes
Graeme Welch
Philip Weston
Robin Weston
Craig White
Howard Williams
Huw Williams
Bob Willis
Jon Wills
Don Wilson
Julian Wilson
Matthew Wood
Ronnie Wood
Matthew Wrecker
Ian Wright
Bill Wyman

Paul Young

Bless you all!

INDEX

West Bruce and Laing 82, 136–7
West, Leslie 82, 136–7
Weston, Paul 128
Wexler, Jerry 84
'Whirlpool' (screenplay) 146–7, 152
White, Michael 116
Williams, Chris 116
Williams, Huw 185
Windfall Records 136

Winwood, Steve 73, 74
Wood, Ronnie 74, 189
Wright, Ian 179, 187–8, 190
Wyman, Bill 182, 186, 189, 190, 192, 221

You and Me 184
Youle, Chris 95

Zimmerman, Gary 177